PRAISE FOR *THE RESILIENT CULTURE*

'Resilience is more needed than ever, and so is this book. *The Resilient Culture* cuts through common myths, presenting resilience as a dynamic skill we all can build and benefit from.'
Jan Artem Henriksson, Executive Director, Inner Development Goals Foundation

'This book is not merely recommended; it is an indispensable resource for 21st-century leaders seeking to navigate the complexities of today's environment.'
Michael Hagemann, Global VP, Change and Transformation Engagement and Enablement, DHL

'Offers a powerful new way of thinking about resilience, one that resonates with the needs of our time. It is realistic, insightful, funny and innovative. A joy to read.'
Michael Bunting, keynote speaker and author of *The Mindful Leader*

'A must-read for leaders and employees alike. An insightful guide to turning adversity into strength in today's fast-paced world.'
Khaled El Gohary, Leadership and Capacity Building, Prime Minister's Office, United Arab Emirates

'Offers compelling research, vivid examples and practical strategies that turn resilience into a competitive edge, proving it's not just a wellness concept but a pivotal business strategy. Essential reading for any leader!'
Christian Greiser, C-suite coach, strategist and author

'Delivers answers and inspiration to get started on workforce resilience.'
Eivind Slaaen, Head of People and Culture Development, Hilti

'Offers discoveries from decades of work with business and concrete action plans so organizations know where to begin.'
Tina Weilmuenster, Head of Learning and Talent Development, European Space Agency

'The methods, evidence and ideas that the authors put forward are rigorous, time-tested and have the capacity to support powerful change. Read this book. Put even a few of its key ideas into practice. And see things get better.'
Michael Chaskalson, Founder, Mindfulness Works

'From debunking previous myths to introducing a new perspective on communal resilience, this work is an essential guide to enhancing our ability to navigate life's challenges and create organizations that allow people to flourish.'
Stefan Tuegend, Global Mindfulness Lead, Novartis

'Presents a compelling new view of resilience – one rooted deep in our human relational nature and our capacity for regeneration.'
Thomas LeGrand, Lead Technical Adviser, Conscious Food Systems Alliance, UN

'Contains all you need to know about resilience, and why organizations do well to offer resilience training at all levels – including to the top leaders.'
Gertrud Ingestad, former Director General, HR and Security, European Commission

'This brilliant book on resilience not only dissects its various elements but also equips us with essential resilience skills to thrive. Timely and imperative, it's a must-read for all.'
P V Ramana Murthy, author, consultant, lawyer and educator

'Today we work less, more safely and securely, better paid and with more say than ever before in human history. And yet work is making people increasingly ill. There are a thousand things that individuals and organizations can do to remain resilient. The authors explain these with unusual clarity.'
Frank Dopheide, Founder, Human Unlimited

'A great book that will inspire you and make you think! There are lots of helpful and easy-to-apply tips for readers to use themselves and for their own organization.'
Christine Senkel, Vice President, Corporate Human Resources, Faber Castell

'When a team of highly recognized experts summarize all their knowledge and research in a book, it is already worth reading. If these experts also have in-depth experience in these topics, then it is a must-read.'
Petra Martin, Head of Center of Competence Leadership, Bosch

'A must-read for every organization, every company, every team and every individual.'
Daniela Wiesler, Head of Media Training, DW Academy

The Resilient Culture

How collective resilience leads to business success

Chris Tamdjidi

Liane Stephan

Silke Rupprecht

Michael Mackay Richards

KoganPage

First published in Great Britain and the United States in 2024 by Kogan Page Limited

2nd Floor, 45 Gee Street
London
EC1V 3RS
United Kingdom

8 W 38th Street, Suite 902
New York, NY 10018
USA

www.koganpage.com

Kogan Page books are printed on paper from sustainable forests.

© Awaris, 2024

ISBNs
Hardback   978 1 3986 1832 9
Paperback   978 1 3986 1830 5
Ebook   978 1 3986 1831 2

British Library Cataloguing-in-Publication Data
A CIP record for this book is available from the British Library.

Library of Congress Cataloging-in-Publication Data
Names: Tamdjidi, Chris, author. | Stephan, Liane, author. | Rupprecht,
   Silke, author. | Richards, Michael Mackay, author.
Title: The resilient culture : how collective resilience leads to business
   success / Chris Tamdjidi, Liane Stephan, Silke Rupprecht, Michael Mackay
   Richards.
Description: London ; New York, NY : Kogan Page, 2024. | Includes
   bibliographical references and index.
Identifiers: LCCN 2024015132 (print) | LCCN 2024015133 (ebook) | ISBN
   9781398618305 (paperback) | ISBN 9781398618329 (hardback) | ISBN
   9781398618312 (ebook)
Subjects: LCSH: Organizational resilience. | Corporate culture. | Success
   in business. | BISAC: BUSINESS & ECONOMICS / Management | BUSINESS &
   ECONOMICS / Organizational Behavior
Classification: LCC HD58.9 .T365 2024 (print) | LCC HD58.9 (ebook) | DDC
   658.4/013—dc23/eng/20240515
LC record available at https://lccn.loc.gov/2024015132
LC ebook record available at https://lccn.loc.gov/2024015133

Typeset by Integra Software Services, Pondicherry
Print production managed by Jellyfish
Printed and bound by CPI Group (UK) Ltd, Croydon, CR0 4YY

To Saskia, Rosa and Hannah. May you grow and flourish, each in your own beautiful way, and be resilient. To all who have lost their sense of resilience, may you reconnect to your own deep, basic healthiness and have trust in your innate resilience skills – Chris

A heartfelt appreciation to all the clients from whom I have learned so much. Without their receptiveness and openness, the wisdom shared in this book wouldn't have been possible – Liane

To Fritzi and Milo, may you be able to remain kind, open and caring in a complicated world – Silke

To my wife, Sophie. Thank you for your endless patience and support when I immerse myself in writing projects. I couldn't do it without you – Mike

CONTENTS

List of figures and tables xiv
About Awaris xvi
About the authors xvii
Foreword xviii

Introduction: Facing up to modern challenges to resilience 1

1 Dispelling common resilience myths 16

The origin of resilience in the workplace 17
Resilience in the workplace: celebrating the overloaded worker 18
Myth one – Resilience is about endurance 20
Myth two – Resilience is a trait; some have it and some don't 21
Myth three – Resilience comes from our upbringing and is fixed 22
Myth four – Resilience is someone else's responsibility 23
Myth five – Resilience is too complex to be causally understood 24
Looking beyond resilience myths 26
Key chapter takeaways 26
Notes 26

2 Navigating our inner landscape 28

Our nervous system and arousal 28
Stress, eustress and distress 30
Human emotions, the mesolimbic system and valence 30
Business reality and shifting between the four states 35
The natural patterns of life and work 37
Too many workers are stuck in the stressed zone 38
Overstimulation and exhaustion 40
An emerging 'chilled' generation? 42
The 'bore out', 'burnout' or 'lie flat' generation 42
Resilience: the ability to cycle through states 43
Key chapter takeaways 45
Notes 46

3   **12 key resilience skills** 48

Towards a fuller understanding of resilience skills 49
Which resilience skills are most effective? 53
Assessing resilience skills 60
Understanding our resilience skills balance: the resilience battery
     analogy 61
How we use resilience battery profiles 65
Do resilience skills work? 66
Which skills impact resilience the most? 67
Key chapter takeaways 69
Notes 70

4   **Resilience competencies and profiles** 71

The three resilience competencies 73
Which resilience competencies can help with work and personal
     stressors? 76
Distribution of resilience competencies 78
How competencies combine to make resilience profiles 79
The challenges facing those with low resilience 81
The authors' competencies 82
Important takeaways for organizations 84
Key chapter takeaways 84
Notes 85

5   **The role of mindfulness in resilience** 86

Why are the thinking and feeling brains becoming more
     disconnected? 87
The evidence for mindfulness in the workplace 89
Understanding the mechanisms of mindfulness 91
Physiological intelligence 92
Struggling to focus 92
More than just relaxation 94
Using heart rate variability as a window to neurophysiological
     regulation 97
Lack of mind–body integration 97
Every company needs mindfulness 100

... and leaders need mindfulness too 100
Embedding mindfulness as a foundational capacity 101
Key chapter takeaways 102
Notes 103

6 **Developing our resilience skills** 105

Tackling these growing workplace wellbeing crises 107
The benefit of focusing on resilience skills 108
How to train resilience skills – a five-phase process 110
So how long does this take? 116
What have we learnt by working with businesses? 119
The secret hack: all the benefits without the effort? 120
Key chapter takeaways 121
Notes 122

7 **From 'I' to 'we': The importance of business culture** 123

Our nervous system is social too 125
How does neuroception work in the workplace? 127
The social fabric of work: a crucial component of resilience 128
Leaders and managers play a crucial role in creating the business
    culture 130
The power of the workplace culture 134
Business culture is a crucial aspect of resilience 137
Key chapter takeaways 139
Notes 140

8 **How to build resilience skills at the business-wide level** 141

Personal resilience skills have a limit 142
Organizations and individuals are mutually responsible for
    resilience 144
Building up organizational resilience skills 146
Building business-wide attention management 151
Targeted interventions are needed 156
Organizations must take responsibility for building skills and healthy
    behaviours 157
Key chapter takeaways 158
Notes 159

9 Team resilience skills 160

Successful teams are defined by their skills and habits 161
Building team emotional intelligence and psychological safety: through
   regular practices and habits of interaction 162
Mastered practices make a difference 169
Some team skills matter more than others 171
A five-step process towards improved team resilience 173
Key chapter takeaways 176
Notes 177

10 The importance of having resilient leaders 179

Resilience is on the radar, but putting it into practice isn't 180
Cultivating resilience intelligence in leaders 185
Leading for resilience 187
Key chapter takeaways 190
Notes 191

11 Why resilience is a business responsibility 193

Resilience is a business responsibility, not just a wellbeing officer's
   responsibility 194
Resilience requires building resilience skills, not a symptom-treatment
   approach 197
Resilience is a shared responsibility – it's neither an individual's nor
   an organization's responsibility alone 198
Making businesses responsible for resilience 199
Key chapter takeaways 200
Notes 200

12 Anchoring resilience in organizations 201

Step one: working with an appropriate group size 201
Step two: getting management on board 202
Step three: starting with individual resilience screening 203
Step four: looking at staff-wide data 205
Step five: selecting shared priorities with management 207
Step six: consistent individual resilience skill building 208
Step seven: building business-wide resilience skills in parallel 209
Step eight: measuring outcomes 211

Towards resilient business cultures 211
Key chapter takeaways 213
Notes 214

Epilogue: A letter to a business leader 215

Appendix I: Why wellbeing approaches fall short compared to skill-building approaches 217
Appendix II: The physiological, psychological and behavioural outcomes of our three resilience competencies 222
Appendix III: Our approach to implementing organization-wide resilience interventions 224

Index 227

LIST OF FIGURES AND TABLES

FIGURES

Figure 0.1   Global workforce stress is rising 4
Figure 0.2   Global anxiety and negative affect are growing 4
Figure 2.1   Stress is not always bad: low stress, eustress and distress 30
Figure 2.2   Map of our inner landscape and the circumplex model 32
Figure 2.3   Calm, eustress and distress on the map of our inner experience 33
Figure 2.4   Shifting between the four states is vital for resilience 35
Figure 2.5   Natural cycles of stressed, growing, regenerating and letting go 38
Figure 2.6   Narrowing the window of tolerance through excessive stress 39
Figure 2.7   Resilience: being able to shift through states 44
Figure 2.8   Learning to let go and regenerate is needed to restore balance 45
Figure 3.1   Resilience skills can be trained at four levels 51
Figure 3.2   We've identified 12 resilience skills within three connected domains 54
Figure 3.3   Resilience battery profiles 61
Figure 3.4   Stress temperature: stress load vs stress level gives the resilience battery drain rate 62
Figure 3.5   Resilience battery level, and recharging and drain rates 63
Figure 3.6   Three different resilience battery profiles 64
Figure 3.7   Resilience skills help us regulate stress 67
Figure 3.8   The top four predictors of high resilience 68
Figure 4.1   Resilience competencies and their mastery: high-level view of overall resilience competencies 78
Figure 4.2   Low resilience is the most common outcome 80
Figure 5.1   Mindfulness research has outstripped many other fields 91
Figure 6.1   The five phases of learning a skill: an integrated learning process to cultivate resilience 112
Figure 6.2   Practices as the basis of skill building and new behaviours 116

Figure 6.3   Wellbeing and compassion can be trained **119**
Figure 6.4   Practice frequency is related to greater impact **120**
Figure 7.1   Workplace culture is more important than strategy in retaining employees **136**
Figure 7.2   There's never too much psychological safety **137**
Figure 8.1   Limits to individual resilience **143**
Figure 8.2   Different stress factor resilience profiles exist **145**
Figure 8.3   Organizational factors also impact engagement and wellbeing **156**
Figure 9.1   Work is becoming more collaborative: change in tasks performed by US workers relative to 1980 **161**
Figure 9.2   Team habits predict collective intelligence **163**
Figure 9.3   Interaction habits are becoming increasingly important: psychological safety is necessary for high-performing teams **166**
Figure 9.4   Teams with resilience skills have lower burnout **169**
Figure 9.5   Collaborative teams are twice as innovative **170**
Figure 9.6   Resilient teams are significantly more psychologically safe, more motivated and highly effective **171**
Figure 9.7   Teams that process emotions well are five times less likely to suffer burnout **172**
Figure 9.8   The training impact on habit change **175**
Figure 10.1   Leadership style is related to employee burnout and job satisfaction **181**
Figure 10.2   Managers demonstrate higher resilience skills, which may influence their stress management ability **184**
Figure 11.1   Stress impairs employee flourishing **194**
Figure 11.2   Performance declines as perceived stress increases **196**
Figure 11.3   Perceived stress impairs performance **197**
Figure 12.1   Chronic stress decreases for both genders over their lifetime **206**
Figure 12.2   Prioritizing skill development: which skills might require more attention? **208**

TABLES
Table 4.1   Three main resilience competencies: statistical analysis shows a clustering of skills **73**
Table 4.2   Resilience competencies **77**

ABOUT AWARIS

Since being founded in Germany in 2009, Awaris has had a clear mission: to strengthen the mental, emotional and collaborative capabilities of people in companies. It supports teams and leaders in learning the inner development skills needed to overcome modern workplace challenges in areas such as resilience, sustainable performance, collaboration and leadership. And in doing so, we hope, it transforms hearts and minds for the better.

Awaris has worked with 250 businesses and trained 50,000 employees since 2012. These businesses include Bosch, Audi, HSBC, Hilti, Deutsche Bahn, SNCF, L'Oréal and Novartis, and members of parliament in the EU and UK, among many others. This book is based upon resilience statistics we've collected from over 2,000 people, 150 teams and 30 organizations. It builds on our ongoing commitment to reviewing the latest scientific research on resilience, and on some of the conclusions outlined in our own in-house research.

Ultimately, this book is the culmination of Awaris spending over a decade refining the best methods to build resilience at the individual, team and organization-wide levels. We're delighted to share it with you.

ABOUT THE AUTHORS

Chris Tamdjidi is one of two joint managing directors of Awaris. He has over 30 years of mindfulness experience. This includes leading a network of 70 mindfulness centres for seven years and spending almost a year on retreat over his lifetime. He has a deep, embodied experience of mindfulness and has led resilience projects for more than 50 organizations. He also brings extensive corporate and analytical skills, coming from his seven years working at the Boston Consulting Group, and his MBA and physics degrees from the University of Texas, Austin, and Imperial College London, respectively.

Liane Stephan is the other joint managing director of Awaris. She has over 40 years of mindfulness and systemic thinking experience. She's one of the most experienced practitioners in the field in bringing mindfulness and leadership together. She's a systemic coach (IF Weinheim Institute for Systemic Training and Development), sports scientist (German Sports University Cologne), certified psychotherapist (Fitz Perls Institute Hückeswagen) and the author of numerous books on coaching and family therapy. Liane's background has given her a deep understanding of how people and systems function. She has led resilience and leadership development projects for over 50 companies with Awaris.

Silke Rupprecht was director of research at Awaris. She has a PhD in psychology from Leuphana University of Luneberg, a master's in educational science, psychology and counselling from the University of Cologne and a bachelor's degree in social and economic communication from Berlin University of the Arts. Silke has published numerous research articles on mindfulness and leadership, having completed a post-doctorate in mindfulness in the workspace at Radboud University. She has also worked as a product developer for the Jonny Wilkinson Foundation and for the Mindfulness in Schools Project. She teaches mindfulness research at the University of Oxford Mindfulness Centre.

Michael Mackay Richards is an editor at Awaris. He has an MSc in international relations and BSc in politics, both from the University of Bristol. He writes economic and political research for the research arms of both *The Economist* and Fitch groups and, before going freelance, he worked in the City of London for seven years. He's also a trained mindfulness instructor, passing with distinction from the British School of Meditation. He has practised mindfulness for almost a decade.

FOREWORD

Imagine a comprehensive, research-packed compendium of the key capacities an organization can cultivate to create a culture that values resilience while promoting engagement, creativity and collaboration at all levels. On this empowering journey we are offered succinct packets of actionable knowledge and steps to build the crucial elements that demonstrate in practical terms what leaders can use to make the interactions *between* members of their organization create an atmosphere of inspiration and cooperation that reduces stress, enhances a sense of commitment and belonging, and provides a safe environment. It is these essential aspects of organizational culture – the ways we interact with one another in group settings – that let our brains function to their optimal abilities and enable our collective intelligence to thrive.

But you may be wondering why the 'culture' of an organization matters so much? Why focusing on resilience, as proposed here, is more useful than the more common attention, if any at all, leaders may put energy into to wellbeing? What makes the important and unique idea of 'we-silience' that our creative authors encourage us to consider so helpful?

The answers to each of these foundational questions are in the pages of this deeply considered, carefully crafted and extremely useful book. From the point of view of interpersonal neurobiology we can understand the systematic programme illuminated here in *The Resilient Culture* as a roadmap that allows anyone working within an organization to inspire the leadership that in turn allows each member of a group to make an important contribution to their community or organization. The research shows that when a designated leader is given these tools, the organization will be much more likely to be a place people feel devoted to supporting, creating more collaboration, more creativity and a sense of security. When we belong, we all prosper. The profit of such an approach is win-win-win: at each dimension of the organization, the seeds of strength are sown and the system itself is enabled to self-organize optimally. By honouring differences and promoting linkages inherent in we-silient practices, the crucial integration of complex systems is catalyzed and the flexibility, adaptability, coherence – resilience over time – and energy is released to allow this emergent property to blossom.

The human mind is both fully embodied and relational. What this means is that understanding how the nervous system functions – suboptimally in conditions of distress, threat and disconnection and optimally in times of workable challenge, engagement and the belonging of connection – helps each member of a team take responsibility for how workloads are handled and goals achieved. For someone with designated leadership responsibilities in that organization, working to guide employees under their management within a department can greatly facilitate how tasks are distributed and results monitored within timeframes and workloads that make the culture of that group work well.

For those in a position to oversee how departments and their divisions work within a larger organization, knowing these inner neurological insights into how mental processes, such as attention, motivation and memory, operate will greatly assist in managing the distribution of work tasks and the attainment of larger goals while monitoring the pulse of what is working well and altering course as needed. This book provides the core curriculum for understanding such neurological foundations and then applying them in everyday work life. Within the window of tolerance we achieve optimal outcomes. But when stress overwhelms our capacity to cope, we move to either side of that range by moving into states of chaos or rigidity – neither of which is helpful in working well individually or as a collaborative team. In this book, you'll learn not only about this window of tolerance, but how to build on other insights from neuroscience that will enable you to cultivate a culture that optimizes social connection and clear focus while minimizing states of distress.

On the relational level, you'll learn how to understand deeply that we humans are not only built with an inner neural system that helps us focus and function well, but that this same bodily system is also social. As our mental life – how we focus our attention, recall important data, keep an open and creative perspective to new possibilities, and imagine innovative ways of handling a challenge – is both embodied *and* relational, we can see that the suggestions to focus on organizational *culture* is not a side commentary; it is, in fact, the central point. As social beings with minds that function within our social connections, our brains are literally hardwired for a sense of safety and belonging. When we feel connected, we work collaboratively and creatively. When we feel secure, we become committed to the group in which we belong. We 'give it our all' and feel a sense of pride in the group outcome of our collective efforts. This is what a resilient culture cultivates.

It is an honour to invite you on this important and engaging journey in these challenging times on our planet. Take in these words of wisdom about we-silence and you will have the key knowledge and skills to create a resilient culture that will be an empowering experience for all of those fortunate to belong to your organization.

Daniel J Siegel
Executive Director, Mindsight Institute
Founding Co-Director, Mindful Awareness Research Centre
and former Co-Principal Investigator, Centre for Culture, Brain and
Development, University of California, Los Angeles

Introduction: Facing up to modern challenges to resilience

Participants from the private and governmental sectors gathered at the World Economic Forum (WEF) Annual Meeting in Davos in early 2023. They discussed a world affected by unprecedented crises and an increasingly perilous-looking future. They focused on rising geopolitical tensions, climate change, social instability and the potentially profound disruption set to emerge from artificial intelligence (AI) technologies.

The consensus was that these challenges are unavoidable – they simply cannot be ignored. Nor will they simply disappear. And as part of the answer to these challenges, we'll all need resilience. More resilience for our communities, business structures and digital systems. The WEF said, 'Facing a world of continuous, overlapping disruptions, leaders are recognizing resilience as the imperative condition for securing a sustainable, inclusive future.'[1]

It's worth reflecting on this a little. We're facing an unprecedented era of transformation in the coming decades. AI systems will develop at an exponential speed. They'll transform many parts of work and the world. We must decarbonize our businesses, restructuring global supply chains and industries to meet ambitious net zero targets. All the while, geopolitical uncertainties and shifting great power dynamics are making the world less predictable. Change is coming, and we can't avoid it.

While facing these challenges, we have to also acknowledge that our working lives have perhaps never been as stressful. Constant emails mean we can never truly switch off. We often work in hybrid teams, blurring the line between home and the office. Smartphone apps compete for our attention. It's clear that leaders and employees in organizations face many challenges.

We can face this uncertainty with fear or with courage. If we have confidence in our ability to learn and change, then we might view some of these upcoming changes with excitement, realizing that opportunities are opening up in the green economy, and in the AI sector too. On the other hand, if we remain stressed or paralysed in the face of this oncoming change, then the disruptions will be more painful and destabilizing than is perhaps necessary.

Where we live and what we do will impact the role we play in driving some of these changes and how much we'll be affected by them. Our personal agency might be limited in some cases. But what we do have control over is how we'll face these challenges and how we react and relate to them. And in the main this will be determined by how resilient we are as people.

But being personally resilient is no longer enough.

We need organization-wide, shared resilience. **Modern challenges demand truly resilient cultures, or 'We-silence', as we call it.** This means strengthening the resilience of our human systems. Of our teams, departments, communities and entire businesses. Developing a shared ability to handle stress, change and learn. The goal is to shift our human systems, helping ourselves and our organizations become more resilient as a whole. Whether the future scares or excites us might depend on how resilient these systems are.

Humans are wired to be adaptable

Despite many of these anxieties over rising stress and over the future, it's important to remember that humans are highly adaptable. Proof of this is in the way working habits were revolutionized by the Covid-19 pandemic, and by the spread of the internet in the decades prior to this. As humans, perhaps our biggest evolutionary advantage is that we're collaborative and adaptable. We succeed not because we outcompete other humans, or animals for that matter; we succeed because we collaborate and adapt.[2] This is the core of who we are. We're nature's ultimate learning machines,[3] hardwired for learning and growth.

These traits are anchored into the very structure of our bodies and brains.[4] Most animals are born with 80 to 90 per cent of their brain's wiring completed at birth. A horse can run within a few hours of being born – and so the wiring for running must be ready at birth. Evolution has led humans to be born when our brains aren't fully formed, partially so that babies can better fit through the birth canal during childbirth. So, we're born with our brains incomplete, the wiring less fixed than in other animals. Around 30 per cent of our brain structures and neurons are present at birth.[5] Our brains are formed throughout our lives, through interactions with our fellow humans. They're neuroplastic and can change over time.

This provides us with massive advantages. Someone born in the Sahara could in theory be a research scientist in the Amazon rainforest or Antarctica 25 years later. A giraffe born in the Sahel today, on the other hand, is unlikely to have such success. It simply doesn't have the adaptability (nor the legs suited to slippery Antarctic ice). A child born today might in the future find career success in a completely different environment from their home culture and climate. With all the changes on the horizon, they'll probably need to.

It's easy to see how children adapt and learn naturally. From learning to walk to installing a new app on their smartphone, they're constantly adapting. In addition, they quickly change their states, including their mood and energy levels. Learning and adaptation are in their very nature, like breathing. In fact, it's more of an anomaly when children don't learn or master new skills. All of this makes them naturally resilient.

Indeed, when children stop learning, stress, trauma or exhaustion are often responsible.[6] This can happen to children in school, or when their family environment isn't supportive. And even as adults excessive stress and in some cases trauma can also make us less liable to learn and adapt. We need to be able to regulate our stress levels and our emotions to learn and grow – as we'll see in Chapter 2.

Global stress has reached unprecedented levels

Stress is natural. It's a healthy response to situations which require more resources from us. When faced with something stressful, our minds and bodies mobilize resources for breathing, our muscles and other systems necessary for the fight, flight or freeze responses.[7] Other systems necessary for learning, digestion and social connections are downregulated, or even shut down.

This reaction makes sense when we see a snake. We don't need to engage in a complex, emotionally resonant conversation with it. Nor do we need to understand its motivation. After all, it's a snake. We'd do well to run away, and fast. So, stress is valuable for heightened performance, focus (to an extent) and strength in specific situations.

It is chronic stress, continual stress without recovery, which leads to problems. It's bad for our health and for our cognitive and collaborative faculties.[8] So it should concern us that global chronic stress has been growing in recent years, particularly in the workforce. At Awaris, we've spoken

FIGURE 0.1 Global workforce stress is rising

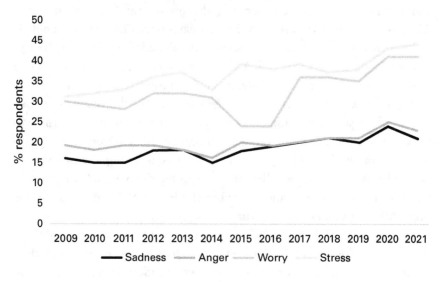

SOURCE *State of the Global Workforce: 2022 Report*[9]
Respondents were asked: 'Did you experience the following feelings a lot during the day?'

FIGURE 0.2 Global anxiety and negative affect are growing

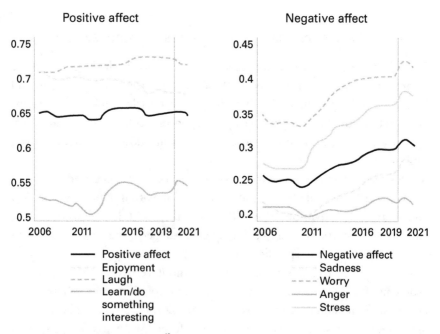

SOURCE *World Happiness Report 2022*[10]
Global trends from 2006 to 2021.

to thousands of employees and worked with hundreds of businesses in the last decade. And from our direct experience, we'd say that workers have never been as stressed as they are today. Indeed, we estimate that 30 to 40 per cent of the employees we've worked with typically have elevated stress scores – scores that bring them close to burnout.

Our observations have also been backed up by a Gallup global survey, which found that average global workforce stress levels have increased by almost 50 per cent in the last 15 years (see Figure 0.1).

This data is mirrored in several other surveys including the *World Happiness Report 2022,* which has shown an ongoing increase in global negative affect and anxiety in the workplace (see Figure 0.2). Interestingly, this has coincided with the spread of smartphones, social media and 'on call' email culture. We doubt it's a coincidence.

What does it mean to be resilient?

We are organic beings, subject to change. We experience day and night. We cycle through winter, spring, summer and autumn. We work and rest, raise families and socialize with friends. The changeability of our lives is natural. In fact, it could be said that change is the only constant in life.

Change impacts our behaviour, minds and physiology. Some changes might be welcomed, while other changes might be stressful and anxiety-provoking. Resilience isn't about toughing it out. Resilience is about how we adapt to such changes. And to do this, Awaris believes resilience requires being able to shift our internal states. In other words, true resilience is a skill or set of skills. Resilience arises when we're able to shift from high arousal (stressed) to low arousal (recovery) states, and vice versa.

For example, at times we need to be able to shift to a heightened energy state, to master a complex work challenge. Or, when there are fewer immediate pressures, we need to be able to shift into a regenerative state – healing damage to our systems, allowing more room for socializing and rest. Given the reality of our finite mental and energetic resources, resilience demands being able to shift states and our energy consumption, depending on what our environment presents us with. Unfortunately, too many individuals and businesses are always focused on performance, without a break. They believe they can't rest or relax, and remain stuck in the stress state for too long.

Collaboration: the blind spot of global business leaders

From our work with hundreds of business leaders, we've found many believe their businesses survive or succeed simply because they outcompete their competitors. In one such case, Chris was working with an automotive supplier in southern Germany a few years ago. He was meeting with a manager called Matthias, who led a team of over 200 people in product development. They sipped coffee in an airy room on the third floor. It had large windows, offering views over the extensive factory and to the forests beyond that.

As with any automotive supplier, competition and cost pressures were intense. After they sat down, the manager told Chris that his team was under significant pressure. While he was concerned about some in the team, he was also frustrated that many were sick or didn't seem to understand the seriousness of the situation. Matthias felt that they needed to be tougher, but also clearer about their boundaries. Chris could tell that these challenges were impacting Matthias: he was tense, impatient for Chris to 'get' his problem. Impatient for Chris, as the expert, to come up with a way to make his extended team more resilient.

'We're facing so many challenges at the moment,' Matthias said. 'The future of our business is under serious threat. Automotive companies want more share of the vehicle production process to protect their employees and margins, and there are more new entrants than I can count. It's been very stressful. The competition has never been this intense. We have to match them in speed and innovation. Given the urgency of the situation, I've made it clear to my employees that they each need to be more accountable for their own performance. Business is all about competition, you know, and we're in a very challenging situation.'

Chris nodded and said he understood. After a short pause, he said 'Do you really think business is *all* about competition? Would it be outlandish to say that collaboration could be more important for you right now, given that you need to pull your team together to face this new challenge?'

'Well, I know that collaboration is important,' he said uncertainly, before quickly adding, 'but there's no use in collaborating and feeling good if the competition is going to put us out of business. So, we need to be gearing ourselves up for a real challenge. Our business was more protected in the past. But many of these new entrants don't play by the old rules. We need to push through this challenge, then we can focus on collaboration again.'

There was a short pause. Chris and Mattias sipped their coffees. They both momentarily looked out of the window, gazing over the ongoing activity within the factory boundaries, and the distant green forests beyond that.

Chris restarted. 'I'm going to disagree with you here, if that's okay,' he said, smiling. 'My experience is that improving collaboration is many times more important than fixating on competition. And that, in fact, most of what organizations do is based upon collaboration and teamwork, rather the competition.'

The manager didn't look convinced. In Chris's experience, this reaction was par for the course with conversations he'd had with other managers. So, he continued. Chris asked him what percentage of his business's success he felt was due to collaboration and what percentage was due to competition. Matthias said, 'I'd estimate that our success is 60 per cent competition and 40 per cent collaboration, or thereabouts.' Chris was used to hearing many leaders and managers saying it was a 50:50 split, or in some cases that their organization's success was 30 per cent due to competition and 70 per cent due to collaboration. So, this manager's view wasn't massively out of kilter with the consensus.

Chris continued with the next part of the exercise and asked Matthias to pull out his phone. He looked a little confused – perhaps concerned Chris was about to get them to take a selfie or something – but then cautiously obliged.

'Okay,' Chris said. 'Can you please open your work calendar? Now, count the hours of work events this week in which you are really competing with someone and scribble them down in one column in your notepad. After this, write down all the events in your calendar where you are collaborating and put them in another column.'

Matthias spent the next few minutes trawling through his calendar and stopping occasionally to write in his notepad. After a short while, he said 'Okay... Ah, I see where this is going,' delivered with a wry smile.

Matthias flipped the notepad around so Chris could see it. The 'collaboration' column was full. It had perhaps 45 entries. The 'competition' column? Only one entry. 'I might have got my percentages a little bit off,' he said laughing.

'Don't worry, everyone does,' Chris said. 'We've run this calendar exercise hundreds of times. And I'd say we've rarely met any manager who can find more than one event which is really about competition in their weekly calendar. Actually, through running this exercise, we've found that more than 95 per cent of what leaders do is collaborative, even with their customers, suppliers, stakeholders and other industry players. And these were all people who thought they spent their entire working lives competing!'

Matthias looked a little relieved to find out he wasn't the only one.

That's not to say that competition isn't part of our working reality. It is. But most of what we do at work is based on collaboration, and the fixation on competition undermines this. Chris continued. 'One more point. Do you think we collaborate best when we are stressed or when we're more relaxed?'

'Yes, collaboration is key... but... we can't afford to relax,' said Matthias. Despite what we'd just discussed, somehow it was still difficult for him to fully accept the importance of collaboration, or that it also required relaxation.

'Without focusing on effective, *sustainable* collaboration, you'll be selling your organization short,' Chris said. 'Collaboration requires presence, care, emotional resilience and relaxation. Allowing your workers to get too stressed would also end up sending your employees on a path to burnout, which really isn't good for anybody.'

Chris and Matthias wrapped up their conversation and bade each other farewell. They pledged to pick up this conversation again at their next training session, due in a few weeks' time. On the walk back to Chris's hotel, strolling through a park, he had a few minutes to reflect. In conversations like these with business leaders, he could see the impacts that a misplaced fixation on competition was having on managers personally, as well as on their teams. In situations like this, it was perhaps inevitable that workforce stress and burnout would surely follow.

A narrow focus on competition fits with the misconception that resilience is endurance or toughing it out. But we believe this thinking is flawed, in two key ways. First, it doesn't reflect the reality of why businesses succeed. Second, it creates incentives for workers to be too stressed for too long, which causes more problems for the business down the line.

So why are so many business leaders misunderstanding the reality of stress and competition? Usually, it's because these leaders are themselves too stressed most of the time. Stress traps them into fixed mindsets[11] and can make them overly competitive,[12] even when they don't need to be. With stressed leaders heading up most organizations, it's no surprise that the language of business is often too focused on competition.

As we'll attempt to show in this book, this is an outdated way of thinking. And it is a way of thinking which must be replaced with a move towards resilient cultures, as the example below highlights.

The impact of too much stress: a team exercise

When we work with businesses, we demonstrate how allowing workers to be stressed for too long is bad practice, and inevitably leads to suboptimal business outcomes in many surprising ways. To do this, we take a group of 10 to 30 people and divide them into three groups. We give each group the same challenge, but different conditions to tackle it.

With **group one**, we describe the task or challenge that they must master, and also explain that this will be a test of their ability to handle stress. We tell them they have to be tough and they can't take a break from the task. If they really can't carry on, then they can give up. We leave the rest up to them. We usually underscore this message by delivering these instructions with a stern look and arched eyebrows, channelling the spirit of tough bosses from our collective unconscious.

For **group two**, we describe the challenge they have to carry out and also the duration of time it'll take. We encourage them to relax whenever they want to, and once they've relaxed, say they can simply carry on with the challenge.

With **group three**, we describe the challenge and its duration. We encourage them to relax whenever they want to. We also encourage them to notice how the strain of the task affects them, and to share insights among themselves on how they can minimize their felt strain as they fulfil the challenge.

We've run this exercise hundreds of times. Naturally, like all good challenges, it goes on for longer than expected and the strain the participants feel is real. Interestingly enough, the outcome is almost always the same, as we describe below:

- **Group one** – the 'stress group': The participants stand in a line, looking strained and not speaking, as they fulfil the task. They carry on, experiencing increasing stress and even pain. Over time, some give up with a frustrated or resigned expression. Others start complaining about the exercise or point to other groups they think are cheating. This is always the group that questions who we are to have given them such a challenge, and it is the only one that complains about others. Those who give up feel defeated. On average, this group gets a fulfilment score of 70 per cent in the challenge – primarily because some have given up. Those who gave up feel unhappy about letting the group down.

- **Group two** – the 'regeneration group': The participants usually stand in a circle, in contact with each other, chatting, working on the challenge. They communicate and take pauses whenever they're tired. They carry on indefinitely and don't give up. They don't have to be motivated; it's natural for them to hold their responsibility. They don't complain or criticize the other groups. When asked about their experience, they usually say they enjoyed it and could have carried on for longer. On average this group gets a fulfilment score of over 90 per cent in the challenge.

- **Group three** – the 'learning group': They also stand in a circle, chatting, fulfilling the challenge and pausing. They carry on working on the challenge and don't give up. They don't complain or criticize other groups. They experiment with many ways to fulfil the challenge, and usually learn to minimize the degree of strain they experience. When asked about their experience, they usually say they enjoyed it. That they could have carried on for longer and enjoyed learning from each other. On average, group three gets a fulfilment score of over 90 per cent in the challenge.

After the exercise, we bring all three groups together and summarize the key takeaways:

- **Group one:** The 'stress group' displays symptoms of poor communication, negative outlook, burnout and irritation. And their performance is usually the poorest. They also communicate poorly and learn nothing. Trying to maintain 100 per cent performance without emphasizing recovery has many unintended negative consequences, both on completing tasks to a good standard and also on communication, health, learning and connection.

- **Group two:** The 'regeneration group' has the same challenge, but also the condition of relaxation and self-regulation. They have much better performance than group one and enjoy their work more. They can continue indefinitely. They naturally communicate and remain connected.

- **Group three:** The 'learning group' also fulfils the same challenge, but under the condition of relaxation and self-observation. They have equally high performance to group two, but they also become a learning team, optimizing their approach to the challenge as they fulfil it. They communicate, remain connected and learn. The other groups offer no learning insights, whereas this group learns simply from the task of self-observation.

Following these conclusions, group one members are often silent and are the ones most struck by these learning takeaways. They feel foolish that they fell into this mode of competitive and stressed behaviours. Groups two and three are more cheerful, but also reflective. They're surprised how much better the outcomes were for groups that prioritized relaxation.

We then ask the leaders to reflect on these learning outcomes. A lot of them are surprised by how easily they've fallen into the patterns of group one in the past, and how group one patterns inhibit team performance, communication, collaboration and learning. Liane remembers one institutional leader at the European level discussing this with a colleague, who said: 'I can't believe we've being doing things this way for so long. To be honest, we've been working like group one for many years, and this does now look to be suboptimal.' Separately, a research and development director once said: 'I knew recovery was important for staff wellbeing. But I always saw performance and relaxation as separate things, and the employee's own responsibility. Now I'm not so sure.'

We usually reassure these leaders that they aren't alone. Most modern businesses are led like group one, sadly, whereas in an ideal world they should function like group three. Clearly, sustainable performance, collaboration and learning are what modern work requires, and are more important than short-term performance. Prolonged stress isn't generally conducive to team or business success. And this is what we often find ourselves needing to highlight to our clients, even those who have started taking wellbeing more seriously in recent years.

Wellbeing isn't enough

You'd think we might celebrate the massive growth in wellbeing departments, initiatives and recommendations in recent years. Indeed, one report estimated that the global corporate wellness market was worth $61.8 billion in 2022, up from negligible levels a couple of decades ago.[13]

While we agree that an increased focus on wellbeing is an important step in the right direction towards building resilient business cultures, it's also clear that the wellbeing drive in modern workplaces hasn't worked. The data simply says stress has got worse,[14] even with this tremendous expansion of wellbeing initiatives. Perhaps modern workplace stress would be even worse without this growth in wellbeing initiatives? It's hard to say. But what we can say is that a focus on wellbeing alone isn't enough, given the challenges businesses face.

Below, we outline why a focus on wellbeing falls short:

- **Wellbeing is often an afterthought.** Mindsets haven't shifted enough, and many leaders and organizations continue to focus too narrowly on high performance. They talk about performance, measure it and reward it. In contrast, wellbeing is usually an organizational afterthought. Despite exponential growth in recent years, wellbeing budgets are still typically less than 1 per cent of salary costs and around 0.3 per cent of overall business costs.[15] This implies a limited effort to balance performance and care, or to focus on wellbeing anywhere near as much as performance.

- **Wellbeing initiatives fail to convince executives of the link between performance and care.** While definitions vary, wellbeing is generally described as a state that aids recovery and is associated with positive emotions. Those who support wellbeing initiatives often do so because they worry about stress and view wellbeing as an antidote to it. Others, however, sometimes view wellbeing as somehow anti-performance. At present, wellbeing initiatives fail to provide a compelling explanation of how they support both performance and care. Indeed, they don't encompass the inseparability of performance and care.

- **Wellbeing is a state, not a skill.** Wellbeing is merely one of a number of important physiological states, which include stressed, growing, regenerating and letting go. In the face of ever-increasing workplace challenges, the ability to balance and shift states – not just to reside in wellbeing – is required to combat stress effectively. Wellbeing interventions are normally focused on getting to a state of wellbeing, without being clear on how to train the skills to recreate that state. Many wellbeing interventions create a nice, temporary state. There are cheerfully bizarre ones, like inviting puppies to the office for staff to have their 'Awww' moment. But this state is temporary. It doesn't teach staff the skills of shifting states for the future. And in some cases, it might leave unusual stains on the carpet. (See Appendix I for more details on why wellbeing interventions fall short compared to skill-based interventions.)

- **Focusing on wellbeing might not always be realistic.** The simple fact is that global stress will continue rising in the coming years, based on the challenges we're facing. No amount of wellbeing will prevent stressful situations from arising, which is why the skill of shifting states and an emphasis on resilience have never been more important.

We don't doubt that wellbeing departments are important, particularly those adopting preventative approaches to reducing stress and improving wellbeing. For modern businesses to cope with a rise in stress in the coming years, there'll also need to be a shift to more targeted interventions. And a significant percentage of these need to be targeted at building individual and organizational resilience.

Shifting from 'I' to 'we'

With wellbeing interventions falling short, businesses too focused on competition and stress at unprecedented levels, we at Awaris believe a new approach is needed. We have written this book because we care deeply about humanity's ability to be resilient in the face of our world's upcoming changes.

A wise person once noted that moving from illness to wellness is a shift from 'I' to 'we'. Similarly, we call for a change in the approach to resilience. When people speak about resilience, they usually talk about individuals who somehow endure. But what's often ignored is that a lot of our resilience comes from our social connections, at the 'we' level. From collaboration, rather than competition.

For human resilience to flourish, we need to include the team, the organization and the social level. This is what we mean when we talk of building resilient cultures, and of **We-silience: resilience at the level of the entire organization, the whole system.** And in the rest of this book, we'll outline what we've learnt and what you need to do to build truly resilient working cultures yourself.

This book will chart a path for improving team and organizational resilience. It will look at some of the myths around resilience. It will explain the importance of understanding mind and body states, and how shifting between these physiological states is the key to resilience. We'll explain which discrete skills allow us to regulate different systems in the mind and body, and the importance of embedding a culture of long-term skill development. We'll sketch out the key habits and skills which make teams resilient, and map out how organizations can firmly embed them into their workflow, as well as in the very fabric of their business and their private lives. The book will conclude by looking at how the sum of our resilience habits can make our team, work and community cultures more resilient, creating happier individuals and better organizations.

In reading this book, we hope that you, the reader, will be able to join us on this journey, moving from resilience to We-silience. Let's go.

KEY CHAPTER TAKEAWAYS

- Businesses face unprecedented challenges in the coming years but aren't well-placed to deal with them.

- Managers overvalue short-term performance goals at the expense of having stressed staff, without realizing how much stress inhibits sustainable performance.

- Business leaders overstate the importance of competition and undervalue the importance of collaboration, contributing to burnout and stress in the workplace.

- The rising levels of stress in organizations suggest that the recent growth in wellbeing interventions hasn't worked, and that the language of wellbeing needs to shift from wellbeing as a state to resilience as a series of skills.

- For companies to achieve sustainable performance it also requires a change of focus, from resilience at the 'I' level to the organization-wide 'we' level. This change in focus will increase the chances of building resilient working cultures.

Notes

1 World Economic Forum (2023) Seizing the momentum to build resilience for a future of sustainable inclusive growth, www3.weforum.org/docs/WEF_Resilience_Consortium_2023.pdf (archived at https://perma.cc/GH2H-HVBR)

2 Rushkoff (2016) Evolution made us cooperative, not competitive, *Medium*, https://medium.com/team-human/evolution-made-us-cooperative-not-competitive-60704d8fe49d (archived at https://perma.cc/JPA6-BRZL)

3 T Stafford (2022) Why are we so curious? BBC Future, www.bbc.com/future/article/20120618-why-are-we-so-curious (archived at https://perma.cc/H29K-2ZZP)

4 D Eagleman (2021) *Livewired: The inside story of the ever-changing brain*, Canongate Books, London

5 J Gilmore, R Santelli and W Gao (2018) Imaging structural and functional brain development in early childhood, *National Review Neuroscience*, **16** (19), pp. 123–37, www.ncbi.nlm.nih.gov/pmc/articles/PMC5987539/ (archived at https://perma.cc/AF69-EC3S)

6 H Lebow (2022) How can childhood trauma affect learning? *Psychology Central*, https://psychcentral.com/ptsd/complex-ptsd-trauma-learning-and-behavior-in-the-classroom#trauma-and-the-brain (archived at https://perma.cc/3LPS-V4Z9)

7 Harvard Health Publishing (2021) Understanding the stress response, www.health.harvard.edu/staying-healthy/understanding-the-stress-response (archived at https://perma.cc/7KRX-9SF9)

8 P Morgado and J J Cerqueira (2018) The impact of stress on cognition and motivation, *Frontiers in Behavioural Neuroscience*, **12** (326), www.frontiersin.org/articles/10.3389/fnbeh.2018.00326/full (archived at https://perma.cc/Y7XB-CP6A)

9 Gallup (2022) *State of the Global Workplace: 2022 Report*, www.gallup.com/workplace/349484/state-of-the-global-workplace.aspx (archived at https://perma.cc/8FBX-6EKX)

10 J F Helliwell, R Layard, J D Sachs, J E De Neve, L Aknin and S Wang (2022) *World Happiness Report 2022*, https://happiness-report.s3.amazonaws.com/2022/WHR+22.pdf (archived at https://perma.cc/33AC-CDYW)

11 T Smeets, P van Ruitenbeek, B Hartogsveld and C Quaedflieg (2019) Stress-induced habitual behaviour is moderated by cortisol, *Brain and Cognition*, **133**, pp. 60–71, www.sciencedirect.com/science/article/pii/S0278262618300460 (archived at https://perma.cc/2F3W-EVE3)

12 L Goette, S Bendahan, J Thoresen, F Hollis and S Sandi (2015) Stress pulls us apart: anxiety leads to differences in competitive confidence under stress, *Psychoneuroendocrinology*, **54** (April), pp. 115–23, www.sciencedirect.com/science/article/pii/S0306453015000335 (archived at https://perma.cc/SJV2-RYUQ)

13 International Market Analysis Research and Consulting Group (2023) Corporate wellness market: global industry trends, share, size, growth, opportunity and forecast 2023–2028, www.imarcgroup.com/corporate wellness-market (archived at https://perma.cc/PW6U-DAQQ)

14 M Rigo, N Dragano, M Wahrendorf, J Siegrist and T Lunaum (2021) Work stress on rise? Comparative analysis of trends in work stressors using the European working conditions survey, *International Archives of Occupational and Environmental Health*, **94** (3), pp. 459–74, www.ncbi.nlm.nih.gov/pmc/articles/PMC8032584/ (archived at https://perma.cc/8H2H-58QW)

15 J Overton (nd) Understanding corporate wellness program costs as investments, Limeade, www.limeade.com/resources/blog/corporate-wellness-program-costs/ (archived at https://perma.cc/56P5-UX9W)

1

Dispelling common resilience myths

In an average year, Chris interacts with people from over 70 companies. While each company is different and faces unique challenges, when it comes to stress, things are pretty much the same. When he meets teams in person, he often finds himself in a room full of stressed people. He can see it in the tension in their bodies. In the way they stand. He notices people quickly becoming uncomfortable, even if he pauses speaking for a few moments to consider what someone's just said. Rather than spending a few torturous seconds without stimulation, phones are whipped out of pockets, messages are checked or people just become restless.

If meeting online, this stress is still clear for Chris to see. He can see it in how attendees' eyes move – darting from side to side, or up and down, as they attempt to understand what he's saying, while simultaneously replying to emails (spoiler alert: probably doing both tasks sub-optimally).

Whether meeting in person or online, some other key themes emerge. When managers talk, they say they'd like to make 'them' (meaning everyone else in the business) more resilient. Managers normally want to ensure that everyone understands that their business is facing unprecedented pressures, and people must become stronger (and faster, ideally). From what managers say, it's clear that they deeply care about the continued success of their business and remain 100 per cent focused on this. At the same time as demanding a relentless focus on performance from their staff, managers often confess that they feel frustrated and helpless when faced with rising burnout and stress in their teams. They say they're at a loss as to what to do.

When Chris listens to HR, health and safety or wellbeing officers talk, they say they feel compassion for the stress and struggles of some of their employees. They'd like to make 'them' (meaning managers this time) understand that their relentless focus on performance is coming at a high cost.

Naturally, there are managers and HR professionals who are themselves stressed. They say they're struggling to maintain their performance, their façade, and even to keep it all together. There are those who 'own' their stress, conceding that they feel weak and defeated sometimes. They say they'd like to be stronger and more resilient, but also want to have space to *feel* their stress.

Sometimes, in situations like this, Chris tries to get a sense of the mindset in the room or online. To do this, he simply suggests everyone should 'just relax'. This has an interesting effect. Manager types might roll their eyes. Their facial expressions imply they think Chris is a little dim-witted or slow (a criticism he hopes is just limited to this exercise). They say, sometimes politely, sometimes impatiently, that he can't possibly understand the reality of their business, and they can't see how relaxation is relevant. HR teams tend to stiffen a little. As if they're not sure if Chris has really *understood* how much people are struggling. His 'just relax' comment makes it seem like he's taking these problems too lightly and is oversimplifying things. And finally, those who're struggling with stress often have a look of panic on their faces. They're scared that if they relax, in some way, they might fall apart altogether.

Some of these reactions are underpinned by their own valid experiences. But these interactions all highlight a series of much bigger misunderstandings when it comes to stress and resilience. Relaxation is a necessary skill and becomes increasingly important the more we experience stress. But when Chris mentions it, most individuals seem to think that relaxation means simply 'a short break from stress' or 'giving up on performance', rather than learning skills to regulate our stress. And business leaders think Chris is undermining their relentless focus on performance. Part of these misunderstandings reflects a profound confusion about what resilience actually is in the first place.

The origin of resilience in the workplace

The field of resilience has been developing for close to 300 years. The origin of the word 'resilience' in modern usage comes from materials science. In this definition, resilience means 'the power or ability of a material to return to its original form, position, etc, after being bent, compressed, or stretched'.[1] It was also used commonly in physics, where Francis Bacon used the term to refer to a variety of physical processes.[2] It was also later used in applied mechanics. In recent decades, resilience has also been seen more commonly in physiology, biology and ecology.

In psychology, the roots of resilience can be traced back 50 years. Psychologists studied children who came from troubled backgrounds with a high risk of psychopathology. At first, the research was deficit-focused, looking at what caused trauma in the children. Among these children, they realized that some didn't develop any psychopathological disorders and grew up surprisingly healthy and without mental health disorders.[3] These children were often deemed 'resilient'.

Researchers tried to understand how some children emerged from their trauma relatively unscathed, and so replaced their deficit-focused research approach with a strength-focused one. They examined the positive variables that contributed to good outcomes and resilience in the at-risk children. Overall, until perhaps 10 years ago, this research was focused on fixed traits in the children, or factors in their history which made them resilient in the past. It wasn't until more recently that this research moved on to look at how these children could learn to be more resilient *now*, which is closer to where Awaris's interest in resilience lies.

Clearly, resilience has had a multitude of meanings, in a number of different contexts. As a result, people should be forgiven for misunderstanding what resilience should *actually* mean in the workplace.

Resilience in the workplace: celebrating the overloaded worker

In the workplace, cues on resilience have mistakenly been taken from these other fields. Employees who endure heavy workloads and stress have often been lauded as 'resilient', with admiration. Think of the drained employee, bags under their eyes, on their fifth coffee of the morning, boasting about how late they stayed at the office last night during a meeting (and later struggling to stay awake in it). Employers have expected workers to be resilient according to outdated definitions of it, and in doing so have contributed to a massive rise in stress levels in the past few decades. A trend made worse by an expectation for workers to be contactable via email at any time of day and, sometimes, on the weekend.

Continued workplace stress can lead to numerous negative outcomes. Long-term stress can impair health, cognitive function and emotional regulation.[4] Those who work in stressful settings are at a higher risk of anxiety, depression, secondary traumatic stress and burnout. Organizations with stressed staff will struggle to retain them, morale will suffer, and performance will, eventually, too.

Despite this, the resilience discussion in the workplace has remained marginalized. Often, it's not really taken seriously, or it's viewed as a single, one-off event, like a plaster on a wound. Or, even more disappointingly, it has been limited to simply building more resilient IT or business systems. As a result, it's no wonder the corporate world is starting to lag behind some other sectors, which are beginning to develop a better idea of why some humans are resilient. These include developments in trauma therapy, the treatment of people with attention deficit disorder (ADD)[5] and advancements in neurophysiology. They're all shedding light on the neurophysiological systems involved in regulating our internal states.

CASE STUDY

A conversation we've had many times...

Company: 'We're worried about the resilience and wellbeing of our staff and want to do something at the upcoming company offsite. We heard that X is a good thing to help people and wondered whether you could lead a virtual session on this topic.'

Awaris: 'Yes, happily, how much time did you have in mind?'

Company: 'We've managed to secure 30 minutes from management for the session.'

Awaris: 'Ah. That's interesting. Have you tried that before?'

Company: 'Yes, we had a good session of Y last year. People really enjoyed it.'

Awaris: 'Interesting. Did that help? Did their stress levels go down?'

Company: 'Well, it was nice at the time, but things seem to have got worse in the last year.'

Awaris: 'So would you like to do something like that again?'

Company: 'Yes!'

As this understanding has matured, psychologists and researchers have been able to design interventions to help people learn regulation skills that most of us have but aren't often aware of. So, there's an emerging knowledge about how people can regulate their own internal state, at the physiological level, and how to train this ability.

In the workplace, however, confusion and misunderstandings about resilience remain quite widespread. The five most common we see are:

1 Resilience is about endurance.

2 Resilience is a trait; some have it and some don't.

3 Resilience comes from our upbringing and is fixed.

4 Resilience is someone else's responsibility.

5 Resilience is too complex to be causally understood.

We'll now look at each of these resilience myths in turn.

Myth one – Resilience is about endurance

It's not surprising so many people think resilience is about endurance in the workplace, given the word's multiple uses in different fields. Other factors have also contributed to this view in the workplace setting – in particular, the idea of the 'hero leader', employees avoiding any talk of being stressed, and the projection of toughness by business leaders.

Being stressed tends to make us drop potentially resilience-boosting behaviours and just suffer what we're going through. This contributes to the myth that resilience is merely endurance. It's well established from behavioural science that chronic stress makes us perseverative. This is laid out in the book *Behave* by Robert Sapolsky:

> These stress effects on frontal function also make us perseverative – in a rut, set in our ways, running on automatic, being habitual. We all know this – what do we typically do during a stressful time when something isn't working? The same thing again, many more times, faster and more intensely.[6]

As the famous quote goes: 'Insanity is doing the same thing over and over and expecting different results.'

This description coheres with what we've seen on the ground at Awaris, in our work with hundreds of teams – most of which were stressed. As stress increases, teams tend to adopt behaviours which make them even more stressed. They drop restorative ones which could make a big difference and repeat the very habits which are making them stressed in the first place. Unfortunately, this negatively impacts team performance, with the 'most stressed' or 'hardest-working' team members being praised for their efforts.

This is clearly the wrong way to think about resilience. Resilience isn't about endurance. It's about the ability to shift your state in response to stressors. But a further important part of resilience is being able to shift the external environment we're in, too. Changing the state we're exposed to is as important in being resilient. This can include simply saying 'No' to a task or getting out of the house and going for a walk.

Myth two – Resilience is a trait; some have it and some don't

In many companies we've worked with, we hear the same thing time and time again when we talk with employees about the leadership of the firm. 'Mrs X is naturally tough.' Or 'Mr Y is known for his ability to endure. He gets by on only five hours' sleep.' This perceived toughness is seen as a badge of strength, and as an immutable trait – and a desirable one for many businesses. There's often a feeling that workers might think 'Mrs X and Mr Y have these traits, the rest of us don't. And this is why these two are in positions of power, and we're not.'

But when we dig deeper, we usually find that this isn't quite the whole story. Liane had a telling conversation with a senior institutional leader recently in a virtual town hall, in front of the leader's team members. To the crowd, the leader described himself as 'someone who just happened to be tough'. And confessed that he 'probably wasn't a good example of someone who actively engages in resilience behaviours'. Liane quizzed him on this. After a long pause – and her continued prodding – he revealed that he did three things that helped him. First, he took time to breathe deeply during the day. Second, he made sure that he was home with his family for dinner daily (even if he had to work again afterwards). Third, he went to the gym a few times a week.

Smiling, Liane highlighted to him that he was actually engaging in three strong resilience behaviours: conscious breathing, social connection and movement and exercise. 'This is perhaps why you're as resilient as you are,' she said. He looked surprised. And then acknowledged that he didn't even realize that these were resilience behaviours. 'I've just kind of done them automatically for as long as I can remember.' The large number of people on the call also looked surprised. Having chatted with some of the firm's employees previously, Liane knew they'd always seen him as one of the naturally tough ones. So hearing that he did breathing exercises regularly to help with stress resonated with everyone.

While there are indeed inherited traits which impact resilience, this plays only a partial role in explaining someone's resilience. Some studies have shown that 40 per cent of the variance in a person's wellbeing comes from lifestyle and choices and 30 per cent comes from their genetics.[7] From working with more than 500 leaders, we've seen that their resilience usually reflects things they regularly do, often unconsciously, which shift their neurophysiological state. In other words, they engage in resilience skills.

Myth three – Resilience comes from our upbringing and is fixed

This third misunderstanding is at least based upon some kernels of truth – that a person's resilience is influenced by nature and nurture, with nature referring to an individual's genetic makeup from birth and nurture referring to their upbring and environment, including the workplace.

Clearly, there's a genetic component to resilience (nature). Some studies have identified certain genes that are associated with resilience, such as the brain-derived neurotrophic factor (BDNF) gene. This gene is involved in neuroplasticity and the development of new neurons in the brain.[8] However, like in almost all aspects of human psychology, genetics play only a partial role in determining an individual's resilience. Environmental factors also play a role (nurture). A supportive and nurturing childhood environment can help individuals develop resilience, while a stressful or traumatic one can hinder their development.

For many people, high levels of workplace stress can also hinder the development of their resilience. In contrast, we've seen many examples of how a supportive workplace culture, positive relationships with colleagues and opportunities for growth can all help individuals develop their resilience.

While nature and nurture both play a role in determining an individual's resilience, our view is that resilience is not a fixed trait. **Resilience can be developed and strengthened over time through intentional effort and practice.** Individuals can develop resilience through learning resilience skills and building a support network. Their genetics and upbringing don't need to determine their resilience outcomes permanently.

At this point, it's worth sharing something about our own resilience journeys. Liane had a difficult childhood, which included multiple instances of trauma. And so, her upbringing (nurture) didn't help her resilience. She instead had to train herself to be resilient, perhaps helped by the fact that her genes (nature) seemed to equip her with some of the facets of resilience. She was a naturally skilled and highly competitive athlete growing up. She's one of the people who takes easily to any form of meditation. And she's exceptionally emotionally astute and has more energy than most people 20 years younger than her. However, she also pushes herself too much at times, sometimes crashing.

Chris grew up in privileged surroundings. He can sleep standing against a wall, regenerates easily, and often feels relaxed, owing partially to his supportive upbringing (nurture). He's able to remain resilient through ongoing relaxation and recovery. However, Chris isn't tough naturally (nature), nor so naturally gifted at sports or meditation practices. While his nature was perhaps less naturally resilient than Liane's, his nurture didn't deal him any difficult cards. And he's since had to work hard at mind–body training and fine-tuning his emotional regulation, training his resilience skills to help him bounce back easily.

Both of us could today be described as highly resilient people, despite our very different natures and upbringings. This highlights two things. First, how important it is for us all to figure out our own resilience profiles, given how individual everyone's resilience profile is. Second, that we can work with our upbringings and natural dispositions; resilience isn't fixed.

Myth four – Resilience is someone else's responsibility

Another common misguided assumption is that resilience is someone else's responsibility. We've seen and heard this too many times to count in our work with businesses. The general themes in these conversations are outlined below:

- **Management:** 'Our staff must become more resilient, particularly the junior ones. I simply don't understand young people nowadays. They just don't seem tough. If I think back to my generation and how hard we had it back in the day, no wonder we're so much stronger than they are.'

- **Junior employees:** 'The workload is too high. It's just continual, one thing after another, with no respite. I've resigned myself to being stressed and unhappy while I work. Until the leaders of this organization change, nothing will. It's just one long grind.'

- **Human resources:** 'The employees are struggling. I'm having lots of conversations with those who are really stressed. Some are talking about leaving. They need help. I can't get management's attention on this, they aren't interested. It feels like there's nothing we can do.'

All these responses, while normally rooted in some degree of lived experience, offer an incomplete view of the picture. At Awaris, we see resilience as being everyone's and every department's responsibility. And so, our responses to the above, in conversations, town halls and many other situations, usually go something like this:

- **To management:** 'Resilience is a crucial skill that all people, teams and organizations need. Whether you think younger workers are less "tough" isn't relevant. The fact is that excessive work stress severely hampers resilience and team performance. Management needs to create the right conditions for resilience to develop in their teams – and this first means managers becoming consciously resilient themselves.'

- **To employees:** 'Stress is an ever-present part of life. You have no alternative but to cultivate your resilience skills. And this goes beyond the workplace. You're guaranteed to face stress in your private lives and continual change. They'll never go away. Indeed, these pressures are only likely to become more intense with the changes on the horizon for the world.'

- **To human resources:** 'We understand that your staff feel stressed. And that management will often resist change. But organizations need to be resilient. Workers need to be able to change their internal states from stressed to growing to regenerating to letting go [as we'll discuss more in the next chapter]. This will be a key hallmark of organizational culture in the decades ahead. One that will make a crucial difference for sustainable employee performance, engagement and retention. Just as HR departments have developed a deep understanding of how to build organizational skills, resilience will need to become a strength too. So, this is worth highlighting to management.'

Myth five – Resilience is too complex to be causally understood

Another misconception is that resilience is too complex to be completely understood. And part of this does make sense. After all, we're humans, who as individuals are already unfathomably complex. Making matters more confusing, we're embedded in highly complex social and organizational systems. And there is a potentially vast number of skills and methods which could be used to help us become more resilient. Because of this complexity, it's understandable that there are numerous models for resilience. And these models aren't exactly succinct.

Let's look at one such model. The American Psychological Association suggests '10 ways to build resilience':

1 Maintain good relationships with close family members, friends and others.
2 Avoid seeing crises or stressful events as unbearable problems.
3 Accept circumstances that cannot be changed.

4 Develop realistic goals and move towards them.

5 Take decisive actions in adverse situations.

6 Look for opportunities for self-discovery after a struggle with loss.

7 Develop self-confidence.

8 Keep a long-term perspective and consider the stressful event in a broader context.

9 Maintain a hopeful outlook, expecting good things and visualizing what is wished.

10 Take care of one's mind and body, exercising regularly, paying attention to one's own needs and feelings.[9]

Piece of cake, right? Perhaps not. Let's be honest. Most of us might struggle to implement *one* of the above suggestions, let alone all 10 of them at the same time. It's no wonder many are left with the feeling that resilience is simply too complex to be actionable.

That's not to say there's not some merit in the model. The goals it sets are admirable. What's also good is that it treats human resilience as a holistic topic, covering mind, body, relationships and outlook. However, this model (and many others) might leave people with more questions than answers. It, like other models, gives few clues as to how one might train towards reaching these goals, or how much time it would take for someone to do this.

There are literally dozens of such resilience models. They all share some or all of these deficiencies:

- They don't address all the relevant skills and mind–body systems.
- They don't clearly distinguish between the behavioural, psychological and physiological levels of interventions.
- They don't adequately explain causal mechanisms.
- They aren't statistically validated.
- They aren't actionable.

Although resilience is indeed complex, we still think it's possible for it to be causally understood, especially when we look at resilience skills. At Awaris, our resilience model focuses on the causal relationship between shifting our internal states and resilience. It highlights what mind–body skills should be addressed. The model is statistically validated and actionable. And it is much more specific than the rather vague 10-step programme mentioned earlier, which most people would struggle to follow as it's currently outlined.

Looking beyond resilience myths

Armed with a basic understanding of the five common resilience myths, and how they manifest themselves in modern workplaces, we can now look at what they can be replaced with. We believe we've developed an approach to building resilient business cultures which is effective, actionable and causal; that identifies the shifts individuals and teams need to focus on.

Being able to shift your state first requires an understanding of your physiological makeup – or your inner landscape, if you will. And this will be the focus of the next chapter.

KEY CHAPTER TAKEAWAYS

- Materials science and early research on resilience have coloured our understanding of resilience in the workplace.
- Resilience isn't about endurance. It's about being able to shift our internal states and our environment in response to the challenges we face.
- Resilient people are often precisely this because they engage in resilience behaviours, even if they don't realize it.
- Resilience is trainable at any age. The forces of nature and nurture need not define your resilience profile permanently.
- Resilience isn't someone else's responsibility. Resilience is the responsibility of every part of an organization.
- Resilience is multifaceted. We must understand it at the causal and trainable levels.

Notes

1   Dictionary.com, www.dictionary.com/browse/resilience (archived at https://perma.cc/8Z6E-DQB3)
2   S Gößling-Reisemann, H Dieter Hellige and P Their (2018) The resilience concept: from its historical roots to theoretical framework for critical infrastructure design, *ARTEC Forschungszentrum Nachhaltigkei*, **217** (June), https://media.suub.uni-bremen.de/bitstream/elib/4775/1/217_paper.pdf (archived at https://perma.cc/ML5J-86Y8)

3 S Gößling-Reisemann, H Dieter Hellige and P Their (2018) The resilience concept: from its historical roots to theoretical framework for critical infrastructure design, *ARTEC Forschungszentrum Nachhaltigkei*, **217** (June), https://media.suub.uni-bremen.de/bitstream/elib/4775/1/217_paper.pdf (archived at https://perma.cc/ML5J-86Y8)

4 B S McEwen (2017) Neurobiological and systemic effects of chronic stress, *Chronic Stress*, **1** (1), pp. 1–11, www.ncbi.nlm.nih.gov/pmc/articles/ PMC5573220/ (archived at https://perma.cc/WH5H-WDHW)

5 B van der Kolk (2014) *The Body Keeps the Score*, Penguin Random House, London; G Mate (1999) *Scattered Minds: The origins and healing of Attention Deficit Disorder*, Vermillion, London

6 R M Sapolsky (2017) *Behave: The biology of humans at our best and worst*, Penguin, London

7 J M McGinnis, P Williams-Russo and J R Knickman (2002) The case for more active policy attention to health promotion, *Health Affairs*, **21** (2), pp. 78–93, https://doi.org/10.1377/hlthaff.21.2.78 (archived at https://perma.cc/VC47-BJCG)

8 K Niitsu, M J Rice, J F Houfek, S F Stoltenberg, K A Kupzyk and C R Barron (2019) A systemic review of genetic influences on psychological resilience, *Biological Research for Nursing*, **21** (1), pp. 61–71, https://pubmed.ncbi.nlm.nih.gov/30223673/ (archived at https://perma.cc/7L5F-FA76)

9 American Psychological Association (2011) Building your resilience, www.apaservices.org/practice/good-practice/building-resilience.pdf (archived at https://perma.cc/QND5-E776)

2

Navigating our inner landscape

As human beings, we have learnt to respond to different situations. In situations where we had to fight or flee, we'd suddenly need to mobilize a lot of energy to ensure our survival. In contrast, other situations require less energy, for example sleeping or spending time in a familiar social group. Our bodies also respond differently depending on whether we're mobilizing this energy to avoid something negative or to work towards an expected reward.

We're primed to respond to most situations in generally automatic ways. This helps us respond to situations quicker and using less energy. Just imagine, for example, if you had to consciously move each individual muscle in your leg to run from an angry dog or a snake (you wouldn't get far). Or if you had to command your saliva to get going before you bit into a chocolate cake. If we had to do this, some of us might simply choose to keep drooling all the time. Ready at any moment for a chocolate cake, despite the social cost, rather than potentially missing out on it.

These automatic responses involve two important systems in the human body: our nervous (sympathetic/parasympathetic) and reward (mesolimbic) systems.[1] To truly understand resilience, one must understand both how these systems work and what we can do to impact them.

Our nervous system and arousal

The amount of activation or arousal in our body is governed by our stress system (the kind of arousal needed to escape menacing animals, that is). This functions primarily through our nervous system, and its connections to the brain and body. The **autonomic nervous system** (ANS), a branch of our central nervous system, plays an important role in translating an external stress trigger into a response. The ANS directly innervates tissue through the nerves. This is triggered through signals from the brain, either from direct stimuli or from our internal processing.

The ANS is composed of the parasympathetic nervous system and the sympathetic nervous system. These two branches have opposing effects on your physiological state. Learning how to navigate between them is a crucial step in building resilience.

The activity of the **sympathetic nervous system** drives what's called the 'fight or flight' response. The fight or flight response to stress involves an increased heart rate and breathing, and the release of energy into our blood system.[2] Cortisol and adrenaline are released into the blood, priming us for action. This is usually referred to as allostasis, an adaptive response to external challenges, allowing our bodies to maintain stability through change. While certain bodily systems are activated, others are deactivated, to save energy during stressful events. These include digestion, regeneration and aspects of immune system function.

The **parasympathetic nervous system**, or 'rest and digest' response, regulates recovery and rest. It involves a slowing heart rate and deeper breathing. It includes increased activity in the digestive and immune systems, as well as general healing processes.[3] The parasympathetic nervous response helps us maintain homeostasis, the state of balance among all the bodily systems needed for the body to survive and function correctly in the long term. Specifically, in slowing down the heart rate, decreasing blood pressure and activating digestive processes, the parasympathetic nervous system helps in the conservation and restoration of energy. By managing these functions, the parasympathetic nervous system ensures that the body's internal environment remains stable and functions efficiently during calm and non-stressful conditions.

The parasympathetic nervous system ensures a return to homeostasis. It thus conserves and restores energy, after a threat's been warded off (barking dog), or after energy has been expended for a reward (converting the chocolate cake to energy). Returning to balance also includes reconnecting to our social group. Our relations with family, friends and acquaintances are just as important for our survival. And so, the meaning of homeostasis can be extended to include our social systems. It can be said that our survival depends on us tending to our energy, bodies and social bonds. Crucially, being resilient must show up at this deep physiological level, via our ability to regulate our inner states to adapt to stress (allostasis) and re-establish the homeostasis of our systems.

FIGURE 2.1 Stress is not always bad: low stress, eustress and distress

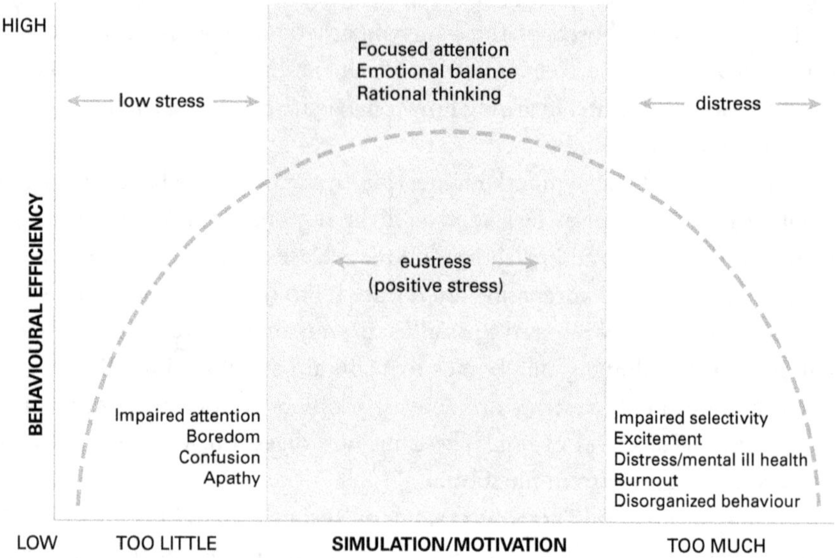

SOURCE Yerkes-Dodson model[4]

Stress, eustress and distress

While our stress wiring is designed for fight or flight situations, and is a little archaic, it's still relevant in our everyday life. Stress can increase our ability to perform well in numerous ways, and so isn't always bad. We speak of 'eustress' when stress is at the right dosage.[5] In contrast, too much stress or stress over a prolonged period is called 'distress'. Distress is bad. It blocks us from engaging in homeostatic activities and from returning to physical, mental and social balance. Too much time in distress can have numerous associated negative health, cognitive and social impacts.

Figure 2.1 highlights how the balance of stress works in practice.

Human emotions, the mesolimbic system and valence

The stress system isn't the only one which impacts our resilience. We also experience a range of emotions – automatic responses – which fundamentally encourage us to move towards or away from something. We can classify emotions as positive and negative. The term used to describe this is the **valence of the emotions.**[6]

Emotions are also rooted in our physiological energy systems. They motivate us and coordinate the many systems in our body towards either getting a goal (the next piece of chocolate cake) or avoiding something (the fifth piece of chocolate cake). As such, they're also deeply connected to the body's energy balance. In fact, some neuroscientists have gone as far as to say that emotions are nothing more than expressions of our body's energy budget and the situations we face. When faced with a situation, our brain assesses millions of pieces of data, from inside and outside the body. Within the body, the brain processes your metabolic rate, heart rate, temperature, muscle tension and state of the digestive system, among many other things. From outside the body, the brain assesses the degree of the challenge faced and amount of energy required to deal with it.[7]

From the combination of these two vast sources of information and our previous lifetime experience, the brain makes predictions and readies our body and mind to respond both to the energy demand of the situation (partially indicated by our nervous system arousal) and to the expected reward of the situation (the emotional valence of the situation). We might find ourselves happy, excited, tense, sleepy, gloomy or angry. These emotions represent responses to the situation we face and the current energy budget of our body.

You can test this prediction system on yourself with the following simple experiment:

- On a day when you feel full of energy and positive, scan your email inbox and tune into your bodily response. Look for an email from someone which will likely represent a challenge. Do this without reading the whole email. Allow your brain to unconsciously predict what will happen. See how your body responds. How does your breathing, heart rate and general feeling within the body change?

- On a day when you're tired or stressed, scan your email inbox. Tune into your bodily response when you see a similar email. Again, don't read the email itself – just notice your body's prediction and reaction to it. How do you feel? What's happening inside the body? What thoughts do you have?

Thus, we see that emotional responses aren't fixed – they depend on what state we're in. In the first scenario, you might have noticed that the email didn't elicit a strong reaction. The mind predicted that you'd be able to respond easily to the email and deal with it effectively. There was likely no major change to how your body felt or the state of arousal that was activated to deal with the situation.

In the second example, however, the response might have been different. The mind, sensing you had less energy, could have felt that the energy available might not be enough to deal with this situation, and started worrying. 'Have I done something wrong? Have I made a mistake? I'm so busy, I don't have the time to deal with this.' And then the body might have responded with an increased heart rate, shallower breathing and feelings of anxiety. Or, alternatively, it might have tried to marshal more energy and increase arousal.

In other words, our emotions have a profound impact on our mind and bodies. Which emotions we experience is dependent on the **valence** (expected energy gain or loss) and the degree of **arousal** (stress activation or energy cost) of a situation. The assessment of the valence of emotions involves our mesolimbic pathway. The mesolimbic pathway, also called the reward pathway, is a dopaminergic pathway in the brain.

Scientists have studied emotions for many years and have come up with a way of classifying them, called the circumplex model of emotions.[8] It maps emotions according to their degree of valence and arousal (see Figure 2.2).

FIGURE 2.2 Map of our inner landscape and the circumplex model

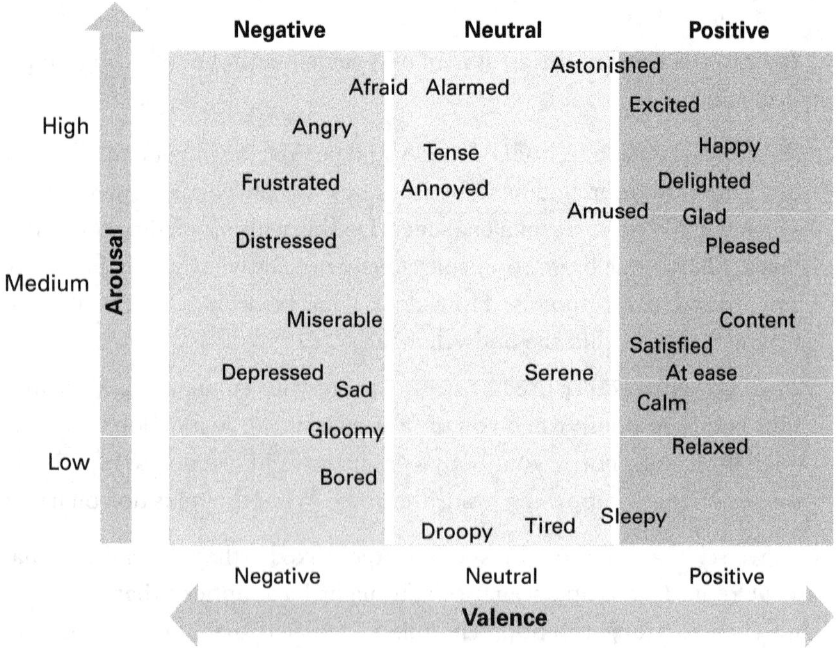

SOURCE Adapted from the circumplex model

FIGURE 2.3 Calm, eustress and distress on the map of our inner experience

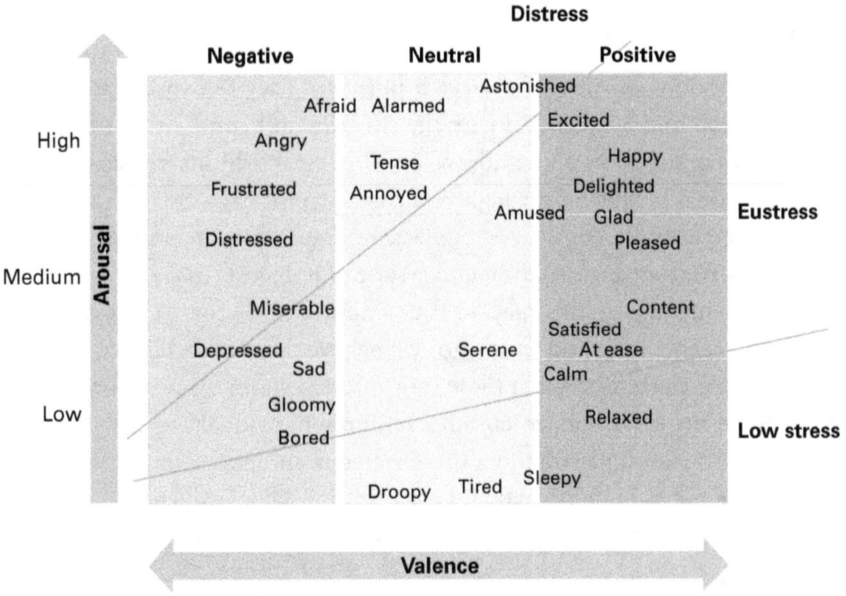

SOURCE Adapted from the circumplex model

We can combine this map of emotions with the model of eustress and distress mentioned earlier. It creates Figure 2.3, which outlines the emotions we typically experience in three different states: low stress (calm), eustress and distress.

There are some key takeaways from the map of our internal states:

- First, the line separating eustress and distress is slanted upwards to the right. This is because when we're expecting a reward, a higher amount of arousal doesn't necessarily cause distress. Think of looking forward to a squash game or feeling excited about going on vacation. This means the eustress region gets wider as your state becomes more positive.

- Second, negative valence states tend to be in the distress zone – this part of the map represents both high arousal (energy activation) and low expected reward. So, this isn't a state we want to spend too much time in. For that reason, it's a negative stress state.

- Third, low energy negative states like sadness or boredom aren't necessarily distress. They are important. Temporarily withdrawing from an activity or our engagements is sometimes necessary for reflection and introspection. We learn and recover in this state. This is something that's underappreciated, particularly when thinking about resilience. We'll look at this in more detail below.

All the emotions on this map serve a purpose. They're expressions of the state we're in and help us deal with the situation at hand – either to quickly respond to a situation or withdraw, or to re-establish our physical, social and emotional wellbeing through homeostatic processes. So even anger or fear, while generally considered unpleasant emotions, can provide us with the energy to change a situation and return to homeostasis.

We can summarize this map in four important internal states: stressed, growing, regenerating and letting go. We believe that true resilience requires us to be able to shift between these four internal states. As a starting point, creating resilient workplace cultures requires individuals to get better at doing so. And so, understanding these states is an important first step that needs to be taken in individual and organization-wide resilience journeys.

We can summarize these four internal states, shown in Figure 2.4, below:

- **Stressed** – High arousal and negative valence. This is a common state in modern workplaces. High arousal is often due to task urgency, complexity or high workloads, combined with some kind of threat or potential perceived loss. This is increasingly likely to be experienced regularly as part of working life, especially in negative environments, with high-urgency tasks, or tasks with high risks or costs associated with them. This is valid for a short period of time, but not healthy for a long period. It's not useful for people to get stuck in this state – they'd expend energy with insufficient reward. Getting stuck in the stress zone for too long is where the symptoms of chronic stress show up. Being stressed is a state of intensity, and high performance for a brief period of time and high energy use.

- **Growing** – High arousal and positive valence. An expected reward activates us. We're more likely to learn, grow and perform well in this state. We're expending energy for some future benefit, and so this still involves a short-term homeostatic imbalance. This is a state of learning, with heightened intensity but also with an expected reward. Equally, it could be mapped to what's commonly called 'thriving'. This is naturally an ideal state to be in. But because it's still high energy, the energy cost outweighs the rewards after a while, even with positive valance. In this case, we'd move into a stressed state.

FIGURE 2.4 Shifting between the four states is vital for resilience

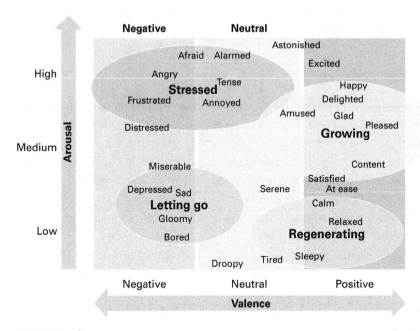

SOURCE Awaris

- **Regenerating** – Low arousal and positive valence. We feel safe, we can relate to others in a calm way, and thus can regenerate and gather energy or strengthen social bonds. This is an important zone, one where we are recuperating energy, healing and strengthening connections. It most closely resembles a zone of wellbeing.

- **Letting go** – Low arousal and negative valence. A perceived threat or loss is present, and it's time to let go, unlearn and withdraw. This can be an important state to shift into as part of being resilient. In today's world, we forget about the importance of letting go, letting be and not acting. Homeostasis also involves getting rid of unwanted things from our system, and this is what being in this state helps us do.

Business reality and shifting between the four states

Let's look at these states from a point of view of business performance, and especially with a view of neuroplasticity and learning. In the modern workplace, being able to learn and adapt is a crucial aspect of success – many businesses compete on the rate of learning. Individual employees also need to be able to learn and adapt. Our ability to learn and grow is the basis for us being able to function well and succeed.

Stressed

There will always be tasks with high urgency, complexity or load. We need to bring high energy and focus to these tasks. These are moments of high performance. So, it's necessary for us to be stressed for a brief period in order to perform well at these tasks. High arousal in this state can also promote learning. However, precisely because of this high arousal, individuals are more likely to learn avoidance or self-centred survival behaviours. The brain is wired to remember threats for survival purposes and to automate future responses based on this.

We saw in our exercise in Chapter 1 how easily people fall into non-conscious, narrow-perspective and stressed states. In addition, prolonged states of negative high arousal can be detrimental to brain health and impede learning. So, overall, in today's economy, which so emphasizes learning and adaptability, we don't want to spend too much time in this state.

Growing

This state is increasingly important in the modern knowledge economy, as it's conducive to both task engagement and learning. The high arousal of the nervous system can amplify the encoding of memories, especially when associated with positive outcomes. Positive emotions such as curiosity and excitement can motivate exploration and interest, and can enhance information retention. It's not hard to see how being in such a state would be beneficial in a workplace setting (as opposed to being too stressed or disengaged).

The anticipation of reward boosts dopamine associated with motivation and learning. It also strengthens pro-social behaviours. This is wired into our evolutionary make-up. When we do something with a positive outcome, we'd do well to remember it, so we can repeat it often.

Regenerating

There's been an increasing recognition that time for regeneration is important for health. But it's also important for learning. Learning in this state can be subtle and more prolonged. This includes reflection, consolidation and the integration of previously acquired information. This can also include calm states, such as those during mindfulness practices or deep reading. Both can enhance learning through focused attention and reduced distraction. And naturally, in sleep, when we're completely at rest, there's deep learning as information from short-term memory is encoded into long-term learning.

To avoid burnout at work, as a key component of resilience, there's perhaps no more important state than regenerating.

Letting go

This state isn't optimal for performance or new learning. A low-energy, negative state, such as feelings of depression or apathy, can decrease motivation and attention. This makes it harder to acquire or retain new information. However, letting go can be beneficial if seen as a time of active unlearning, of letting go of behaviours and activities which no longer serve us. This is a blind spot for many people and companies. They're often loath to let go of products, processes, key performance indicators (KPIs) or behaviours. However, letting go is necessary for learning. It is also a healthy part of the cycle of resilience.

Seeing how these neurophysiological states impact both performance and learning underpins how important it is to not get stuck in one state for too long, but to be able to navigate through all of them. While being in the stressed zone is necessary at times for performance, being there all the time is suboptimal – for performance, learning and health outcomes. Growth, which has many positives, also can't be maintained permanently. A growth mindset, which emerges from the inner state of growing, is one of the four natural zones in life, but also comes with a higher energy cost. It must be balanced with sufficient regeneration and times of letting go. And equally, just being in the regeneration or the letting go zones won't be sufficient if we want to perform and learn. These zones need to be balanced by times of heightened activation.

All four zones are responses to our external challenges. The more we can navigate through these zones, the more we'll be able to respond well to challenges and become more resilient in the workplace.

The natural patterns of life and work

These four states are experienced as part of working life. It's normal to cycle through them (see Figure 2.5). You regenerate during a good break or

FIGURE 2.5 Natural cycles of stressed, growing, regenerating and letting go

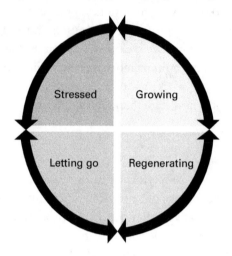

SOURCE Awaris

when you sleep (if you get enough). You let go after a project which doesn't go well – you might struggle with it for a while, but eventually you accept the outcome and let go. At times you need to be stressed – highly activated and alert to ensure that a complex or urgent task gets done in a timely manner. The stress gives you impetus to hit the deadline. And there are times when you're fully absorbed in a rewarding task or project, and feel you're learning and growing.

Nature goes through similar seasons of spring, summer, autumn and winter. Just as cycling through the seasons is natural, so our own cycling through the states is natural, and an expression of resilience. Problems occur when you get stuck in one state or have difficulty navigating through the states.

Too many workers are stuck in the stressed zone

Unfortunately, most people don't have the ability to shift readily between these states. It makes it impossible for them to be resilient. Over the past 10 years, we've worked closely with our partner Firstbeat to undertake stress assessments with our clients. We've used this physiological data for more than 20 companies and over 2,000 participants. Working with this data, we've helped participants identify several unhealthy pathways or patterns.

And in doing so, we have pinpointed what they need to do to strengthen their resilience skills.

Our most notable finding is that too many workers get stuck in a stressed or distressed state, or spend a high percentage of time in this state. With the Firstbeat assessments, we've regularly seen people who spend 70–80 per cent of a typical day in this state. This has several main consequences, and – spoiler alert – few are good:

- **Being stressed weighs on health and bodily resources.** A high stress state is where we consume resources and aren't recovering. This leads to a deterioration of bodily resources. Firstbeat works with many of the leading football teams (including Arsenal, Manchester City, Liverpool, Bayern Munich and Werder Bremen) and Olympic teams in multiple disciplines, all over the world. Working with over 100,000 people annually, they've amassed an incredible depth of data. This data clearly documents the decline in bodily resources which accompanies prolonged time in stress activation. Liane has worked with people who for months had this pattern in the workplace. It was as if she was seeing them age before her eyes, as ongoing stress hampered the necessary daily regeneration processes.

FIGURE 2.6 Narrowing the window of tolerance through excessive stress

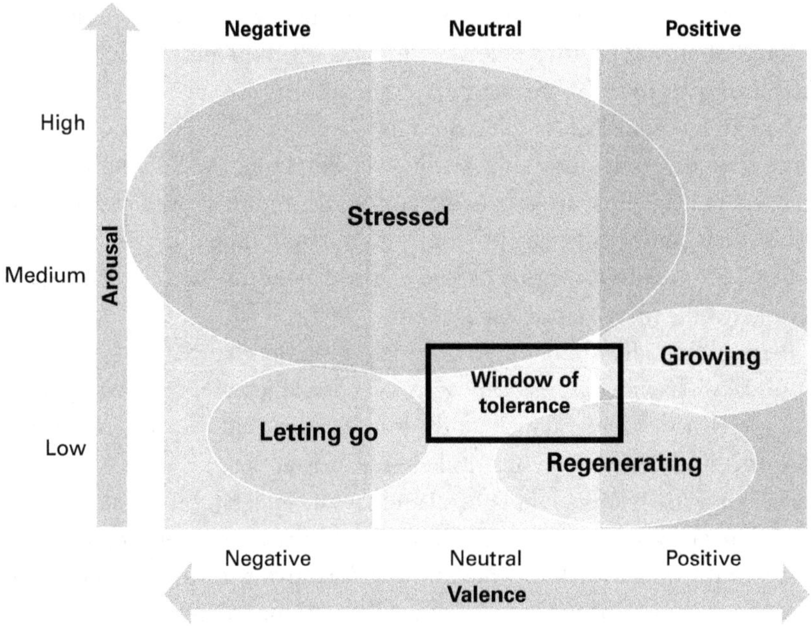

SOURCE Awaris

- **The ongoing state of distress has negative mental and social consequences.** Our mental state and our social connections can suffer too. This last point is often massively underreported – but if you ask many highly stressed people, or even busy highly successful people, they lose their friends or their time with friends first. So, distress has a high physical, mental and social cost.

- **Getting stuck in distress ends up narrowing our 'window of tolerance'.** [9] The window of tolerance is the region in which we function well and can regulate our state. In Figure 2.6, we see that the window of tolerance gets narrower if the stress zone is larger. In such a scenario, individuals are more likely to get stuck in distress, or respond to situations that normally would not require a stress response with a high degree of arousal.

Overstimulation and exhaustion

A recent trip to China highlighted some of the challenges faced by individuals continually under pressure. While in Suzhou at a business school, Chris was leading a session on balancing performance and care for people in business. He had a conversation with a smart and analytical person in a break between sessions. The man told Chris he had a lot on his plate. To cope, he said, 'I play at least two hours of video games per day when I get home. It's a source of strong positive emotions for me – a dopamine rush, I guess – which I only seem to get through video games.'

'You aren't alone,' Chris said. 'But this is a wider issue. For you, it's video games. For others it's drinking alcohol or watching TV. But the theme is often the same. People are too stressed at work, and then need to find ways to shift their state – either by other arousal or by zoning out.'

'Oh, I see,' said the worker. 'I know friends who use alcohol, so I guess playing video games isn't as bad.'

'Perhaps not. However, you're missing out on the chance to engage in the full range of learning states, removing the chance for you to learn to relax, or to socialize or reflect. Which, in the long term, would help you regenerate more effectively, boosting your resilience,' Chris added.

The young man looked thoughtful and said he understood. He said he was 'looking for new ways to get social time and other forms of regeneration. But I know that gaming works for me for now. And giving it up all at once could make my stress levels even worse without something to replace it.'

They shook hands, and Chris wished him all the best, knowing his problems certainly weren't unique. Like this young man, many people in the modern working world cycle between high arousal states (work stress followed by excitement) and 'zombie-ing out'. This could be by playing video games, self-medicating with alcohol or watching mindless trashy television. Often, people who behave in this way might not experience a healthy balance of zones. They don't spend time in the growing zone. The arousal level in the excitement zone is too high for proper learning, digesting or any conscious regeneration. Thus, they're in danger of not learning and growing. They use these crutches as coping mechanisms, to get some semblance of balance in their lives.

Later that day, Chris reflected. He'd heard stories like this time and time again. It reminded him that so many of us are fundamentally overstimulated. We're addicted to stimulation, in some ways. And indeed, Chris knew that he was no exception. For him, there are two things he notices when he's tired, and when he's been overstimulated for too long. First, he reaches for his phone a lot, looking for something, anything, to distract him. Second, when he *really* stops, he notices how tired he is. He notices that he's actually using the stimulation from the phone as a way of keeping himself awake.

A few days later in Shanghai, Chris observed the following scene. He went alone to have dinner at a local restaurant, with delicious-smelling noodle specialities. From what he could see, he was the only foreign person in the restaurant. Once he'd managed to communicate his desire to eat (which wasn't easy given his lack of Chinese), he sat down. He then figured out how to use the QR code to open the menu and order the food he wanted. He began to settle and look around.

In front of him, there were three other tables, all full. One table had two parents and a 10-year-old. Another table had four adults, all in their mid-thirties. And another table had three people, two in middle age and a young adult. On each table, **every single person was on their mobile phone.** They were consuming stimulus while they (absent-mindedly) consumed their food. Chris remembers thinking that they surely can't have been paying any attention to the flavours of the delicious food that they were eating.

The next day, Chris boarded a domestic flight to Taiyuan. As he walked down the aisle, most of the other passengers were already sitting in their seats. Pretty much everyone – at least 80 per cent of them – were on their mobile phones. Chris sat down. Shortly after this, the captain asked people to turn off their mobile devices. Within five minutes, most people on the plane were asleep. Once they stopped stimulating themselves, their tiredness took over and they collapsed. Their lack of true regeneration time became apparent. They were cycling from stressed to exhaustion and back again. Weibo, sleep, repeat, perhaps.

The only ones who stayed alert were the people aged over 65, who didn't seem to have this addiction to stimulus and the associated exhaustion. A win for the luddites.

An emerging 'chilled' generation?

As a response to the ongoing high stress in our societies, there is a small cadre of people who are focusing on remaining chilled. Prioritizing their wellbeing. Being 'chilled' (likely their emphasis, particularly if they're from California) is a low arousal positive state. It's one which is good for healing, and most closely resembles regeneration. But it's not a state where we learn from new experiences, or rise to challenges, or deal with difficult issues we might be facing. There are real challenges in life. There are times to be careful, or even to be angry, and to respond to negative consequences.

Focusing on being 'chilled' is perhaps a sensible response to heightened negativity and stress. But it's not a balanced state. And in the workplace, if someone's boss asks them to meet an upcoming deadline, and they respond by simply 'chilling' and miss it, their career progress will likely be chilled, too.

However, on the more positive side of things, a new emphasis on work–life balance and wellbeing from many young employees is a good thing. It's an expression of the rejection of getting stuck in the stress zone, a zone of ongoing high arousal with low reward or fulfilment.

The 'bore out', 'burnout' or 'lie flat' generation

There is a particular phenomenon in China called the 'lie flat' generation (躺平, táng píng). This refers to a social phenomenon whereby young people choose to opt out of highly competitive and demanding societal norms. The concept of 'lying flat' involves a minimalist approach to life, rejecting the rat race and embracing a lifestyle with fewer desires and ambitions.

Chinese culture has traditionally placed a high value on hard work, competition and achievement. However, this has led to high levels of stress, burnout and a perceived lack of fulfilment, despite the pursuit of success. The 'lie flat' movement can be seen as a counter-response to this environment, a natural response to too much time spent in high stress negative valence, where individuals choose to disengage from societal pressure to constantly strive and achieve. It's different from the 'chilled' movement since it's connected less to positive reward. It's almost as if a generation of people perceive themselves to have no access to positive reward (regeneration or growth), and they're stuck in the low arousal negative valence zone of letting go.

Parallels can be found in other societies as well. Japan has a similar phenomenon known as 'hikikomori'. Here, individuals withdraw from social life, often staying in their homes for extended periods. While different in its expression, it similarly arises from societal pressures, high expectations and the stress of conforming to rigid societal norms.

In South Korea, the intense pressure for academic and professional success has led to high levels of stress and mental health issues among the youth. The concept of 'Hell Joseon' has emerged (Joseon is a pejorative term used to describe the fall of the Joseon dynasty, which fell before Korea was formed). The term is a critique of the highly competitive and pressurized workplace and societal conditions in Korea. This is what happens when workers and even societies are stuck in the stressed state for too long.

Resilience: the ability to cycle through states

So, we now should have clarity about what we mean by resilience. Resilience isn't the ability to endure high stress states or to tough it out. It isn't only regeneration. It isn't avoiding low energy negative states and always being positive. Resilience isn't wellbeing, or always trying to return to a state of low stress.

Resilience is the fundamental ability to shift between states (see Figure 2.7). Being able to adapt to situations. Having a healthy balance of responding to external situations. Being activated sometimes, even being stressed sometimes. But, crucially, being able to return to learning and regeneration states when needed. It is the ability to shift from stressed to growing to regenerating to letting go.

FIGURE 2.7   Resilience: being able to shift through states

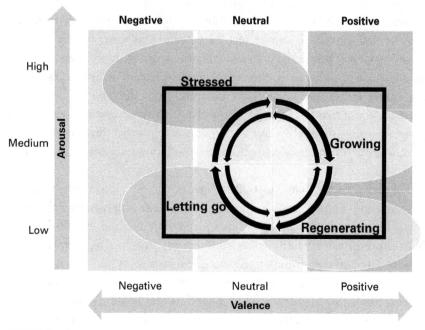

SOURCE Awaris
A broad window of tolerance allows for self-regulation.

Someone who has a high degree of resilience skills can remain within their window of tolerance (or they can have a wide window of tolerance, the zone in which they can self-regulate). On a daily or weekly basis, perhaps, they can circulate through these zones of their inner experience. In being resilient, they can move consciously through these states, as required by the external situation they find themselves in.

There are also times when other pathways are healthy and necessary for resilience. When someone's been stuck in the stressed state for too long, we've observed that it's not possible for them to go directly from stressed to growing, or to easily circulate between the states. They've been pushed out of their own window of tolerance. Their own resources are too depleted. Instead, they need to cycle through letting go and regenerating first, before entering the growing phase. This is natural, like the seasons.

In sum, resilience demands we learn to cycle between stressed, letting go, regenerating and learning. Not just for the individual, but at the 'we' level, we need to be able to move through these zones. The ability to shift states is needed

FIGURE 2.8 Learning to let go and regenerate is needed to restore balance

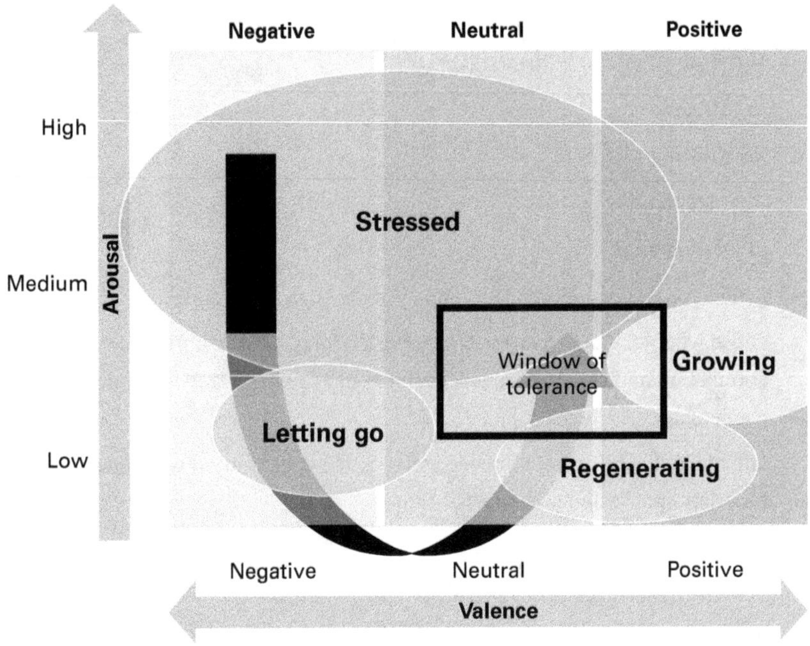

A form of the U Process can be necessary for getting back into our window of tolerance.

at the organization-wide level to build resilient cultures. Those who can't do this will get stuck in certain states. This can include crises: situations where businesses must go through some form of U Process[10] – letting go of people, processes, demands or resources before the new can emerge (see Figure 2.8).

With this in mind, the next chapter outlines 12 key resilience skills which can help individuals cycle through these states, and which can extend to entire organizations.

KEY CHAPTER TAKEAWAYS

- The amount of arousal in our bodies is governed by our stress systems. The parasympathetic nervous system drives a 'fight or flight' response, the sympathetic nervous system a 'rest and digest' response.

- Emotions are rooted in homeostasis, an attempt to restore the body's energy balance. Whether these emotions are positive or negative is described as the valence of these emotions.

- Understanding the valance and intensity of an emotional state is a crucial first step in being able to shift your state, and thus becoming more resilient.
- There are four core human states:
  a. stressed
  b. growing
  c. regenerating
  d. letting go
- Resilience is the ability to shift and cycle through these states.
- Those who get stuck in stress states for too long, or cycle through stimulation and exhaustion, will perform sub-optimally and will find life challenging.
- The ability to shift through these states at the organization-wide level is the foundation of resilient business cultures.

Notes

1 A Alcaro, R Huber and J Panksepp (2007) Behavioral functions of the mesolimbic dopaminergic system: an affective neuroethological perspective, *Developmental Brain Research*, **56** (2), pp. 283–321, https://doi.org/10.1016/j.brainresrev.2007.07.014 (archived at https://perma.cc/4FPR-NGLL)

2 D Padgett and R Glaser (2003) How stress influences the immune response, *Trends in Immunology*, **24** (8), pp. 444–8, https://doi.org/10.1016/S1471-4906(03)00173-X (archived at https://perma.cc/PR8E-QK69)

3 J N Langley (1921) *The Autonomic Nervous System*, W Heffer and Sons, Cambridge

4 R M Yerkes and J D Dodson (1908) The relationship of strength of stimulus to rapidity of habit formation, *Journal of Comparative Neurology and Psychology*, **18**, pp. 459–82, https://doi.org/10.1002/cne.920180503 (archived at https://perma.cc/PQF7-U2JJ). While the Yerkes-Dodson model provides a foundational understanding of the relationship between stress and performance, modern research advocates for more nuanced and individualized approaches to optimizing performance through stress management and emotional regulation. See, for example, E J Calbrese (2008) Stress biology and hormesis: the Yerkes-Dodson law in psychology: a special case of the hormesis dose response, *Critical Reviews in Toxicology*, **385** (5), pp. 453–62, https://doi.org/10.1080/10408440802004007 (archived at https://perma.cc/6UKE-44Q4)

5 A M Rossi, P L Perrewé and S L Sauter (2006) *Eustress and Hope at Work: Accentuating the positive, in stress and quality of working life: current perspectives in occupational health*, Information Age Publishing, Greenwich, CT

6 N H Frijda (1986) *The Emotions*, Cambridge University Press, Cambridge

7 L Feldman Barrett (2017) *How Emotions Are Made: The secret life of the brain*, Macmillan, London

8 J A Russell (1980) A circumplex model of affect, *Journal of Personality and Social Psychology*, **39** (6), pp. 1161–78, https://doi.org/10.1037/h0077714 (archived at https://perma.cc/GEE6-VGRY). Also see J Posner, J A Russell and B S Peterson (2008) The circumplex model of affect: an integrative approach to affective neuroscience, cognitive development, and psychopathology, *Development and Psychopathology*, **17** (3), pp. 715–34, https://doi.org/10.1017/S0954579405050340 (archived at https://perma.cc/3AAK-M652)

9 D Siegel (2020 *The Developing Mind: How relationships and the brain interact to shape who we are*, Guildford Press, New York, NY

10 'Theory U', also known as the 'U Process', is a change management method and the title of a book by Otto Scharmer. Scharmer, together with colleagues at the Massachusetts Institute of Technology (MIT), conducted 150 interviews with entrepreneurs and innovators in science, business and society. They then extended the basic principles into a theory of learning and management, called Theory U. See Society for Organizational Learning (2007) *Theory U: Leading from the future as it emerges*, https://fosterwhatmatters.com/wp-content/uploads/2012/07/Theory_U_2page-Overview-.pdf (archived at https://perma.cc/B5YC-LNVT)

3

12 key resilience skills

We've dispelled some enduring resilience myths and we have made it clear that resilience isn't about endurance. It isn't some mysterious, mystical state of being. Instead, resilience arises when we learn to regulate the intensity of stress activation and the valence of that activation in our work and lives. We are resilient when we can regularly shift through the four physiological zones of life: stressed, growing, regenerating and letting go.

Being able to shift our state is a skill – or, more accurately, a series of skills. When we speak about skills, we refer to **specific learnt behaviours or actions that individuals can perform with a degree of proficiency.** They're often acquired through training, practice or life experience. Skills are typically measurable and observable, and individuals exhibit different degrees of proficiency in them. Examples of skills include programming, public speaking, project management, operating machinery or being able to complete a Rubik's cube in 10 seconds (despite our admiration for this skill, we're not sure this is the most relevant to learn). Skills are often categorized into different types, such as technical skills, soft skills or transferable skills.

This view of skills fits well with our experiences as long-term meditation practitioners. In effect, mindfulness encompasses many skills, among them skills in attention regulation. When Liane and Chris began practising (too many years ago to mention without feeling very old indeed), we weren't particularly good it at. We'd try to focus on our breath. But almost immediately – perhaps after a few seconds – we'd get distracted by a mundane thought, such as what we'd be having for breakfast, or other thoughts too boring or not suitable to publish in print. We'd completely forget that we were supposed to be following the breath.

We'd nobly strengthen our resolve to follow the breath again, vowing never to let the mind wander again. And yet, before we'd even finished this internal vow, the mind had done its own thing again. We'd be thinking about lunch later or start formulating an alternative response to a letter we sent weeks ago (no, not an email: we're old – or wise – enough to remember the pre-email world).

However, with daily practice, over weeks, months, years and decades even (dare we say it), we've become more proficient. Mind wandering still occurs, but much less frequently. As our skills of meditation and attention grew, over the years we've also developed a deeper sense of how our bodies and minds are interrelated. Just as scientists do in the lab, we've observed our inner states, our stress arousal, the valence of our emotions and our energy budgets. Through practice, we've noticed how these states influence our behaviours deeply, and how our behaviours in turn influence them.

Put simply, mindfulness practice is a skill like any other, which you can master over time. It's a set of skills that impacts the body and mind, which can help us become more resilient. We'll write more about mindfulness later.

We believe a skill-based approach to resilience has several advantages:

- Skills can be assessed and trained.
- We can see which skills are widely distributed among employees and where there are gaps, and also understand which skills have the most impact on outcomes.
- Skills are easier to define and target. In the ill-defined view of resilience as endurance, there's no realistic way to judge whether someone could handle a challenge or not, other than to hope they can just grin and bear suffering.
- We can also realistically acknowledge the limits of skills. While someone can exercise regularly, contributing to their resilience, it doesn't automatically mean they can run a marathon. In the world of skills, we have a reasonable sense of their limits.

Towards a fuller understanding of resilience skills

Awaris has worked with 250 businesses and trained 50,000 employees since it was founded in 2012. Which, having trained many of them personally, we can attest is *a lot* of people. We've spent the last two years in particular digging into the science of resilience. As part of this, we've collected data from over 2,000 people, 150 teams and 30 organizations on resilience.

From the outset, it was clear we needed to understand how skills show up at the physiological level – how skills impact our landscape of arousal and valence, and what skills in turn affect this. This, interestingly enough, is now the same approach scientists in the lab are taking to understand resilience. Several recent papers have attempted to explore the neurophysiological, the neurochemical and even the genetic levels of resilience.[1]

To develop a systematic understanding of resilience skills, we considered the existing literature, as well as our own experience helping organizations become more resilient. Several clues guided our research:

- **Skills, not states:** We see resilience as a series of trainable skills, allowing us to shift our state. Thus, we were looking to identify skills, not states like wellbeing, and to understand which interventions could help train these skills.

- **Looking for physiological impact:** We're biophysiological beings. Our bodies have 30 trillion cells, and we need to regenerate around 200–400 billion cells daily. This ongoing healing process is central to being resilient, and our resilience skills had to support this process. So, for each resilience skill, we checked whether it had a measurable impact on our biophysiology, impacting us on a cellular level. We knew we had to identify skills that affected our homeostasis (the balance between our bodily systems); that moved us around the map of our experience; and that impacted our stress arousal levels and the valance of our experience, as we've explained in the previous chapters.

- **Skills can be trained at three levels:** Skills are broad. They can be trained at the behavioural, psychological or physiological levels. A neurochemical level also exists, but it is hard to train directly (see Figure 3.1).

Let's explain simply. We can **behave** differently (behavioural level), and this impacts our response to stimuli and our internal state – for example by going to sleep earlier. We can also **think** differently (psychological level), which can also impact our response to stimuli and our bodies on deep levels. And as we get more skilled at internal regulation, we can apply interventions that directly target the **nervous system** ((neuro)physiological level). Finally, advanced meditators are known to be able to directly impact their own **hormone levels** and their flow in the body (neurochemical level). Locating these skill levels has helped us understand how different resilience interventions work, as well as assessing their effectiveness on our biophysiology.

FIGURE 3.1 Resilience skills can be trained at four levels

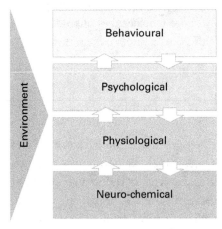

Behavioural – How we behave and act, our observable activity and our aggregate responses to internal and external stimuli.

Psychological – Our approach to an issue, perceptions, feelings, thoughts and motivations arising from and driving responses to internal and external stimuli.

(Neuro)physiological – Our physiological and nervous system response to stimuli and behaviour.

Neuro-chemical –The flow of hormones and regulatory processes in the nervous system and body.

SOURCE Adapted from Wu et al (2013)[2]
All impacted by our environment – the stresses and strains we live with.

To understand how we can train skills at different levels, it is time for an example. Someone, let's call him Mark, struggles with ongoing anxiety. He has an excessive workload and Zoom fatigue. He isn't getting enough sleep. He spends most of his day at work looking at screens. And when he gets home, he spends a few more hours looking at screens, filled mainly with close-up pictures of friends' and strangers' faces on social media, while getting his dopamine and attention systems hijacked.[3]

One day at work, Mark receives a rude email. Angry and stressed, he almost sends back a nasty response. But before he presses send, he stops. He takes a breath to calm himself. He simply notices and accepts his thinking processes, tiredness and frustration – and, eventually, realizes it'd be unwise to respond angrily. He resolves to sleep on it and reply in the morning when he's calmed down. He's exhibited the skill of emotional regulation, in part through breathing exercises.

This is a form of emotional regulation, one of many resilience skills. But such a form of regulation could look different for different people:

- One person might find they feel better after a brisk 15-minute walk.

- A second person might shift their perspective to calm down. They remember the person who emailed them has just lost their mother and is going through a tough time. They realize it's not about them.

- A third person, like Mark, might apply breathing exercises and mindfulness practices.

- A fourth person could drink an alcoholic drink to calm down. It works at the time, but they feel hungover the next day. Plus, as they drink another glass of wine, and then another, they start to wonder whether they should send an angry email response after all – to give this boss a piece of their mind.

The first three examples are resilience skills in action. All demonstrate different forms of emotional regulation to get from a stressed state to a neutral or regenerative state. The fourth example is a suboptimal way to do this, clearly.

Emotions are how the body's energy changes in relation to the challenges we're facing. They activate the limbic system. This leads to bodily changes, including to muscles, blood flow and pain sensitivity. Strong emotions usually include activation of both the nervous system (sympathetic arousal) and the endocrine system (hormones such as cortisol or dopamine). Skilful emotional regulation has to impact both systems. So how did emotional regulation work in the earlier examples, in relation to the three skill levels mentioned earlier?

- **Person one shifts things at the behavioural level.** They leave the difficult situation and go for a walk. Crucially, this shifts the body's energy state. The brain perceives more energy in the body, and the magnitude of the problem in relation to the body's energy level declines. This in turn leads to a downregulation of the nervous and endocrine systems. The rhythmic movement of the body while walking loosens tight muscles. The fresh air and nature help with general relaxation. The application of this behaviour, specifically going for a walk, leads to shifts in the person's thinking and physiological state.

- **Person two shifts things at the psychological level.** They empathize with the person who's just lost their mother. By changing their mindset, their brain sees the problem as less important and doesn't need to activate the nervous and endocrine system as intensely. They don't bother to respond to the nasty email. A change in perspective and thinking leads to behavioural and physiological shifts.

- **Person three shifts things at the physiological level.** They use breathing and mindfulness practices to do this. They slow their breathing, drop negative thinking patterns, and notice unease in their bodies, simply letting it be. Calmer nervous and endocrine systems help them choose not to send a nasty email back. This is a physiological intervention leading to shifts in psychology and behaviour.

- **Person four drinks alcohol.** This is a direct intervention at the neuro-chemical level. Alcohol leads to some degree of relaxation and drows-iness, and slows anxious thinking. But this isn't a sustainable long-term behaviour at work (indeed, even if you work as a sommelier, you're expected to spit the wine out). If a 'tipping point' of inebriation is reached, person four might be tempted to do something they later regret.

Which resilience skills are most effective?

By applying the first three lenses – shifts in behaviour, psychology and phys-iological activation – we searched for the most impactful resilience skills. So, we reviewed the literature to find skills that were:

- **Measurable** – with a quantifiable impact at the neurophysiological level. There's an emerging body of evidence for the neurophysiological and neurochemical levels of resilience.[4]
- **Trainable** – that could be adopted and show improvement through train-ing. We reviewed several meta-studies, one of which concluded that 'resil-ience-promoting interventions significantly improved resilience relative to controls'.[5]
- **Variable** – which exhibited a statistical variance across people. This vari-ance exists and is clearly evidenced in multiple studies.[6]
- **Relevant and actionable** – that were relevant and actionable in working life. Here, we focused primarily on the skills needed to adjust our internal landscape, based on the requirements of modern knowledge work and supply-chain environments.

Based on these assumptions, we've identified 12 resilience skills (see Figure 3.2). They're divided into the physical, mental and emotional, and social domains. These are the 12 skills that we teach to clients when we work with them, to help their workers become resilient. And, in doing so, contributing to more resilient business cultures, where teams and the wider business are more We-silient as a whole.

We give a brief explanation of these 12 resilience skills below, explaining how each skill impacts our physiology and health outcomes and examples of behaviours that we can engage in to build or strengthen that skill.

FIGURE 3.2 We've identified 12 resilience skills within three connected domains

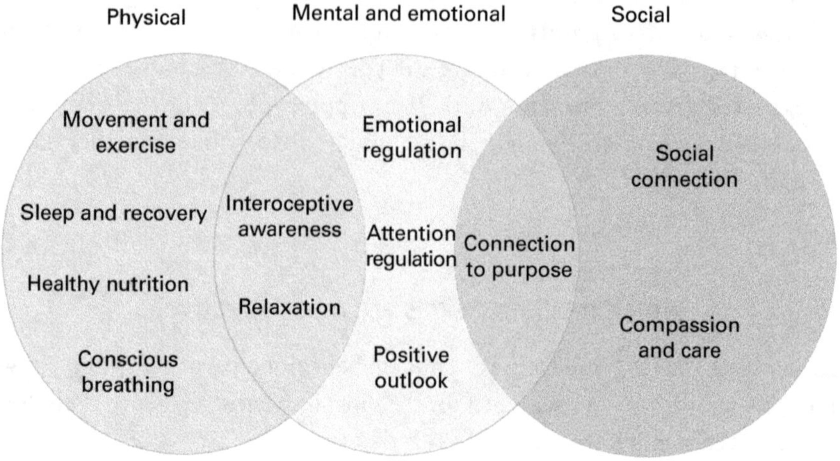

Physical   Mental and emotional   Social

Movement and exercise

Sleep and recovery

Healthy nutrition

Conscious breathing

Interoceptive awareness

Relaxation

Emotional regulation

Attention regulation

Connection to purpose

Positive outlook

Social connection

Compassion and care

SOURCE Awaris

1 Movement and exercise:

   o **Definition:** The ability to move and exercise with sufficient regularity and intensity, activating cardiovascular and muscular systems regularly.

   o **Physiological impact:** Leads to improvements in muscle, heart and lung health. Strengthens nervous, immune and digestive system function and mood. Initially heightens nervous system activation but leads to increased relaxation and positive mood after exercise.

   o **Behaviour:** Regular and sufficient exercise for endurance, power or flexibility, in the form of sport, walking, yoga, fitness training, etc. Moderate intensity cardio exercise 30 minutes daily, five days per week, or intense training and a combination of flexibility and resistance training.

2 Sleep and recovery:

   o **Definition:** The ability to sleep with sufficient regularity, duration and quality.

   o **Physiological impact:** Activates repair of bodily systems, regenerates tissues and strengthens immune system function. This leads to better mood, lower stress, improved cognitive function and overall health.

   o **Behaviour:** Regular and sufficient sleep and rest, supported by good sleep hygiene. This potentially includes sleep diaries, sleep labs, sleep trackers, planning pauses and recovery during the day.

3 Healthy nutrition:

- o **Definition**: Eating healthy food in the right quantity and of the right composition. Eating the right nutrients.
- o **Physiological impact**: Can lead to better overall health, including improved heart and digestive health, better mood and a strengthened immune system.
- o **Behaviour**: Regular, healthy, balanced and moderate eating, with some understanding of nutrition. Adoption of healthy eating behaviours such as interval fasting or mindful eating.

4 Conscious breathing:

- o **Definition**: The ability to regulate the breath consciously. Breathing in a manner to optimize respiratory efficiency, oxygenation and energy levels.
- o **Physiological impact**: Leads to better energy, mood and immune system function. It also reduces stress and emotional imbalances.
- o **Behaviour**: Regular, deep, slow breathing, primarily through the nose, supported by mindfulness, breathing exercises, posture and yoga.

5 Relaxation:

- o **Definition**: The ability to consciously shift nervous system activation, from sympathetic to parasympathetic activation.
- o **Physiological impact**: Leads to reduction in stress, improved heart function, sleep, concentration and tone of vagus nerve. Leads to overall improvements in health, immune system function, energy and mood.
- o **Behaviour**: Regular and frequent moments of relaxation – even amid activities. Reading, being in nature, doing something peaceful, digital detoxing, mindfulness practices or compassion practices.

6 Interoceptive awareness:

- o **Definition**: The ability to sense and respond appropriately to internal physiological signals (interoception). Being able to sense physiological state/limbic system activation, and the valence of that activation.
- o **Physiological impact**: Enables improved stress and emotional regulation, and better physical and nutritional health management. Leads to many improvements in self-regulation, as well as physical and mental health.

o **Behaviour:** Pausing to notice inner state. Reflecting, writing a diary, receiving coaching, reflecting on one's life story and mindfulness practices.

7 Attention regulation:

o **Definition:** The ability to regulate and maintain attention and manage distractions. Having the skill of maintaining cognitive focus on an activity, with high stability and low effort and distractedness.

o **Physiological impact:** Leads to a better ability to work effectively, improved work–life balance, learning and decision making. Also reduces stress and improves emotional regulation.

o **Behaviour:** Single tasking, reducing potential distractions, digital detoxing, working in quiet spaces or mindfulness practices.

8 Emotional regulation:

o **Definition:** The ability to regulate our emotions for optimal physiological, behavioural and social wellbeing. Regulating emotional state by noticing, suppressing or reappraising emotions, feelings, thoughts and physiological states.

o **Physiological impact:** Leads to less anxiety, negative thinking and mental ill health. Also improves mood, interpersonal relationships, decision making, self-confidence and life satisfaction.

o **Behaviour:** Naming or talking about emotions. Shifting one's perspective. Going for a walk, cognitive control or reframing, breathing deeply, keeping an emotional diary or mindfulness practices.

9 Positive outlook:

o **Definition:** The ability to perceive the positive in situations and remain realistically optimistic. Being positive, cultivating happiness and a positive outlook.

o **Physiological impact:** Leads to strengthening of reward pathways in the brain and improved emotional regulation. Reduces stress, improves awareness, attention, memory retention, interpersonal relationships, immune system function and sleep. Has multiple other health outcomes, including longevity.

o **Behaviour:** Appreciating the little things, gratitude journalling, savouring experiences, taking time for things, mindfulness practices and compassion practices.

10 Connection to purpose:

- o **Definition:** The ability to give meaning to experiences, and to remain connected to a greater purpose in life.

- o **Physiological impact:** Giving meaning to experiences or connecting to a less self-focused purpose can lead to a heightened ability to prioritize actions, deal with setbacks and maintain a positive outlook. This has positive impacts on immune system function, emotional regulation, attention regulation, interpersonal relationships and brain and body health.

- o **Behaviour:** Reflecting on life experiences. Keeping a diary, receiving life coaching, practising mindfulness and contemplation practices.

11 Social connection:

- o **Definition:** The ability to connect to people on a cognitive and emotional level. Frequently engaging in that connection, to have a sense of belonging. The ability to understand and feel what others are experiencing, and, in doing so, mirroring their experience in our own brains.

- o **Physiological impact:** Leads to emotional resonance, better social relations, improved collaboration and a sense of belonging. Also leads to improved emotional regulation, sleep and recovery. Other benefits include less stress, anxiety and mental ill health.

- o **Behaviour:** Spending time with friends and family, pets, social evenings with friends, listening well and deep dialogues.

12 Compassion and care:

- o **Definition:** The ability to feel others' suffering. A willingness to help others. The ability to activate our care/oxytocin and reward systems in relating to others.

- o **Physiological impact:** This can lead to a reduction in stress and improvements in multiple dimensions (heart health, mood, cognitive control, mental wellbeing and immune system function). Also leads to improved interpersonal relationships, greater care for others (which in turn improves others' mental and physical health) and a better sense of satisfaction and meaning.

- o **Behaviour:** Compassion practices, perspective shifts, conflict resolution, mentoring, charity work and helping others. Random acts of kindness.

All the above skills have direct physiological correlates. This means they end up affecting the activation of our nervous system, our hormone (endocrine) system, our reward (dopamine) system, our care (oxytocin) systems or many other bodily systems. This in turn impacts many other aspects of our physical, mental or emotional health. Crucially, these skills are trainable either at the behavioural, psychological or physiological levels. And as a result, they're eminently relevant to working life.

As authors, we'd love to claim that we've mastered each and every one of these skills. That we never get stressed. That we float around in a state of constant, productive euphoria, employing these 12 resilience skills as we please, like expert resilience ninjas. But alas, we need to be honest. We're human. We have strengths and weakness when it comes to these skills. For Liane, she's naturally sporty, highly skilled at meditation and has a strong connection to purpose. But she's not the best sleeper and is partial to the odd cake or two, and the occasional cute puppy video online (or 10). Chris sleeps like a lion, has good breathing, and considers himself to be a positive person. But he likes a Haribo every now and then, isn't as naturally gifted at meditation as Liane, and prefers solitude to social connection.

Below, we summarize Chris's and Liane's strengths and weaknesses when it comes to Awaris's 12 resilience skills.

1 Movement and exercise:
   o **Chris:** Not a natural. There was never a danger of him playing for the German national football team. But he trains often and has developed his exercise skills.
   o **Liane:** Natural athlete who takes easily to any sport and is still competitive.

2 Sleep and recovery:
   o **Chris:** Natural talent. Maintains good sleep hygiene.
   o **Liane:** Sometimes struggles with this.

3 Healthy nutrition:
   o **Chris:** By nature, a bit of an unhealthy appetite. Generally eats healthily now, especially due to his wife and two daughters. Weakness: Lindt.
   o **Liane:** Generally, a healthy appetite, but often forgets to take the time for healthy eating.

4 Conscious breathing:

- o **Chris:** Generally good posture and deep breathing.
- o **Liane:** Always has good posture.

5 Relaxation:

- o **Chris:** Relaxes easily and naturally.
- o **Liane:** More fiery, less naturally relaxed. Has worked on this.

6 Interoceptive awareness:

- o **Chris:** Initially poor, not a natural talent. Has worked on this.
- o **Liane:** Complete mastery in interoceptive awareness. Has been a body worker and has done extensive training.

7 Attention regulation:

- o **Chris:** Generally pretty good but sometimes slips into fragmentation.
- o **Liane:** A good single tasker, but also uses phone excessively and thus gets fragmented.

8 Emotional regulation:

- o **Chris:** Not naturally good at this. Generally used to suppress or ignore emotions. Has worked to integrate them more.
- o **Liane:** Complete mastery of emotional regulation. Also uses emotional expression consciously to shift situations.

9 Positive outlook:

- o **Chris:** Generally positive, affable and sees good in people. People sometimes ask what the secret is.
- o **Liane:** More alert to risks and problems, can get caught in negative thinking.

10 Connection to purpose:

- o **Chris:** Generally connected to purpose.
- o **Liane:** Very strong on maintaining connection to purpose.

11 Social connection:

- o **Chris:** Often weak. Enjoys social contacts, but also prefers quiet time in nature and isolates himself.
- o **Liane:** Strong, gives and gets a lot of energy from social situations.

12 Compassion and care:

- o **Chris:** Reasonably strong in self-compassion, but doesn't express care to others so strongly.

- o **Liane:** Sometimes more self-critical but also strong in extending care and compassion to others.

So, the truth is out. We're not perfect. We have our strengths and weaknesses. But so does everyone. The point isn't to be perfect in these 12 resilience skills (good luck trying to master them all in one go, seriously). It is instead to each understand our resilience profiles. To try to develop skills in the areas where we are weak, to become more resilient. And if this is done at the team and organization-wide level, to start imbuing a sense of We-silence across the whole business, building a resilient working culture.

Assessing resilience skills

'But how am I supposed to know my own resilience profile? How am I supposed to know what my strengths and weaknesses are?', you might be thinking. Based on this list of 12 resilience skills, we've developed an assessment tool for use with our clients. It takes about 8 to 10 minutes to fill out, and generates a helpful report to help people understand their stress, their mastered skills and those that need attention. It helps people understand their strengths in each of these skills.

Crucially, for each person we survey, we ask three questions about each skill:

- **Engagement in resilience skill.** The first questions asks participants whether they regularly engage in this skill or behaviour. Pretty obvious, but a necessary first step.

- **Ability under stress.** The second question asks whether they can engage in this skill or behaviour while under stress. So, if the first question asks whether someone engages in sports or movement regularly, this question asks if they're able to do this when under stress.

- **Overall competence.** Finally, we ask people whether they feel competent in this skill or not. For example, whether they feel fit and healthy, or able to sleep well or regulate their emotions in general.

This helps us understand an individual's engagement in the skill, including under stress, and their overall skill competence.

Understanding our resilience skills balance: the resilience battery analogy

One way of conceptualizing this is to think of a battery, as shown in Figure 3.3.

In this metaphor, your resilience is a battery charge. The charge level – green, orange or red – is your resilience balance score. We calculate the resilience balance score by giving points for skills you've mastered or regularly engage in. We subtract points for those skills that aren't developed. So, our engagement in resilience-boosting behaviours contributes to the charge level of the battery. In terms of battery size, nature or nurture gives some people large batteries, others smaller ones. But their battery charge level isn't determined by nature or nurture, but by how they engage in resilience skills. How fast the battery drains depends on the stress you're exposed to, and the length of time you're draining it.

The resilience battery drain rate can be thought of as the combination of the stress load (the number of stress factors we're facing) and our perceived stress (how stressed we are by this). Work-related stress factors might include high workload, uncertainty about one's job, conflicts with co-workers or an 'evil' boss (at least in your eyes). Private stressors might include financial worries, conflict with a partner or having to be a caregiver for a family member. These work and private stressors add up to our **objective stress load**.

On the other hand, our perceived stress level is the **subjective stress load**, which is a felt sense of our nervous system arousal and emotional valence (positive or negative) in response to these stressors. The combination of

FIGURE 3.3 Resilience battery profiles

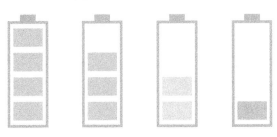

SOURCE Awaris

FIGURE 3.4 Stress temperature: stress load vs stress level gives the resilience battery drain rate

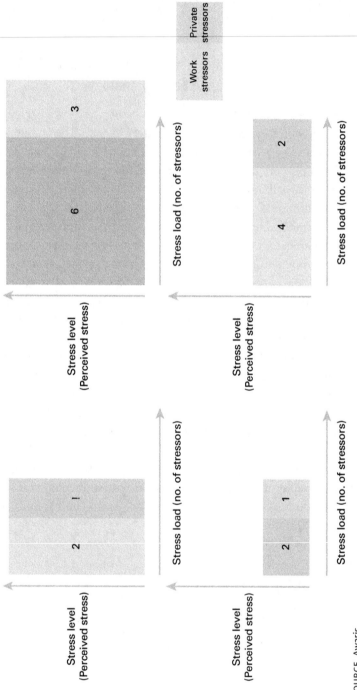

SOURCE Awaris

FIGURE 3.5 Resilience battery level, and recharging and drain rates

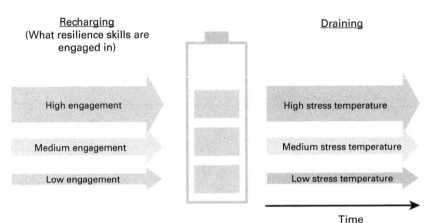

SOURCE Awaris

objective and subjective factors defines our **total stress temperature**. It's important to include the objective stress factors, because even if we don't feel stressed by them, they nonetheless represent a load on our system.

Figure 3.4 shows how our temperature might be, with four examples. The two examples on the right-hand side would imply a fast drain rate, with the top-right hand example being the worst affected.

A combination of our resilience levels, our engagement in resilience skills and our stress temperature gives a total picture of the battery, as shown in Figure 3.5.

To help us understand this further, look at the three example resilience battery profiles in Figure 3.6.

- Person one has a high overall resilience battery charge level. Their rate of discharge is less than their rate of recharging, so their resilience level is rising. They're doing a lot to charge it (with resilience skills), they don't stay in stress for extended periods of time, and their stress isn't too high. However, they don't always apply these resilience behaviours under stress.

- Person two has a very low resilience level, which is declining. They've been stressed for a long time, their resilience behaviours have declined, and so they're not recharging their battery. They're also facing ongoing stress, meaning their rate of discharge is higher than their rate of recharging.

- Person three has a moderate level of resilience, which is stable. They engage in some degree of resilience skills, but not at a high level. They do have an ongoing level of stress, and so they're discharging resilience energy, but also not at a high rate.

FIGURE 3.6 Three different resilience battery profiles

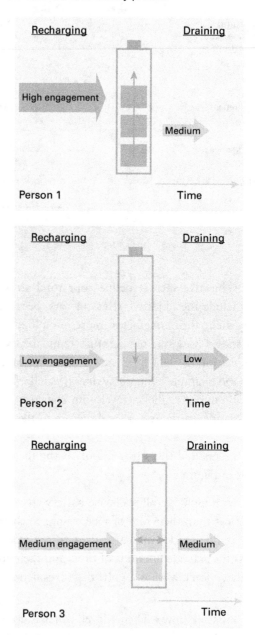

SOURCE Awaris

Maybe now there's a chance to assess yourself honestly. What do you think your resilience battery would look like? How do think your resilience behaviours would hold up to stress? Are you more like person one, two or three?

How we use resilience battery profiles

From this approach, we can generate resilience battery levels for people and profiles of their stress loads. This can help individuals understand how their resilience skills, their resilience levels and their stress temperature are balanced – or, in most cases, how they're unbalanced. And they can learn whether they're recharging or draining their resilience levels. This way of understanding our resilience battery levels helps explain differences in how people respond to stress.

Some examples might help make this more easily understandable. We were once working with a team that was under a lot of pressure, and had been for quite some time. One team member, Jun, had grown up with some challenges. She didn't seem to project strength. However, she was aware of her limits, and had learnt over the years to ensure she rested well, maintained her exercise, engaged in yoga and always took time for her friends.

Almost in direct contrast to her was George, clearly physically strong, and seemingly decisive and confident. Basically, a rock upon whom all his co-workers could rely. He was blessed with a large resilience battery, which seemed full. But over time, we began to notice two things. Jun remained steady and adaptable, and while you could clearly see some of the successive shocks the team faced mirrored in her face when they happened, she always bounced back. This was because she maintained her resilience skills and was careful about not draining herself.

George, on the other hand, while at first epitomizing resilience, didn't bounce back so easily. After some time, he didn't sleep well. He began to be emotionally grumpy, then somewhat cynical and negative. He'd never consciously needed to be mindful of his resilience skills. He simply called on his reserve when he needed it, and recovered enough on the weekend if he was tired. But this time, the ongoing pressure over the months wasn't something he could just brush off. Despite initially having a high resilience level, the ongoing drain of the high stress temperature wasn't balanced by his recharge rate.

Jun didn't have a large battery reserve to begin with, so she couldn't ignore her recharging and had learnt to maintain it well. Perversely, she fared better than George in this scenario. This highlights the power of resilience skills over being 'naturally' resilient.

Do resilience skills work?

You don't just need to take our word or these case studies as proof of concept for resilience skills. One of the first things we ask when we looked at resilience data is whether these skills were relevant. Did learning these skills contribute to resilience or reduce stress? How relevant was their contribution? The answers we've got, taken from 1,200 respondents, are emphatic: engaging in resilience skills strongly correlates with improved resilience outcomes and the reduction of stress.

Look at Figure 3.7. Based on our data, we see that practising resilience skills accounts for 39 per cent of the variance of perceived stress, whereas stressor load explains only 18 per cent. In other words, our resilience skills have a bigger impact lowering our stress levels, and thus our resilience, than the number of stressors we're facing. This correlation only works up to a point, however, as we'll explain in a later chapter.

Q: What is the biggest predictor of perceived stress? Resilience skills or stressors?

A: Resilience skills!

- The Resilience Balance Score predicts 39 per cent of perceived stress – the higher the resilience skills resources, the lower the stress.

- The stressor sum score predicts only 18 per cent of perceived stress.

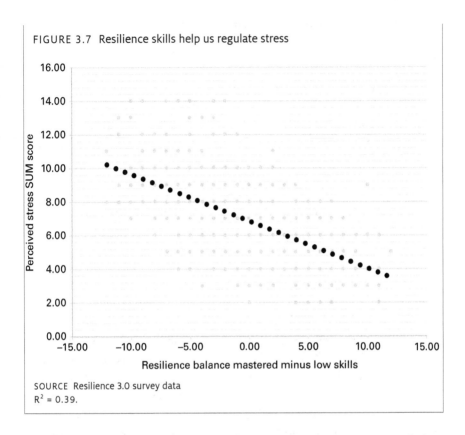

FIGURE 3.7 Resilience skills help us regulate stress

SOURCE Resilience 3.0 survey data
R² = 0.39.

Our data suggests that perceived stress does slightly increase as people face more real-life stressors. But this effect is not as strong as the reduction in stress due to engaging in resilience skills.

Which skills impact resilience the most?

In addition, we also looked at which skills have the highest impact on resilience, according to self-reported surveys. Again, the picture was interesting here. Figure 3.8 shows which four resilience skills had the highest correlation with resilience, and together explained 33 per cent of the variance in resilience in our data.

In the data we do see variances, depending on the population sampled and the stressors they face. Not all stress is the same, and not all people are the same. So, for example, we've found for those working in the legal field, one marked by a high degree of perfectionism and heightened negative thinking, self-compassion and care and a positive outlook were the most

FIGURE 3.8 The top four predictors of high resilience

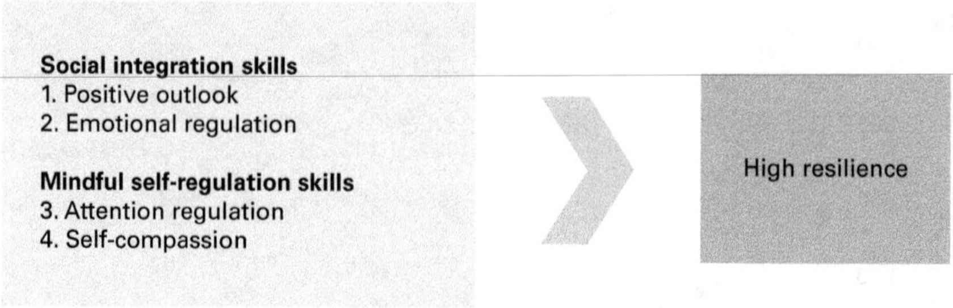

Social integration skills
1. Positive outlook
2. Emotional regulation

Mindful self-regulation skills
3. Attention regulation
4. Self-compassion

High resilience

SOURCE Awaris
All skills correlate significantly with resilience; these are the highest of each cluster. Together
these four skills alone predict 33% of the variance in performance.
N=460 participants of the Resilience 3.0 screening.

predictive skills of resilience. Thus, focusing on self-compassion and a positive outlook shifted the dial the most on resilience in this population.

For HR professionals, we found that their social connection was the most predictive of their resilience, particularly for those in businesses serving a globally distributed population, with high levels of stress regarding change and uncertainty. This was especially interesting since in the post-pandemic period they were working more from home, so they had less direct contact with the population they served. So, their connection to others had suffered, and this was what we focused on in building their resilience.

For managers working under high workloads, their attentional regulation resilience skills were the most predictive of their resilience. Simply, their ability to concentrate and get stuff done had the biggest impact on their own levels of stress. They were also mainly male, with grown children, so their family responsibilities didn't contribute too much to their stress. We tended to find that it was simply their high workload that was the biggest burden for them, which is why working on attention regulation is crucial for managers.

Our data clearly has some important insights. Most notably, it's important to know one's strengths, and to remember they are strengths because we practise them, not because they're unchangeable. They won't continue being strengths unless we continue to practise them. If we sleep well, it's still good to be conscious of sleep hygiene. If we can remain focused without distraction, it's good to practise this regularly, if we don't want to lose attention regulation skills over time.

It's important to work on the biggest weaknesses we have too. Those areas that are clearly our biggest downfalls. For some this might be emotional regulation, for others it might be sleep or social connection. So, together, maintaining our resilience skill strengths and addressing the most pronounced weaknesses is the best path to improving resilience battery scores.

For those who persevere with learning and indeed trying to master some resilience skills, large potential benefits await. These will come in the form of a fuller resilience battery, which might turn from red or orange to green over time. They might find that their engagement in resilience skills slows the rate of battery drain during stressful times. Put simply, you'll gradually become a more resilient person. And you'll also develop so-called resilience competencies, which will be the topic of the next chapter.

KEY CHAPTER TAKEAWAYS

- We view skills as learnt behaviours that can be acquired through training, practice or life experience.

- We see resilience as a series of trainable skills, which must have an impact on our biophysiology to be effective.

- Resilience skills can be trained at three levels: the behavioural, psychological and physiological levels.

- We've pinpointed 12 resilience skills that are measurable, trainable, variable, relevant and actionable. These are: movement and exercise, sleep and recovery, healthy nutrition, conscious breathing, relaxation, interoceptive awareness, attention regulation, emotional regulation, positive outlook, connection to purpose, social connection, and compassion and care.

- We all have a natural resilience level (our battery charge). Practising resilience skills can boost resilience (charge your battery), as well as making us more resilient in stressful times (slowing the battery drain rate).

- Our response to stress and battery drain rate depends on a combination of the objective stress load and perceived stress load.

- Perceived stress increases as people face more stressors, but this effect isn't as strong as the reduction in stress people feel due to practising resilience skills.

- Our surveys suggest that some people naturally gravitate towards some resilience skills compared to others, particularly social connection and positive outlook.

- A further detailed breakdown of our 12 resilience skills is available online.[7]

Notes

1 See F Cathomas, J W Murrough, E J Nestler, M-H Han and S J Russo (2019) Neurobiology of resilience: interface between mind and body, *Biological Psychiatry*, **15** (86) pp. 410–20, https://pubmed.ncbi.nlm.nih.gov/31178098/ (archived at https://perma.cc/4SPE-RWRH); R G Hunter, J D Gray and B S McEwen (2018) The neuroscience of resilience, *Social Work and Neuroscience*, **9** (2), pp. 175–359, www.journals.uchicago.edu/doi/epdf/10.1086/697956 (archived at https://perma.cc/AYH5-QNA2)

2 G Wu, A Feder, H Cohen, J J Kim, S Calderon, D S Charney and A A Mathé (2013) Understanding resilience, *Frontiers in Behavioural Neuroscience*, **7** (10), www.frontiersin.org/articles/10.3389/fnbeh.2013.00010 (archived at https://perma.cc/ZWP9-TSDU)

3 J Hari (2022) Your attention didn't collapse. It was stolen, *The Guardian*, www.theguardian.com/science/2022/jan/02/attention-span-focus-screens-apps-smartphones-social-media (archived at https://perma.cc/CS4J-AKG5)

4 C Osório, T Probert, E Jones, A H Young and I Robbins (2021) Adapting to stress: understanding the neurobiology of resilience, *Behavioural Medicine*, **43** (4), pp. 307–22, https://pubmed.ncbi.nlm.nih.gov/27100966/ (archived at https://perma.cc/U7QZ-6DYU)

5 J Jing Wen Liu, N Ein, J Gervasio, M Battaion and K Fung (2022) The pursuit of resilience: a meta-analysis and systematic review of resilience-promoting interventions, *Journal of Happiness Studies*, **23** (September), pp. 1771–91, https://link.springer.com/article/10.1007/s10902-021-00452-8#auth-Julia-Gervasio-Aff2 (archived at https://perma.cc/X37F-NN83)

6 See L Haskett, D Doster, D Athanasiadis, N Anton, E Huffman, P Wallach, E Walvoord, D Stefanidis, S Mitchell and S Lee (2022) Resilience matters: student perceptions of the impact of Covid-19 on medical education, *American Journal of Surgery*, **224** (July), pp. 358–62, https://pubmed.ncbi.nlm.nih.gov/35123769/ (archived at https://perma.cc/SE6W-7PDV)

7 Resilient Culture (nd) www.resilientculture.info (archived at https://perma.cc/DW9F-Q3N5)

4

Resilience competencies and profiles

We all experience challenges at work. We are sure you have. Perhaps your work's been criticized in front of others, or by your boss. You feel like telling your boss where they should go (trying to pick the best insult or expletive to use). But instead, you just sit there, stewing in embarrassment and anger as your cheeks turn red. Maybe you've spent weeks working on an idea or an initiative, putting your heart and soul into it. Working late often, and even on weekends, to make it as good as it can be. But instead of getting a 'thank you' for your hard work, in a meeting your colleagues only pick out the flaws in it. Not a single person praises you for the effort you've put in, and your initiative is thwarted. Or maybe, despite your best efforts, you've made a mistake. Somehow (incredibly), you made a calculation error in an important spreadsheet. The client points it out, and sadly, your boss is cc'd into the angry email.

Any of these scenarios sound familiar? Well, we compiled data from 900 people who completed Awaris resilience screening from September 2022 to February 2023, to explore situations just like this.[1] Our data showed that 44 per cent of employees were able to remain calm in challenging situations such as these, at least superficially. However, almost 60 per cent of our respondents found it difficult to wind down at the end of the day, hindering their ability to relax and rest. We didn't ask whether anyone responded by telling their boss to get lost, but I'm sure it must have happened at least once.

How come some workers struggle with stress more than others? What determines whether they'll be able to unwind after a stressful day like those described above? As we've mentioned, we view practising resilience skills as a key differentiator which can explain these differing outcomes. When faced with these challenging situations, practising mindfulness, engaging in physical exercise, focusing on social connections or simply getting a good night's sleep, among many other skill options, could make a big difference here in how you bounce back. Indeed, someone who went home after work and engaged in all these skills would likely return to work the next day feeling ready to take on the challenge (even if they still dreaded having to face up to any of the errors they made).

But there is a further level to explore here. In addition to our 12 resilience skills, there's a meta level. A level which we call **resilience competencies**. Resilience competencies arise when people master several resilience skills. They encompass a broader set of attributes that go beyond specific skills. They represent an understanding of the awareness, skills and behaviours that are required to remain resilient, and usually have built up over the years. (We aren't going to promise quick fixes here. Becoming resilient is a lifelong learning journey.)

Identifying these competencies allows us to recognize individuals' **resilience profiles**. The aggregation of 12 individual resilience skills into competencies allows us to find patterns at a higher level, which are easier for us to digest. From here, we highlight three resilience competencies with distinct characteristics and strengths. These are:

1 Mindful Self-Regulation
2 Healthy Habits
3 Social Integration

We found these not just by grouping them as we saw fit, but by doing a statistical factor analysis on the 12 skills and seeing how they grouped.

Knowing which resilience competency type you or your employees are can help in developing targeted interventions. Resilience competencies also provide an insightful summary of the specific resilience challenges an organization faces, and enable us to provide specific recommendations on how best to address them. Table 4.1 shows how our 12 resilience skills cluster together into these three main resilience competency types.

As Table 4.1 shows, the **Mindful Self-Regulators** tend to perform well in the resilience skills of conscious breathing, relaxation, self-awareness, attention regulation, emotional regulation and positive outlook. Those with **Healthy Habits** master skills of physical exercise, recovery and sleep, healthy nutrition and relaxation. The **Social Integration** group are most likely to display the resilience skills of emotional regulation, positive outlook, sense of purpose, social connection, and compassion and care.

Let's look at these three resilience competencies in more detail. (For more details about the physiological, psychological and behavioural outcomes of these competencies, see Appendix II.)

TABLE 4.1 Three main resilience competencies: statistical analysis shows a clustering of skills

	Competencies		
SKILLS AND BEHAVIOURS	1. Mindful Self-Regulation	2. Healthy Habits (energy management)	3. Social Integration
Physical exercise		•	
Recovery and sleep		•	
Dietary habits		•	
Conscious breathing	•		
Ability to relax	•	•	
Self-awarness	•		
Attention regulation	•		
Emotional regulation	•		•
Positive outlook	•		•
Sense of purpose and meaning			•
Connection to others			•
(Self-) compassion and care	•		•

The three resilience competencies

1. Mindful Self-Regulation

Frequency: 26 per cent of surveyed people have this competency.

Core characteristics:

- regular practice of relaxation and breathing techniques
- high self-awareness and internal focus
- strong ability to refocus attention and stop rumination
- high self-compassion, low negative self-talk
- able to say no to excessive demands, are aware of what they can handle

Those in the Mindful Self-Regulation competency category are characterized by an application of mindfulness techniques and practices. People who score highly in this competency are three times more likely to agree that they regularly engage in relaxation or mindfulness practices, such as yoga or meditation. They tend to invest time in developing the skills of internal regulation. They're more likely to notice sensations in their body, regulating their stress early before it becomes overwhelming.

They can lower the impact of negative self-talk which often accompanies stressful situations (eg 'I'm a failure', 'People don't like me' or 'I can never get things right') by responding with self-compassion. For example, they are four times more likely to agree that they give themselves care and tenderness when going through a tough time. These skills benefit Mindful Self-Regulators during the working day: they're less likely to be easily distracted and find it easier to stay focused on a task.

Greatest impact on: job performance due to a superior ability to focus, and lower levels of chronic stress. Strong abilities to internally manage difficulties and shift internal states. However, people who score high solely in this resilience competency can be over-reliant on coping with things on their own, in an increasingly collaborative and interdependent work environment.

2. Healthy Habits

Frequency: 24 per cent of people have this competency.

Core characteristics:

- prioritizes healthy habits
- values feeling fit and energetic
- eats the healthy option at lunch
- regularly engages in sports and physical exercise
- sleep is a priority

People who score highly in the Healthy Habits competency typically have established routines they follow, no matter what. While most people tend to drop healthy habits in stressful times, those in the Healthy Habits competency double down on them. They prioritize exercise, healthy eating and sleep, especially when they are stressed. One way of thinking about healthy habits is that they correspond closely to the competence of energy management – people who maintain good healthy habits remain vital and have good energy.

Because of their healthy habits, less than 10 per cent of people in this competency said they struggled to keep their diet healthy and balanced in the past month, compared to a third of other respondents. Those in the Healthy Habits competency are 2.7 times more likely to have a regular bedtime routine. They've established several habits that make them feel good and stick to them. As a result, 81 per cent of those in this competency cluster agree they feel fit, compared to just 22 per cent of those outside the cluster.

In terms of their inner landscape, these people aren't so aware of their inner state beyond the aspects of vitality, regeneration and recovery. But because they manage their energy well through sport, sleep and diet, they have healthy movement through the landscape. Because emotional states are expressions of a body's energy budget, they're less likely fall into overly negative emotional states and generally remain positive. Unless, of course, their local gym is closed for maintenance, or they have a newborn and their sleep temporarily goes out of the window.

Greatest impact on: sense of achievement, self-efficacy and stress reduction. People with this competency are typically most confident in their ability to bounce back from hardship in life.

3. Social Integration

Frequency: 46 per cent of people have this competency.

Core characteristics:

- strong connections to people at work
- feels appreciated and accepted by people at work
- supports and cares for colleagues
- can regulate emotions well
- a generally positive outlook
- strongest connection to purpose

A likely trait of those in the Social Integration competency is reaching out to a colleague when dealing with an emotionally charged situation and talking it through. As a result, people with this competency are 2.8 times less likely to feel down for a longer period after a stressful situation at work. They're also three times more likely to 'strongly agree' that they help and support others at work.

A larger percentage of those in this competency type could be described as what organizational psychologist Adam Grant calls 'the Givers'.[2] Givers are more inclined to coach and support others and to be helpful, even at the expense of getting their own tasks done. Depending on the kind of work environment these employees operate in, this can either be conducive or detrimental to their careers, according to Grant's research. In our data, those with the Social Integration competency scored higher in self-rated performance compared to others, suggesting that they find this competency conducive to performing highly (or at least they think it makes them perform better). Finally, they score highest on purpose. An impressive 82 per cent in this competency type agreed that they have a strong sense of meaning and direction in life, compared to just 34 per cent who scored low in this competency.

In the Social Integration competency, we see that those with the competency aren't always aware of their own state. But they can instinctively apply their skills of connection and emotional regulation to stay flexible. By connecting to others, they shift their emotional states, and by being able to regulate their own state they manage to get unstuck.

Greatest impact on: adaptability to change, growth mindset, self-efficacy and performance. However, tendency to prioritize others over themselves can cause problems depending on how highly the work environment values coaching and empowerment. Relying solely on relationships to regulate inner states may not be the most effective way to operate. We found that Social Integrators vary greatly in their ability to relax and get good rest at night. Pairing the Social Integration competency with another resilience competency is advantageous when it comes to sustainably regulating stress.

Which resilience competencies can help with work and personal stressors?

So, what to do with this knowledge? How can knowing your resilience competencies, or the competencies of other employees, help you and the business you work for? For us, we believe this knowledge can help you see which resilience skills and competencies are most useful for managing certain types of stress, and also which ones would benefit from being strengthened. This is a crucial insight. It allows us to create stressor profiles for certain job roles, and then match these to worker resilience competencies. In other words, knowing someone's resilience competency type can help you match people to jobs they'd be well suited for, and to help to identify which skills they might need to best deal with the stressors they're likely to face.

To do this, we asked people which stressors they were currently experiencing, and cross-referenced them with their resilience competency types.

TABLE 4.2 Resilience competencies

NO EFFECT ○	LOW ○	MODERATE ○	HIGH ○	HIGHEST ●

Personal and professional stressors	Resilence competency clusters		
	Mindful Self-Regulation	Healthy Habits	Social Integration
Heavy workload	○	○	●
Unrealistic job demands/ understaffed	○	○	○
Change of responsibility or job ambiguity		●	
Poor interpersonal relationships at work		●	
Challenges of hybrid or virtual work		●	○
Personal stressors and mental health challenges	○	○	○

The work-related stressors included job demands, job ambiguity and poor interpersonal relationships. Personal stressors included going through a stressful life period (such as having young kids, going through divorce or caring for older family members) and experiencing a mental health issue.

Table 4.2 summarizes how those in each core resilience competency type experienced these stressors. Due to the nature of correlational data, we can't be certain of the causal effects. Did the stressors lead to a lowered resilience competency, or does the low resilience competency intensify the experience of stressors? It's hard to say with certainty. That said, there are some interesting relationships between stressors and resilience competencies.

Table 4.2 highlights how the three resilience competencies help people cope with unrealistic job demands, as well as with personal stressors and mental health challenges. Engaging in **Healthy Habits** is the most favourable way to deal with heavy workloads. This perhaps reflects effective energy management. The **Mindful Self-Regulators** tend to cope best with personal demands and mental health concerns. They can manage their attention, emotions, nervous system and inner state, helping them cope with stressful periods at work. **Social Integration** doesn't lower the impact of a heavy workload as much as the other two resilience competencies, but has the strongest effect when coping with change initiatives and uncertainty. These could come in the form of changes in the nature of our work, changing job roles, interpersonal work relationships and the challenges of hybrid work.

Thus, our data suggests that, when going through large change initiatives, focusing on social connection, community building and providing spaces for group reflection might help employees regulate the stress of change the most.

Distribution of resilience competencies

While everyone's different, we also took a stab at seeing which skills and competencies were mastered by the widest percentage of the population. We looked at how much our respondents engaged with them, and how competent they felt they were in these skills. We were surprised to find quite marked differences in this. There were clear differences in the distribution of resilience competencies (see Figure 4.1).

It's good news that people felt they had generally good social connections and were able to see the positive in situations. We found that 81 per cent felt they had good social connections at work, and 73 per cent were generally able to maintain a positive outlook. Overall, people felt that they were

FIGURE 4.1 Resilience competencies and their mastery: high-level view of overall resilience competencies

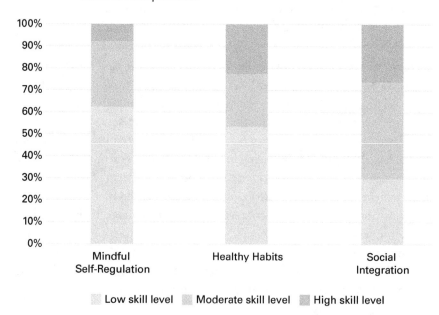

generally stronger in the skills of the Social Integration competency, with around 70 per cent of our participants having a moderate or high level of skills in this competency.

Around 40 per cent of respondents felt they were able to eat healthily and exercise sufficiently regularly. Perhaps this isn't surprising, after so many years of emphasis in public that healthy eating and regular exercise are important. But this data compares well to global surveys, which suggest that 37 per cent of people in the developed world do not exercise enough.[3] This probably reflects our large share of knowledge workers in the sample. Overall, 47 per cent felt that they had a moderate or high degree of skill mastery in the Healthy Habits competency.

Our surveys suggest that people struggle most with the overstimulation of modern life, with only 35 per cent able to manage their attention well, 34 per cent able to feel refreshed and sleep well in general and 27 per cent able to relax. We live in a world where people can't even watch TV without also going on their phone. A world where people sleep with their phones under their pillow, checking them just before bed and as soon as they wake up. It shouldn't surprise us, then, that restfulness for many is elusive. So indeed, only 8 per cent exhibited high skills in Mindful Self-Regulation. A further 30 per cent displayed a moderate degree of skill mastery in this competency.

We can summarize the challenges that people face to their resilience as follows: having sedentary, unhealthy, restless, overstimulated, unaware, distracted, unbalanced, negative, solitary and meaningless lifestyles. Of these, the areas which people have the least mastery concern being over-stimulated, unaware and emotionally unbalanced.

How competencies combine to make resilience profiles

Naturally, people don't always fit strictly into just one competency type. We found that roughly a third of respondents displayed only one of the three resilience competencies described in the sections above. About 17 per cent scored high in two resilience competency clusters, whereas about 10 per cent of super-resilient people scored highly in all three competency types. Interestingly, the largest category in our dataset is made up of people who don't display many resilience skills and don't neatly fit into one of the three resilience competencies. Those in the low resilience category comprise 41 per cent of respondents (see Figure 4.2). This number is in line with recent numbers on the prevalence of high stress in the workforce.

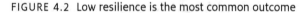

FIGURE 4.2 Low resilience is the most common outcome

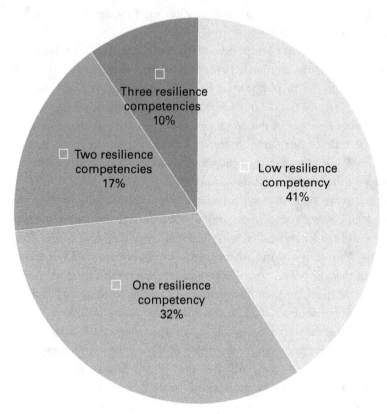

Percentage of respondents categorized in each resilience competency. Respondents can demonstrate more than one competency.

Knowing the percentage of people with low resilience can provide useful insights for organizations. First of all, it can help identify the staff that are most in need of support. People in this category have significantly fewer skills to regulate stress and cope with changes in the work context. Only 1 per cent of them 'strongly agree' that they feel fit, and very few experience restful sleep. As a result, they score more than 10 per cent lower on performance and are three times more likely to experience chronic stress than the average respondent. Second, knowing the percentage of employees lacking any resilience competencies can also provide useful insights into the potential impact the work environment has on people.

Having low resilience should not be viewed as a personal issue – it is also related to the number of stressors experienced at work. When people experience four or more stressors in their private or work lives, they're much more likely to be categorized in the low resilience cluster. We highlight that the 41 per cent of low resilience employees could be at a higher risk of mental health issues. They might be in greater need of organizational and psychological support to help them build up coping strategies.

The challenges facing those with low resilience

It's important to reflect further on this group that currently displays no or low resilience competencies. The emphasis is on 'currently'. The way we compile our surveys, to try to get participants to *really* look at their behaviour in a realistic manner, is to focus on a specific time period. So rather than asking 'Are you generally a positive person?', the question we instead asked was 'Have you generally felt positive in the last month?' And a typical response might be: 'In the last month, even when things were tough, I noticed moments of enjoyment or pleasure in my day (eg when having a cup of tea).' Thus, it's not about criticizing a group of people for not being resilient (which is back to the mental trap of misunderstanding resilience), but recognizing that, at a specific time, 41 per cent of people are having difficulty applying resilience behaviours and skills in their life. This puts them at a higher risk of heightened stress, mental ill health and depression.

There are many reasons why this could be. Perhaps they're going through a difficult patch in their relationship? Perhaps they are recovering from an illness? Maybe they're moving house and don't have time to exercise? Perhaps there are heightened challenges at work? They are working more hours than they usually do, causing them to miss time with friends and sleep less?

Or perhaps they are facing some deeper challenges. Maybe they've experienced trauma in their life and have a dysregulated nervous system, which makes the effective application of any resilience skills more difficult. Maybe they're a member of a minority, and are continually exposed to a heightened level of stressors. Or perhaps they've been facing long-term stress, potentially from work or from their private life, and this has accumulated to the extent that their resilience skills have broken down completely.

Our data implies that it could be a combination of these factors. One telling indicator is the amount of personal and organizational stressors people often face in the low resilience category. People in this category are significantly more likely than people who score high on at least one resilience competency type to suffer from four or more stressors in their private or work lives. These can be work-related stressors such as job demands or job ambiguity, or personal stressors such as mental health issues or taxing family demands.

The key point is to acknowledge that there's likely to be a population of people in any organization who don't currently display resilience skills. We all need to be aware of the need to help them. To approach them with compassion, getting them back in the saddle of their existing positive behaviours or helping to reduce some of the external stressors they face. These results point to the importance of addressing resilience both at the individual and the organizational, We-silience level. **Each organization is only as resilient as their employees who are struggling the most.** We'll turn to what this means for We-silience shortly.

The authors' competencies

Having spoken at length about other people's resilience competency types, it only seems fair that we expose ourselves. In the context of resilience, of course. So, we want to share with you a sense of our own competencies, to see how some of these concepts work in practice.

We both feel like we have two competencies and would thus class ourselves in the higher resilience type. (Given that we've written an entire book on resilience, we're sure that you – the reader – would hope that this was the case.)

Chris seems to have the Healthy Habits and Mindful Self-Regulation competencies. He can handle high pressure and workloads. Despite the fact he often doubles down and gets a lot of work done during the week, he generally doesn't work on weekends or evenings. He never looks at emails outside of work hours (which is a rarity in the modern world). He sleeps well, exercises regularly and eats (fairly) healthily. He practises mindfulness daily, relaxes easily and doesn't overdo it.

Saying that, he does tend to become more solitary in times of high workloads. He loses the depth of connection to friends and family, which isn't so healthy. In addition, while he can generally handle work pressure well without suffering too much, he's often slow to learn new habits and doesn't change easily. He can get stuck in his ways and needs others to nudge him to adapt at times.

Chris wasn't naturally so resilient earlier in his life. When he was younger, he had burnout. It came about in a very challenging work time, when the company he'd founded was struggling with potential bankruptcy and he was also facing a crisis of meaning. His previous strategies of doubling down and working harder weren't working, and he had to learn many self-regulation skills anew. He worked with a therapist over a period of 18 months to build up many aspects of how he lived and worked in a healthy way. In addition, his own longstanding and ongoing practice of mindfulness led to skills in relaxation and conscious breathing, as well as emotional and attentional regulation and self-awareness. The last point is the most notable – he studied theoretical physics in London for his under-graduate degree. He could at the time have been safely described as a 'head on a stick' when he was younger – a thinking mind not aware he even had a body – so wasn't particularly embodied.

Liane also has a good basis in Healthy Habits. She considers herself strong on social-emotional skills, and feels she fits into the Social Integration competency type too. She can handle high workloads, owing to her Healthy Habits, but she does push herself too much. Sometimes her body gives her signals, and she crashes. She remains connected to people, and, in fact, considers herself someone who copes well with change. She genuinely feels she hasn't met any change she didn't like (save for her beloved dog Casiopeia dying). She'll regularly try new habits and new practices, just for the fun of learning something new.

Liane wasn't naturally resilient as a child. She experienced childhood trauma. She suffered from an eating disorder as a young adult, to such an extent that she spent a year in a clinic. She had to completely relearn basic healthy behaviours, including to relax and re-regulate her nervous system. Her extensive body and therapeutic work, also with clients, and her 30 years of mindfulness practice have helped her cultivate these competencies.

To summarize, we'd both say we are resilient, with each of us displaying two resilience competencies. They allow us to deal with stress and pressure – but in different ways. Neither of us is naturally resilient. We've learnt many resilience skills in our life, which we can now rely on as we face the inevitable challenges of our working and private lives. And as it's probably clear, our journey to becoming more resilient wasn't an immediate fix. There's no magic bullet here. Becoming resilient and mastering resilience skills and competen-cies isn't a week-long, month-long or even year-long effort. It's a lifelong learning journey, to take place over decades. But it's one that can be eminently meaningful. It can be hard, but joyful at times. Beautiful even. The path of personal transformation is a noble pursuit – with resilience the goal. And one that we hope, in reading this book, you're taking the first steps on.

Important takeaways for organizations

If you want to run a marathon, it's probably useful to know how good your endurance is, as well as your stride, your emotional state and your ability to endure pain. All of these make up your marathon skills. Equally, if we face challenges at work and in life, it's imperative to know our resilience skills and competencies. We'd encourage everyone to assess their own resilience skills and competencies, as well as their inner emotional landscape, to get a sense of what they might want to work on.

Overall, our deep dive into resilience skills and surveys points to the importance of addressing resilience both at the individual and the organization-wide We-silience level. While those exhibiting one or more resilience competencies may cope with stressors experienced at work, the largest category is people with no resilience skills at all. This could be the result of the unrealistic demands employers expect their staff to cope with.

In terms of reducing stress, there's an intervention that has transformed the authors' ability to cope with stress, as well as in the many businesses we've worked with. In previous decades, this intervention was viewed with suspicion – as an esoteric, 'woo-woo' modality, reserved mainly for hippies and people who burn incense sticks and say 'namaste' a bit too much, whose practitioners would talk nonchalantly about their 'chakras' and 'energy', to the utter bewilderment of many to whom they spoke.

We're talking, of course, about mindfulness, which will be the next topic our attention will turn to.

KEY CHAPTER TAKEAWAYS

- Resilience competencies arise with mastery of specific clusters of resilience skills.

- We highlight three main competency types: Mindful Self-Regulation, Healthy Habits and Social Integration:

  o Mindful Self-Regulators have skills of relaxation, attention and positive outlook, helping them focus and cope with stress. However, they can become solitary in difficult times.

  o Healthy Habits have skills of sleep, exercise and healthy lifestyles, giving them the energy to cope with work stress.

o   Social Integrators prioritize social connection and helping others. This doesn't help them cope with work stressors as much as the other two competencies, but they're adept at dealing with changing job roles and interpersonal relationships.

- You can have more than one resilience competency: 10 per cent of our survey respondents had three resilience competencies, 17 per cent had two, and 32 per cent had only one resilience competency.

- However, 41 per cent displayed no competencies at all and can be described as low resilience. They need to be approached with compassion, and businesses need to support them in coping with work stressors.

- Knowing your own resilience profile, as well as those of employees, is crucial. We recommend that businesses:

o   run resilience screening, to know how best to support employees

o   invest in supporting teams and developing a psychologically safe business culture

o   focus on the 'how' of change initiatives, to improve outcomes

Notes

1 We asked 900 respondents 30 questions about their resilience skills, 12 questions about key organizational outcomes and eight questions about stressors. The answer options were on a five-point Likert scale ranging from 'strongly disagree' to 'strongly agree'.
2 A Grant (2013) *Give and Take: Why helping others contributes to our success*, Phoenix, London
3 R Guthold, G A Stevens, L M Riley and F C Bull (2018) Worldwide trends in insufficient physical activity from 2001 to 2016: a pooled analysis of 358 population-based surveys with 1.9 million participants, *The Lancet*, 6 (10), pp. 1077–86, www.thelancet.com/action/showPdf?pii=S2214-109X%2818%2930357-7 (archived at https://perma.cc/WD3X-JXC4)

5

The role of mindfulness in resilience

Our brains and bodies are amazingly complex systems. Many scientists are convinced the brain is the most complex thing in the known universe. This is not only a structural complexity, with more than 86,000,000,000 neurons in each brain. On average, a single neuron can form thousands of synaptic connections with other neurons. Some studies have suggested that the average number of synapses per neuron in the human brain may be in the order of thousands to tens of thousands. Some scientists have thus claimed there are hundreds more possible neuronal connections in the brain than there are stars in the Milky Way.[1]

Based on this, and despite the direct comparison to computers not being perfect, researchers have attempted to calculate the processing power of a human brain. For example, some estimates suggest that the processing power of the human brain is around 10^{15} to 10^{18} operations per second.[2] That's a one with 15 or 18 zeros behind it. Some have even claimed human brains are still more powerful than the best supercomputers, or at least much more efficient.

Wow – how smart are we?

Now, please calculate 37 × 94 in your head.

Stumped?

This is our dilemma. We have this epic and profound mental processing power, but most of it is not accessible to the thinking or conscious brain. Most of our processing power is used to regulate unconscious processes. Like, for example, how hungry I am (and whether I'd prefer some dried dates or crisps right now). Our body generates around 10^6 bits of information per second – far too much for us to consciously process. And the remaining conscious bandwidth, if we are honest, is often fragmented or poorly utilized. While we read something, we interrupt ourselves to check the football scores. And while we're in a conversation, we ruminate over our weekend plans. We're often not conscious or present in our lives.

For this reason, we can speak of us having a thinking brain and the feeling (or embodied) brain. These aren't so much different parts of the brain, as different networks and processing styles within it. The division between the thinking brain and the feeling brain is a simplification. It describes the functional specialization of different brain regions. The brain is a highly interconnected and integrated organ, and cognitive processes and emotional processes aren't entirely separate. Nonetheless, there are differences:

- **Cognitive processes,** such as logical reasoning, problem solving and decision making, are primarily associated with the cerebral cortex, especially the frontal lobes. This part of the brain is often referred to as the 'thinking brain' because it plays a crucial role in conscious thought processes and executive functions. These functions consume more energy and are quickly shut down in times of stress, to preserve energy and activate survival strategies.

- **Body-related and emotional processes,** on the other hand, involve brain regions like the limbic system. These include the amygdala, hippocampus and other structures. The limbic system is responsible for processing emotions, emotional memories and regulating emotional responses. This region is sometimes referred to as the 'feeling brain' because it's heavily involved in our emotional experiences.

Why are the thinking and feeling brains becoming more disconnected?

In our view, there's an increasing disconnect between these two modes of processing: thinking and feeling. There are several reasons for this.

The first is **technological advancements**. Rapid advancements in technology, particularly in the digital and virtual realm, have changed the way humans interact with the world. Increased screen time, virtual communication and reliance on digital devices can alter the balance between cognitive and emotional experiences, and above all weaken our self-awareness. It's like learning a language. If we don't practise the phonetics and the alphabet of Chinese regularly, we'll lose our ability to speak Chinese. In a similar way, we're training ourselves to recognize tiny visual signals on small screens and give them meaning, while learning to ignore all the signals from our body and forgetting their meaning. We're losing the language of the body. Our obsession with screens is reducing our ability to connect with actual humans, face to face,[3] and has produced a world where, on an average street, people stumble around, eyes glued to their devices, only looking up when they need to cross the road (and even then, not always doing this).

The second factor is **changes in lifestyle and the environment.** Modern lifestyles often involve fast-paced, highly optimized environments, with a reduced variety of sensory experiences. This can influence brain functioning. In addition, urbanization, noise pollution and reduced access to natural spaces also impact our felt sense of the body and how we process our experience. We have less opportunity to practise the skills of mind–body integration in a fast-paced life. Again, listening to the signals from our body initially takes time, just as learning a new language takes time.

Third, we face **rising stress levels.** We cited the evidence for rising global stress levels earlier in the book. Stress causes us to downregulate our felt sense of the body. It also degrades our ability to finely perceive inner sensory signals, as well as outer social and emotional cues. This can also lead to a heightened disconnect between our thinking and our felt senses.

The fourth factor is **changing social dynamics.** Social and cultural changes can influence how individuals express and process emotions. Societal shifts, such as increased focus on individualism or changes in social support systems, are also shaping how we perceive ourselves and others. This inhibits our ability to integrate different styles of processing.

The fifth factor is **challenges to mental health and wellbeing.** The prevalence of mental health issues, such as anxiety and depression, has increased in some societies. These conditions can impact emotional regulation and cognitive functioning, leading to a perceived disconnect between the thinking and feeling brain. Many people don't want to feel how they feel. They prefer to distract themselves from their feelings. The average British person spends over four and a half hours per day on their smartphone[4] – devices with apps designed specifically to distract our attention. We doubt their popularity is a coincidence.

Finally, there are the increasing problems of **sedentary lifestyle and obesity.** A lack of movement and exercise and increases in body weight also lead to a reduction in our mind–body integration and our ability to perceive bodily signals. Many of the skills and behaviours that positively impact our resilience involve physiological processes. Thus, there's a clear need for learning to overcome this divide, to somehow integrate our thinking and feeling brain. While many practices and skills can help with this, we believe mindfulness can play a crucial role here.

While the evidence for mindfulness is strong, due to the above challenges in the modern world, people struggle with practising and becoming adept practitioners. People can often try mindfulness, and not really give it the time needed for it to work effectively. People find it hard, and want to give up, as the example below outlines.

Liane was leading a 20-day online mindfulness sprint for 200 leaders in a global automotive technology firm. It was 25 minutes per day. People were from China, India, Germany and the UK, among others. One person was continually resisting. He was vocal about it.

Ravi: 'Liane, I've tried mindfulness three times now; it doesn't work. I almost feel I'm more anxious and restless after trying this. What's the point if it's not making me calmer?'

Liane: 'Yes, Ravi, this was my experience too when I started jogging. I tried it three times for eight minutes and just got hot and sweaty. I felt tired afterwards. Does this mean jogging doesn't work?'

Ravi looked quizzically at Liane, clearly thinking, 'What a ridiculous thing to say. How can you say jogging doesn't work. It's not supposed to "work", it's exercise…'

He followed the train of thought to its logical conclusion. And then he realized where this was going. Perhaps he was expecting mindfulness to be easy, instantly relaxing and fun. And when it wasn't, he assumed it wasn't working. But when the practice was compared to exercise, it made more sense.

Liane: 'Exercise is often difficult, and often can even hurt. But even if we don't always enjoy it at the time, we *know* it's good for us, and that it can make us feel better afterwards. It takes time to get fit – just as it takes time to learn mindfulness.'

With this in mind, he nodded and said thanks.

The evidence for mindfulness in the workplace

Although many find it challenging, mindfulness has become profoundly more popular in the last decade. When Chris and Liane told people they meditated a decade or two ago, they were used to people changing the subject or nodding vacantly. In one memorable incident, a client of Chris held a senior global role at a German automotive firm. He invited Chris for a private lunch – which was surprising to say the least. This senior executive had wanted Chris to lead the next project at his company. But he'd heard from a partner at Chris's consulting firm that Chris wouldn't be available ... because he was going on a three-month 'retreat' in a monastery.

During lunch, the manager, a dignified and slightly authoritarian person, but who also cared, brought up the subject. It became clear that he was deeply worried about Chris disappearing into a cult, or dropping out of society altogether. Chris laughed and reassured him that mediation was fundamentally mind training and not brainwashing. It took some time to explain this. In the end, it became a touching moment. In part because it appeared to Chris that this senior person was exhibiting the subtle signs of early onset Parkinsons, something that the authority of his role and the power he had to project couldn't allow. There was a moment of mutual recognition and acceptance, a real meeting of minds. The executive came away thoughtful and curious. And they remained in contact over time.

Most people know about mindfulness. Many have even tried it before, using popular apps like Calm or Headspace. Mindfulness is seen as being as normal as yoga or going to the gym. And increasingly, individuals are vaguely aware of the evidence base for the effectiveness of mindfulness. But they perhaps aren't aware of just how strong and expansive this evidence base is. Annually, more than 3,000 research papers are published in journals on mindfulness, compared to fewer than 200 at the turn of the millennium (see Figure 5.1). Papers on mindfulness now outstrip most other psychological interventions, including positive psychology and neurofeedback. It recently surpassed cognitive behavioural therapy too. Many of these journals show how mindfulness reduces stress, improves focus and attention, enhances emotional regulation and promotes overall psychological wellbeing.[5]

There's also strong evidence for the effectiveness of mindfulness in the workplace. A recent meta-review by the National Institute of Health and Care Excellence in the UK looked at more than 150 research studies. The authors concluded: 'Yoga, mindfulness, and meditation were most effective overall in reducing job stress and mental health symptoms and having a positive effect on employee mental wellbeing.'[6]

This is a far-reaching statement – especially given that mindfulness was compared with the impact of leadership mental health training, mental health first aiders, targeted cognitive behavioural therapy, stress management training and other well-known interventions. Another meta-review in 2021 came to a similar conclusion. It stated: 'Mindfulness-based and multi-component positive psychological interventions demonstrated the greatest efficacy in both clinical and non-clinical populations.'[7]

FIGURE 5.1 Mindfulness research has outstripped many other fields

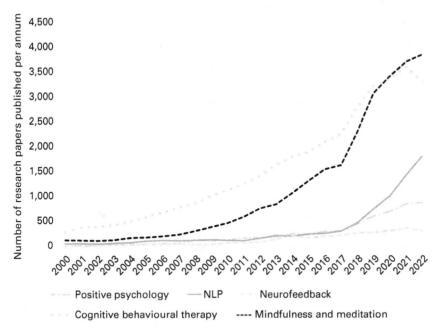

SOURCE Web of Science (2023)[8]

Understanding the mechanisms of mindfulness

At Awaris, we weren't surprised by these results. We'd been working with mindfulness for years. All our staff and trainers are mindfulness practitioners. But it's important to explain here why mindfulness is so effective. Normally, mindfulness is generally communicated in neurocentric language. Discussions relate to the brain, but less so in terms of its connection to our bodies and physiology. But as we've seen in previous chapters, resilience skills impact more than just the brain. Mindfulness practices help us work on ourselves at three levels:

- **Behavioural** – By helping us notice our typically unconscious and automatic behaviours, and consciously practising new ones.

- **Psychological** – By allowing us to notice our thinking processes and fixed mindsets. This enables us to let go of these thoughts or cultivate more purposeful forms of thinking.

- **Physiological** – By regulating our core internal systems through our posture, breathing and the heightened focus we bring to what's happening in our bodies.

A lot's been written about the role of mindfulness at the first two levels: changing visible behaviours and psychological processes (mindset). But the role of mindfulness at the third level – direct physiological regulation – is less well known. Mindfulness can have a profound impact on our bodies, physiological regulation and neurophysiology. The importance of this can't be overstated.

Physiological intelligence

The science of physiology is well established. It encompasses a variety of processes through which the body can detect, respond to and counter changes in internal variables, to sustain life. Our physiology functions to regulate our health, functioning and wellbeing. Most of the time, this happens automatically. Naturally, this encompasses some neurophysiological processes relating to the brain and nervous system, but physiology is wider than this, also encompassing breathing, heart rate and other metabolic processes.

But we can also impact our physiology by the behaviours we engage in. Many people are familiar with this, at least notionally, by engaging in behavioural routines which impact our physiological processes. These can include movement and exercise, hydration and nutrition, sleep and breathing.

An even deeper form of regulating our body exists, through mind–body exercises like mindfulness, visualization and concentration practices. Many high-performance athletes have learnt to regulate their physiology directly in this way. This deeper form of physiological intelligence is opened to us through mindfulness practices. Just as emotional intelligence requires an awareness and ability to regulate our emotional states, so physiological intelligence encompasses an awareness and ability to regulate our physiological states.

There's nothing supernatural about any of this; mindfulness need not be an esoteric pursuit. Mindfulness can encompass a wide variety of practices, including attention and emotional regulation, breathing practices and mind–body practices. It is a pragmatic, effective solution to the challenges of modern workplaces. And, so, our training programmes use mindfulness to help participants learn the skills to do this. But as the example below shows, it's not always straightforward.

Struggling to focus

Chris was once leading a month of daily mindfulness practice online. Tech specialists and engineers from all over the world were taking part. His experience had shown him that some people struggle with settling in to the practice for two primary reasons. First, they have no felt sense of their bodies and no interoceptive awareness. Second, their nervous systems are wound up, and they need to relax before they really engage in skill development.

Since he'd seen this often, especially with cognitively smart people, he was emphasizing in these sessions simply learning to relax as a first step. In several sessions, the same person, a lady called Lisa, essentially asked the same question again and again.

Lisa: 'Chris, I'm struggling to focus. How can mindfulness improve my focus?'

Chris: 'Thanks for asking, Lisa. My experience is that it's not so effective trying to work on focus first. You first must relax the nervous system. Then you can move back into the operating window, before being able to strengthen focus.'

Lisa: 'Oh, thanks. So, I should just relax?' Lisa delivered this with a quizzical look on her face, like I was pointing out the obvious.

Chris: 'Yes. Just relax.'

Lisa: 'Ok, I'll try to just relax. Thanks.' Chris thinks he remembers seeing an eye roll and look of bemusement from Lisa as she said this.

They met again the next day. And still, Lisa was having problems.

Lisa: 'If I relax, I find my mind goes all over the place to deal with the urgent stuff I have to do. So, I don't really relax at all! How does this help?'

Chris: 'Well, it sounds like you aren't relaxing. Try to just follow the outbreath, really feel the outbreath.'

Lisa: 'OK, I'll try it.' She again shook her head ever so slightly.

In the next session, Lisa's struggles continued.

Lisa: 'I just can't seem to focus on the outbreath. I try hard, but I'm not able to focus. Is there something wrong with me!?'

Chris: 'Yes, I think this is what I was trying to say. It sounds like you're trying hard, which suggests a lot of tension. This practice is not about trying hard. It's about relaxing, not trying even, if you will.'

Lisa: 'OK, I'll try to focus on relaxing. And stop trying, I guess.'

It was possible that Lisa's nervous system was dysregulated, so she couldn't relax. She also had a poor amount of interoceptive and self-awareness, so she didn't know what relaxation felt like. Thus, Lisa was in a difficult position. She had no felt sense to guide her to where we were trying to go. Looking for answers, she translated it into the only answer she knew, which was trying hard... to focus on relaxation. Clearly, this was a self-defeating approach.

In the end, Chris taught Lisa a specific breathing style. It helped relax her nervous system. This allowed her to get a felt sense of relaxation in her body, which then became a reference point for her mindfulness practice.

Over time, Lisa was gradually taken in by mindfulness and became more familiar with her nervous system and learning to relax. When we caught up a year later, she said she practised daily. While she still felt stressed a fair bit, she said she could cope with it much better than she used to. 'It's like there's distance between me and my stress,' she said. She now had a tool to 'take the edge off' the stress. And it was a healthier one than her old habit: drinking wine each night to relax.

More than just relaxation

Many view mindfulness just as a practice of relaxation. Indeed, if you Google mindfulness, you'll see many pictures of people in the lotus position, blissing out in a state of ecstasy. And yes, mindfulness is relaxing, but it can be done anywhere; on the train, in a waiting room, in a bathroom cubicle even. It's there, waiting to be utilized, to take the edge off some of life's more stressful moments. But relaxation is only a small part of mindfulness. Fundamentally, it's **a set of practices that help us explore our inner landscape, and learn to strengthen inner skills and the mind–body connection.**

In many modern societies, we're trained to think and function through cognition. While this is important, it can result in people 'overthinking' or getting 'lost in thought'. The average person has a poor understanding of their internal processes, and especially physiological ones.

This awareness can be trained and learnt. A useful analogy here is of listening to an unfamiliar genre of music. Imagine attending a classical concert with someone well versed in the genre. They might recognize so many aspects of the music that would be lost to novice listeners. The mood. The subtle changes in pitch and volume. Which parts of the song the conductor was emphasizing. It's only when we listen to classical music more that we start to recognize patterns. We start noticing subtle shifts and moods in the music.

It's the same with the body. At first, when many people start to practise mindfulness, they don't sense subtle changes in the body. They can think that nothing is happening. As we practise mindfulness over time, we learn to first notice and then regulate our inner states. Below, we'll look at how this works in practice.

The importance of breathing

In mindfulness practice, we usually work with the breath. Given how essential breathing is, it's surprising how poorly understood it is. Our breathing crucially impacts many of our physiological processes. It's the first step into deeper physiological regulation. Lower tissues in the lung have more blood flow. And so there's better transfer of oxygen to the blood when we breathe deeply. Breathing deeply and with a good posture also increases the volume of air taken in. Taken together, deeper breathing allows the breath to slow gradually.

In addition, the lengthening of the outbreath in relation to the inbreath leads to a switch from sympathetic arousal to parasympathetic recovery in the nervous system. This is a great way to shift your state from stressed to letting go to regenerating. Overall, the rate of breathing is deeply connected to our nervous system and our state of mind. We recognize that the breath is a key tool needed to boost individual resilience and wider organizational resilience.

Regulating our nervous system

Using mindfulness practices, we can learn to directly regulate the state of our nervous system via the breath.[9] Not only can we downregulate it consciously – shifting from sympathetic to parasympathetic activity – we can consciously upregulate it. And we can do this not only when practising mindfulness, but throughout the day. This allows us to spend more time in recovery mode, as well as to shift quickly away from stress modes when needed. It isn't hard to see how this could be useful in a workplace setting.

Regulating our emotional state

In addition to the nervous system, we have 'approach' or 'avoid' states in our hormonal systems. Approach is connected to expected reward, avoid to an expected threat. These expectations can lead to shifts in our hormone levels, like cortisol, dopamine and adrenaline. So, we can be positively stressed, looking forward to a pleasant event, or stressed in a negative way (something most people will perhaps feel more familiar with).

Many sportspeople visualize success (positive stress), meticulously going through the stages of a race in their minds to increase their confidence. In a similar way, mindfulness practitioners can downregulate strong emotional states, shifting from a negative to a positive one. These are both important levels of inner physiological regulation, of navigating our inner landscape and moving into the growing zone.

Maintaining focus

Our ability to focus can be trained. Many assume strong focus comes with tension. But when we strengthen our ability to focus, we're able to place our minds on an object with lower effort and higher stability. This means that working with focus strains us less, and we're more easily able to enter flow states. This ability is highly beneficial for deep work.

When reflecting on their personal journeys of mindfulness, Chris and Liane have taken different routes. Liane is naturally sporty and had to relate intensely with her body because of her traumatic childhood experiences. So, she started by building a high level of interoceptive awareness and ability to experience the body. Like a skilled conductor listening to a piece of music, she can become completely absorbed in her bodily experiences, and thus easily rests her mind in the present moment of sensory perception. This ability has also strengthened her naturally high emotional intelligence. She's adept at working with emotions both in herself and in others.

Chris started almost with a deficit in bodily awareness. He tried to work with focus over many years but struggled to develop stability of attention in this route. While he became familiar with the landscape of his mind and mental processes, he was still more often than not likely to be lost in thought.

In one memorable incident, while attending a month-long meditation retreat, he met every three days with Sara, his sage and at times cutting meditation instructor. In each interview Chris brought a new range of questions, options, experiences and insights, which Sara answered patiently and gently, while still trying to steer him in the direction of just resting. Finally, in interview seven, just as Chris was taking a long breath to start explaining all that he'd experienced, Sara cut him off. She said, 'Chris, whatever you're doing, just stop it.'

Somewhat taken aback, he paused – and began to simply notice what was going on. This was an important shift in his practice, simply sitting with the body, resting in the experience of the richness of our sensory experience. Mind wandering, he realized, was not a sign of mindfulness 'not working'.

Using heart rate variability as a window to neurophysiological regulation

In our work with employees, we often use heart rate variability (HRV) measurements from our partner Firstbeat. This helps them open a window into their inner life, and train people to work with their physiology. HRV devices measure the heart rate (for example 60 beats per minute) and the ongoing variance of our heart rate. A high variance is a good sign, indicating a healthy balance between nervous system activity in the sympathetic and parasympathetic systems. The exact values that HRV devices record are translated by Firstbeat into charts. These display the activation of our sympathetic (stress) nervous system against the parasympathetic nervous system (rest and digest).

Many of us spend too much time in sympathetic activation, whether it's because we're stressed, sleep too little, consume too much media or simply can't relax. From our data, we see that many people often spend more than 60–70 per cent of their day in sympathetic activation. While sympathetic activation (the stress response of our body) is in and of itself not bad, too much activation has a negative impact on our body resources and health. Both see the amount of time someone spends in sympathetic activation and the related decline in their bodily resources.

We've worked with thousands of people with HRV devices, helping them learn to separate their inner state from outside influences. In particular, learning to work with their breath and posture, relaxing their nervous systems, downregulating strong emotions and cultivating stable attention and deep work. These have a strong and quick impact on our energy management and vitality and are helpful in our high-intensity working world.

Lack of mind–body integration

The ability to integrate the body and mind, and to cultivate physiological intelligence, is a core aspect of mindfulness. Mind–body integration roots us into our felt sense of being. It strengthens our self-confidence and sense of self-efficacy, at a deep level. At Awaris, we train about 15,000 people per year. We personally see more and more people who seem discombobulated (one of our favourite words in the English language). While people we meet are extremely smart, we perceive them to be both confused and somewhat in a state of mental and physical disorder. And, often, they haven't even realized it.

In our work with over 100 companies annually, we include mindfulness practices in all our interventions. Many people have been deeply appreciative of this, but, in doing so, we've encountered people who struggle with the practice. We thought the following short story might be illuminating (and amusing).

A sensor in our system

Chris was once leading a mindfulness session for a group of senior leaders in a technology company. There were around 50 people in the room, which was a classic, somewhat dry conference room, in which we'd moved the tables to the side to arrange rows of chairs. In the first row sat the CEO, called John. He was clearly on the fence on mindfulness. In a way he wanted to learn it, but he also wasn't sure. There was scepticism.

Chris and the participants did a practice together. Chris invited participants to sit and notice their breath, and to keep their eyes closed or open as they felt was best for them. After a few minutes, he noticed the CEO's head beginning to wobble and bob; John was clearly falling asleep. After the practice, Chris expressed curiosity about his experience and invited him to share. He asked him what he noticed, and the conversation went like this:

John: 'Chris, I've done these mindfulness exercises a few times and I always have the same experience. I fall asleep quite quickly. I don't think this method works for me. What would you recommend? What does this mean?'

Chris: 'I think this means you're tired.'

Silence.

More silence.

Clearly, John was trying to make sense of Chris's (seemingly) completely irrelevant and ridiculous statement. He responded.

John: 'I don't understand? What does that have to do with this? I was talking about the breathing practice not working.'

Chris: 'I think it's working. It's showing you your own mind. You're clearly tired. You need to sleep more.'

John clearly wasn't liking where this conversation was going.

John: 'How does this advice help? I'm trying to clear my mind… and you're telling me that mindfulness is working by putting me to sleep?'

Chris: 'Yes. You probably don't know how to relax, you push yourself continually and might be ignoring your own body's needs. Mindfulness is a mirror to your mind. You should sleep more. You might find that helps.'

John paused and pondered.

John: 'Are you telling me that I don't know what is going on inside of me?'

Chris: 'Yes, it does seem like that. '

Silence.

John: 'So what's the point of mindfulness then?'

Since John was a technological engineer before becoming CEO, and most of the people in the room were engineers, Chris continued in way that might resonate with them.

Chris: 'If you don't have a sensor in the system, you can't regulate the system. What sensors do you have in your mind and body?'

John paused. He got that. 'Are you saying that to regulate my mind and body, see myself in the mirror so to say, I need to have a practice like mindfulness?'

Chris: 'Yes, this is especially true of leaders. If you don't look in the mirror of your mind daily, you won't see yourself. As the boss, many people might not even tell you when you have a bogey hanging out of your nose, let alone comment on how you are performing as a boss. Mindfulness is a sensor. It gives you information, but also allows you to learn to regulate this complex system. You can't shift a complex system by kicking it. You wanted to kick your mind and make it clearer, but given that you were too tired and stressed, that was unlikely to work.'

Every company needs mindfulness

We're going to make a strong statement here – every company needs mindfulness. Mindfulness is a foundational capacity that we'll increasingly need in the future. Interestingly enough, this was also a key conclusion of a meta-review of workplace wellbeing interventions. It recommended businesses '[o]ffer all employees (or help them to access) mindfulness, yoga or meditation on an ongoing basis. This can be delivered in a group or online, or using a combination of both.'[10]

Mindfulness is one of the most, or even *the* most, effective workforce interventions for reducing stress and building wellbeing. This has been established not only in countless studies, and by our own direct experience of working with hundreds of organizations; it's also been demonstrated by the lived experience of literally millions of people who have a regular practice that they've stuck with and deepened – the emphasis being on continuity and depth. In many ways, this is like the impact we expect from sports or nutrition. We have to stick to it, day after day. This will deepen our understanding of it. Only then will it work.

But many companies greet mindfulness with 'Well, we tried that,' or 'We're doing an app,' or 'Management doesn't like it.' They ask their employees to work 65-hour weeks, offer them a free mindfulness session per week, and expect it to solve all their business's problems and make their staff happy. When this doesn't happen, they blame the mindfulness intervention, rather than the way their teams and wider business are operating.

Partially because of this, like all hype cycles, mindfulness seems to be going through a slight dip in its perception in the working place, after its initial explosion. But this is a necessary shift – from mindfulness as a headline to mindfulness as the medicine. Mindfulness practice is a **foundational capacity**, which positively impacts numerous mind–body skills, and, most notably, helps us understand our inner landscape. Without this, shifting our states – and becoming resilient – will be impossible. Sticking with mindfulness builds many strengths, such as openness, self-awareness and self-regulation, and the ability to learn and adapt. Clearly, these are all necessary for success in the future.

… and leaders need mindfulness too

As we mentioned in relation to wellbeing, the evidence is strong that mindfulness is one of the most effective forms of intervention. But there's similar research emerging for leaders. Incorporating mindfulness practices into leadership development programmes, as Awaris does, can offer unique benefits compared to other types of leadership development programmes.[11] These include:

- **Stress reduction and emotional regulation**: Mindfulness practices, which involve focused attention and present-moment awareness, have been shown to reduce stress, enhance emotional regulation and improve overall wellbeing. Leaders who can manage stress and emotions effectively may exhibit more effective decision-making and communication skills.

- **Increased self-awareness**: Mindfulness encourages self-reflection and self-awareness, allowing leaders to better understand their strengths, weaknesses and biases. This self-awareness can lead to more authentic leadership styles and better interactions with team members. They might be less at risk of being described as a 'horrible boss' by employees.

- **Focus and decision making**: Mindfulness practices improve focus and attention. Leaders who can maintain focus are more likely to make thoughtful decisions and prioritize tasks effectively.

- **Enhanced empathy and communication**: Mindfulness practices can promote empathy, by fostering the ability to fully engage in conversations and understanding others' perspectives. Leaders who are empathetic and skilled communicators can build stronger relationships with their teams. In particular, in challenging times, we need empathetic and compassionate leaders.

- **Adaptability and flexibility**: Mindfulness encourages an open and flexible mindset, which is essential for navigating change and uncertainty. Leaders who are adaptable can guide their teams through transitions effectively.

- **Ethical leadership**: Mindfulness practices often align with ethical leadership principles, emphasizing integrity, transparency and concern for the wellbeing of others. Mindful leaders may exhibit higher ethical standards.

Embedding mindfulness as a foundational capacity

Many companies have recognized the importance of mindfulness. They've worked over the course of many years to support their staff with mindfulness training, embedding mindfulness into their working culture. There are many notable examples, including giant multinationals such as SAP, Novartis, Unilever and HSBC. We've been fortunate to work with HSBC for the last seven years, helping them build their global mindfulness champions network and innovating forms of mindfulness training for different audiences.

The HSBC leadership and mindfulness team takes this initiative seriously. They focus on both the quality of the training and the reach of the intervention. A central part of our approach with HSBC has been a seven-module mindfulness training programme, typically stretching over two months, targeted at the challenges of working in a global organization. It's had largely positive outcomes, improving staff wellbeing by over 20 per cent and reducing perceived stress by around 25 per cent in pre- and post-course comparisons. The HSBC mindfulness team has worked to bring this training to over a thousand people per year and the mindfulness champions we trained are delivering it in English, German, Spanish, French, Polish, Mandarin and Cantonese – a real testament to the global reach and inclusiveness of this approach. Fitting for an organization which claims to be 'The world's local bank', to be fair.

Our mindfulness champions training programme includes practice and retreat requirements that have been certified by the British Association of Mindfulness-Based Approaches. It's the first company champions programme that has met its external quality standards and it was awarded the Quality Assessment Mark. Together with HSBC, we've innovated and tested programmes for its senior leaders, the change and transformation community, globally dispersed teams and bank branch staff. In this way, mindfulness has become embedded into the fabric of work. It continues to be one of the most popular programmes at HSBC – and, we think, is a perfect example of how mindfulness can be embedded in an organization. Making its workers less stressed and improving their wellbeing, and helping them become more familiar with their inner states, improving their ability to shift them. Which, as we know, is the foundation of individual resilience.

KEY CHAPTER TAKEAWAYS

- We have both thinking brains and feeling brains.
- The thinking and feeling brains are becoming more disconnected, due to technological advancements, lifestyle changes, rising stress, changing social dynamics and sedentary lifestyles.
- Mindfulness is the best way to tackle these issues and has become profoundly more popular in recent decades.

- It's been found to be the most effective workplace intervention to reduce job stress and mental health symptoms.

- Mindfulness impacts us on the behavioural, psychological and physiological levels.

- Mindfulness helps people regulate their nervous systems and their emotional state and maintain focus, as proved by HRV studies we've conducted.

- We believe every company needs mindfulness, both at the individual and the organization-wide 'we' level, for the above reasons.

- Daily practice, for at least 10 minutes, is the key to success here.

Notes

1   Howard Hughes Medical Institute (2022) Cosmological thinking meets neuroscience in new theory about brain connections, *Science Daily*, www.sciencedaily.com/releases/2022/06/220630134842.htm (archived at https://perma.cc/PL6U-YTY5)

2   Foglets (2019) Computation power: human brain vs supercomputer, https://foglets.com/supercomputer-vs-human-brain/ (archived at https://perma.cc/4EX4-5LKQ); L Smirnova et al (2023) Organoid intelligence (OI): the new frontier in biocomputing and intelligence-in-a-dish, *Frontiers in Science*, 1 (February), www.frontiersin.org/journals/science/articles/10.3389/fsci.2023.1017235/full (archived at https://perma.cc/8PQP-MPM9)

3   Y T Uhls, M Michikyan, J Morris, D Garcia, G Small, E Zgourou and P M Greenfield (2014) Five days at outdoor education camp without screens improves preteen skills with nonverbal emotion cues, *Computers in Human Behaviour*, 39 (October), pp. 387–92, www.sciencedirect.com/science/article/pii/S0747563214003227 (archived at https://perma.cc/27G5-7HLW)

4   J Wakefield (2022) People devote third of waking time to mobile apps, BBC News, www.bbc.co.uk/news/technology-59952557 (archived at https://perma.cc/76A9-6AJS)

5   For an exhaustive look at the benefits of mindfulness, see D Goleman and R Davidson (2017) *Altered Traits: Science reveals how meditation changes your mind, brain, and body*, Avery Publishing, London

6   National Institute for Health and Care Excellence (2022) Mental wellbeing at work, www.nice.org.uk/guidance/ng212 (archived at https://perma.cc/5HXV-NGNQ)

7   J van Agteren, M Iasiello, L Lo, J Bartholomaeus, Z Kopsaftis, M Carey and M Kyrios (2021) A systematic review and meta-analysis of psychological

interventions to improve mental wellbeing, *Nature Human Behaviour*, 5 (April), pp. 631–52, www.nature.com/articles/s41562-021-01093-w (archived at https://perma.cc/AV6L-DX2U)

8   Web of Science (2023) www.webofscience.com/wos/woscc/basic-search (archived at https://perma.cc/79CY-CE4P)

9   Y Y Teng et al (2009) Central and autonomic nervous system interaction is altered by short-term meditation, *Proceedings of the National Academy of Sciences*, 106 (22), pp. 8865–70, www.pnas.org/doi/10.1073/pnas.0904031106 (archived at https://perma.cc/3JRU-8PD6)

10   National Institute for Health and Care Excellence (2022) Mental wellbeing at work, www.nice.org.uk/guidance/ng212 (archived at https://perma.cc/22EU-2NXF)

11   L Llona Urrila (2022) From personal wellbeing to relationships: a systematic review on the impact of mindfulness interventions and practices on leaders, *Human Resource Management Review*, 32 (3), pp. 1053–482, www.sciencedirect.com/science/article/pii/S1053482221000164 (archived at https://perma.cc/33Z3-HTFC); S Rupprecht, P Falke, N Kohls, C Tamdjidi, M Wittmann and W Kersemaekers (2019), Mindful leader development: how leaders experience the effects of mindfulness training on leader capabilities, *Frontiers in Psychology*, 10 (1081), www.frontiersin.org/articles/10.3389/fpsyg.2019.01081/full (archived at https://perma.cc/7RJE-9HZH)

6

Developing our resilience skills

'Don't wish for fewer problems; wish for more skills.'

EARL SHOAFF

In many ways, the last few years have been utterly unique. Prior to the year 2020, most businesses we worked with were reluctant to allow any of their employees to work from home. Even requests to work from home for a day, to let a plumber into the house, were viewed with deep suspicion. Businesses did their best to push back, and to make working from home very much the exception rather than the rule.

Of course, we all know what then happened. The world was plunged into a series of lockdowns. Businesses were forced to accept that they'd simply have to allow their workers to work from home, at least for knowledge workers.

If we review the top trends in workplace wellbeing in the past few years, they have been fundamentally influenced by the pandemic, associated lockdowns and the economic challenges which have persisted since then. In the immediate response to the pandemic, there was grief to deal with, for those who lost loved ones. Others had to deal with anxiety and loneliness amid the shift to working from home, while those in vulnerable groups worried about the potential health issues they might face.

For some, working from home was welcomed. Childless couples talk fondly about a time where they had fewer social plans, got into hobbies like painting and pottery and completed Netflix series marathons. However, those with young children, forced to homeschool them while working at the same time, had to master work and schooling challenges. Many on their own had to deal with prolonged and sometimes deep loneliness or disconnection. Against this backdrop, it's no wonder mental health issues worsened during the pandemic. As a result, mental health awareness and support have intensified in the workplace in recent years, and there's been an increased focus on the loneliness crisis – a crisis which has been rumbling on for a couple of decades, but was thrust into the spotlight during and after the pandemic.

Even after the lockdowns ended, most organizations we worked with continued to allow workers to work from home at least some of the time. A hybrid office and home model suddenly became the norm, completely untested in the modern working world. For many, the flexibility was highly welcomed. Attending Zoom meetings in a suit and tie, while wearing slippers and tracksuit bottoms, was a wonderful novelty. Less commuting meant more time with family (or in bed).

However, this arrangement has resulted in several unique challenges. As work boundaries melted, people working from home found it hard to set boundaries. When your home is your office, the temptation to continue checking your emails and remain 'on call', even on your downtime, increased. It made it harder to switch off. In the workplace wellbeing space, we've notice rising awareness of this problem, and tactics aimed at helping people establish a better work–life balance at home.

Physical exercise has suffered greatly due to hybrid working. For many people, their walk to the station or commute to work represented their only exercise. Now they could sit up in bed, open their laptop, and they were in the office. So, working from home has posed many challenges in terms of movement. Often, home workers don't go outside all day, reducing their exposure to natural light. People sit on unergonomic work chairs. Diets have worsened. It's much easier to turn off your camera on Zoom, grab a few cookies and then return to the call acting like nothing's happened. In a face-to-face meeting, maintaining your composure while doing so would likely be more challenging.

The pandemic has also caused profound economic challenges for households. Western governments splurged on massive social support spending during the pandemic. But in economics, there are no free lunches. These schemes have now ended. The money printed to pay for these schemes – and high global commodity prices – have engineered an inflation and cost-of-living crisis in the world's developed markets. Real incomes have fallen, and household mortgage payments have skyrocketed alongside interest rates.

Alongside these pandemic-related issues, we've seen the 'quiet quitting' and the 'belonging' crises worsen. The years 2021 to 2023 were marked by the Great Resignation. People have felt less engaged in their work or with their colleagues, with an impact on wellbeing and collaboration. The heightened intensity of the pandemic years, piled on top of the ongoing pace of working life, has raised burnout levels across the globe. At the same time, there's been an increased focus on workplace diversity. Inclusivity has become a heightened topic, especially in hybrid work.

Tackling these growing workplace wellbeing crises

Some businesses have taken steps to address these challenges, many of them focusing on rolling out technology for wellbeing. The use of technology has grown massively, with the development of apps, tools and platforms that support employee wellbeing, such as mental health tracking apps, stress management tools and virtual wellness sessions. But it probably won't surprise you to hear that we don't think technology alone is the answer.

Grief. Health challenges. Loneliness. Anxiety and mental health challenges. Deteriorating physical health. The challenges of hybrid working. The cost-of-living crisis. The belonging and quiet quitting crises. The renewed focus on inclusion and diversity. These are huge, pressing issues, which are at least getting more attention. But technology is only part of the answer to such profound workplace challenges. We believe the answer to these challenges will come from resilience skills, as we previously outlined in Chapter 3. Although each of these challenges is unique, the underlying human skills that can help solve them remain the same. This is because these challenges all play out in the same map of our human experience, of our human physiology. Let's take three of them to illustrate this point.

First, we have **physical wellbeing** in the home office. Many people joked about the '19' in Covid-19 referring to the 19lbs of weight people gained on average while working from home. This was not universally true for everyone – some people moved and exercised more, notably the Chinese gentleman who ran and live-streamed an entire marathon in his 40-square-metre apartment, circling around the table and sofa in his living room. Human resourcefulness knows no bounds.

The pandemic was accompanied by a massive decline in global step counts initially, and a big shift in sleep patterns. In addition, people who were unaware of their posture and movement struggled in their home office set-up. In the businesses we worked with, the employees who responded best to these challenges were those who applied their skills of movement, nutrition, rest and recovery and conscious breathing. They remembered to move, eat well, establish clear work boundaries and rest. Their habits made a difference.

Second, we have **financial challenges**. The pandemic and post-pandemic years exacerbated several financial trends in terms of rising housing and living costs. It plunged a lot of people into financial insecurity. There's context-specific support that people can be given, including sound financial advice. But, again, we noticed that skills of emotional regulation, positive outlook and connection to others make a big difference here.

These might not 'solve' your financial worries; we're saying these skills can buttress you against the anxiety caused by them. They can help you weather the inner turmoil caused by financial concerns.

Third, we can look at the **belonging crisis** in more detail. Many companies focused on physical health and safety during the pandemic, ensuring that core work was ongoing. But many businesses simply couldn't predict what damage was being done to the social fabric of their firms – in their teams, in their businesses and even in wider society. This has had repercussions in many aspects of life. It also contributed to employees' lack of engagement and quiet quitting.

Tackling this trend will require investment and time in rebuilding the social fabric of work. The best way of rebuilding the social fabric of an organization is for people to practise their skills of social connection and care. Spending time with each other. Feeling connected. Talking and connecting about matters that are meaningful to the heart and mind. When individuals, teams and leaders invest time and effort in their social connections and express care for each other, the social fabric of an organization is rebuilt, brick by brick.

These three examples show how overcoming key workplace challenges relies on the same human resilience skills – again and again. In the coming years, we'll face further unique challenges, each with their own context and symptoms. We can't prepare for unknown challenges. For example, an AI-driven world in 2050 will be so different to ours now that it's almost hard to conceive of it. But businesses can prepare themselves in a systematic manner for challenges if they choose to focus on training our resilience skills.

The benefit of focusing on resilience skills

As the examples above show, teaching people resilience skills can complement and potentially be more effective than general wellbeing programmes in the workplace. From the companies we've worked with, this appears to be for several key reasons:

- **Empowerment and self-reliance:** Resilience skills empower individuals to navigate challenges and setbacks independently. By supporting employees in developing resilience skills, healthy behaviours and effective stress management techniques, organizations enable them to take control of their own wellbeing. This self-reliance can lead to sustained improvements in mental and emotional health. We've seen in our resilience screening that those with a net negative resilience skills score (more skill gaps than strengths) had an average perceived stress level of 8.3 (out of 10). This is above the threshold level of 7.7 that indicates heightened mental distress and even mental illness. Those with a positive resilience skills balance (more skill strengths than gaps) had a perceived stress score of only 5.4. This is a 35 per cent lower level of perceived stress.

- **Adaptability to adverse situations:** Resilience skills focus on helping individuals to handle adversity and change. To adapt and thrive, even in difficult circumstances. Fundamentally, they're skills of changeability, equipping us with the ongoing ability to handle change. Our data suggests that people with a similar level of external stressors have significantly lower perceived stress if they have high resilience skills.

- **Preventative approach:** Resilience training takes a preventative approach. It equips employees with skills to prevent and manage stress and challenges. This will reduce the likelihood of burnout, absenteeism and other negative outcomes associated with workplace stress.[1] Resilience skills also have lasting effects, as they teach individuals how to approach challenges with a growth mindset and positive outlook. This can contribute to improved overall mental health, not just in the workplace but also in the individual's personal life. Our data also suggests that resilience skills have a significant positive impact on workplace performance, with the skills explaining 20 per cent of the variance in workplace performance.

- **Positive organizational culture:** When employees possess strong resilience skills, they contribute to a more positive and supportive organizational culture. Resilient individuals are better equipped to handle conflicts, setbacks and changes, fostering a healthier work environment. Several studies have shown a strong positive relation coefficient of between 0.35 and 0.45 between resilience and wellbeing and positive organizational citizenship behaviours (such as innovation, collaboration and ethical behaviour).[2]

- **Cost-effectiveness:** Resilience training can potentially be more cost-effective in the long run. It can reduce the need for reactive interventions, such as counselling or medical treatments, to address workplace stress and its associated health effects. For this reason, in a large-scale review of workplace wellbeing interventions, Deloitte found that preventative interventions, in particular training interventions, had a 6:1 return on each US dollar, Chinese yuan or euro invested, which is far higher than restorative interventions.[3]

- **Alignment with organizational goals:** Resilience skills align with the demands of the modern workplace, where change is frequent and challenges are inevitable. By enhancing employees' ability to handle these demands, organizations can improve overall performance and productivity, as we'll show in later chapters.

How to train resilience skills – a five-phase process

As we begin to look at our resilience skills, it's important to remind ourselves that they're skills. They're not states. They are not a simple cognitive understanding of a skill. Skills must be learnt, practised and mastered. Development typically goes through several stages, which are mirrored by neuroplastic developments in the brain and body:

- **Phase one: curiosity:** First of all, we must become aware that such a thing as a resilience skill exists and become curious about it. If you, the reader, have got this far, this implies you're at least at this stage. This opens us up to the field. It directs our attention to the topic, encouraging us to learn more. Fundamentally, this creates an approach state in our minds. For example, we begin to understand what it means to be positive and why it is helpful.

- **Phase two: insight** (the 'aha' moment): When we think about something, or, even better, experience it, we have an 'aha' moment. An insight, a realization. Perhaps we learn something about an experience we've been having, or emotions that have shown up frequently in our lives. Or we feel something that connects to other experiences we've had, and we finally understand the connection. Such an insight is a new series of signalling connections in the brain – like clearing a small track in the dense jungle, leading to a new location. As an example, we could suddenly realize that as a leader we tend to be negative, always focusing on problems, and that this negativity is spilling over into our family life.

- **Phase three: exploration:** The next step is to be willing to experiment with this insight. To have an understanding that this pathway in the jungle will soon be overgrown again, if we don't walk through it again and again. So, it's a willingness to learn, and to take personal responsibility to develop the new skill through repeated training. We've learnt what the skill is, have had an insight about its relevance and, crucially, have realized we can and must take responsibility ourselves for the development of this skill. We understand that being negative isn't helpful. We want to be more positive. We understand we actually have to practise to master the skill.

- **Phase four: practice:** Now we can begin to regularly practise the skill. Whether it's running, changing our diet, cultivating a positive outlook or connecting with people, we have to practise it. If we don't, the skill won't develop. We won't be able to regulate our inner landscape any better than previously. So, first, this requires effort and effective practices which change our state. For example, we agree with our team to start our weekly team meetings with a discussion of what's gone well in the last week, before we jump into the usual unsolved problems. At first it feels strange. But, slowly, we realize these skills lift everyone's mood and make us solve problems quicker. We also notice meetings tend not to drag on too long. The experience is a positive feedback loop, getting us to start enjoying and appreciating this effort. Still, sometimes we forget and drop it.

- **Phase five: habits:** Finally, once we've practised a skill regularly, it becomes easy. It becomes a habit. Automatic, even. What's happened is that our brain has begun to change. New pathways are being created that make repeating this behaviour easier and more likely. We realize that we don't forget to apply the skill, even in difficult situations. Eventually the continual practising of habits leads to trait change.[4] We become habitually positive, or indeed a positive person. Our child calls us a 'happy' mummy or daddy, for the first time that we can remember.

Figure 6.1 outlines the five phases of learning a skill.

We want to lay out two examples of skill development, from the point of view of how the process feels, to highlight this phased approach to learning a skill. One is when Chris started to jog regularly to keep fit, and another is the path of getting a leader we worked with to learn the skill of relaxation.

FIGURE 6.1 The five phases of learning a skill: an integrated learning process to cultivate resilience

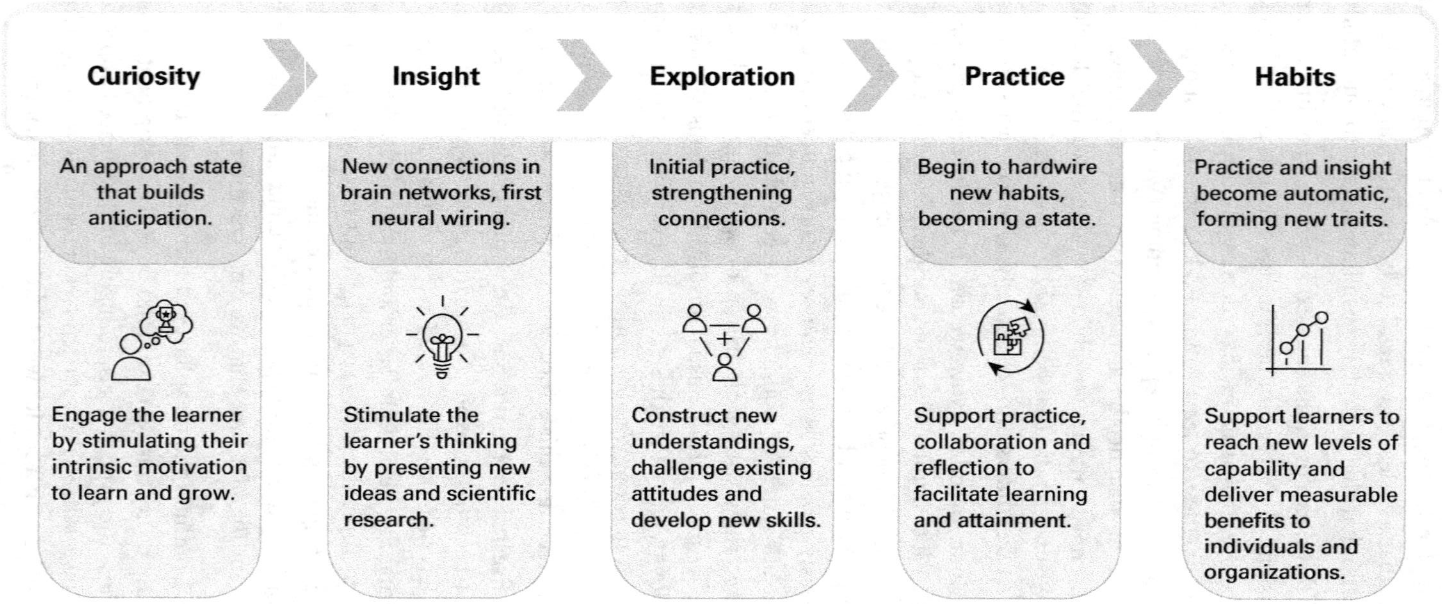

Curiosity	Insight	Exploration	Practice	Habits
An approach state that builds anticipation.	New connections in brain networks, first neural wiring.	Initial practice, strengthening connections.	Begin to hardwire new habits, becoming a state.	Practice and insight become automatic, forming new traits.
Engage the learner by stimulating their intrinsic motivation to learn and grow.	Stimulate the learner's thinking by presenting new ideas and scientific research.	Construct new understandings, challenge existing attitudes and develop new skills.	Support practice, collaboration and reflection to facilitate learning and attainment.	Support learners to reach new levels of capability and deliver measurable benefits to individuals and organizations.

Chris's fight against the flab (or jogging journey, depending on how you look at it)

- **Phase zero: no interest:** Chris was young, reasonably slim and busy working. He didn't think about regular sports much, but did play tennis occasionally. He never thought about getting heavier and didn't watch what he ate or pay attention to sports.

- **Phase one: curiosity:** On a holiday once, while swimming with an acquaintance, Chris found himself in a conversation about weight gain. This friend, Ivan, 10 years older than Chris, made an off-the-cuff remark as his eyes briefly darted down at Chris's slightly pale and quietly expanding midriff: 'Once we reach 30, we begin to put on weight. We lose muscle mass if we don't exercise.' Even though at the time Chris remembers shrugging this off, something about the statement and the look at his belly stuck in Chris's mind. Deep down, he knew there was truth to it. In the next few months, whenever someone brought up regular exercise, his ears pricked up. He listened and asked them about it.

- **Phase two: insight** (the 'aha' moment): Chris once tried to run, but after 15 minutes ran out of steam. He also felt heavy, cumbersome on his feet. For someone who'd tended to be on the slim end most of his life, this felt uncomfortable. He realized what people said about sport was true, as well as the regular accumulation of weight. The 'aha' moment was that this was happening to him.

- **Phase three: exploration:** He began to run occasionally. But it was an effort. It was hard. He'd decided to run once a week on weekends, but it was a lot of effort to change his state from low energy/regeneration to running. He avoided it, sometimes procrastinating because he needed more energy to shift states. He'd even spend many minutes planning his running route, just to avoid starting the run. However, when he ran, he felt good – and, particularly afterwards, he felt fantastic.

- **Phase four: practice:** As Chris practised more, he became a little better. But above all, he enjoyed it. It became easier. He knew it was a reliable way to change his neurophysiological state, from stressed to regenerating. So, when he suddenly had 45 minutes free in a foreign town, he'd put on his running shoes and explore. Not only was running easier, but the skill in changing his state had become stronger, so he naturally had more variance in his states. He was falling in love with the skill.

- **Phase five: habits:** Now, jogging is a habit of Chris's. It requires little effort. He makes sure he walks 10,000 steps a day and has at least 300 minutes of some kind of higher intensity exercise per week, like jogging. He enjoys it, and it's natural. If he doesn't do it, he misses it. A true sign that the habit is embedded in his life.

A leader learns to relax, with some difficulty

Liane once worked with a driven and focused leader, who had substantial responsibilities. Thomasz was leading a division in a global banking firm which that was undergoing a rapid transformation, and he was struggling with burnout in his teams:

- **Phase zero: no interest:** Liane suggested to Thomasz once that it was important to relax and recover. Thomasz was in his mid-forties, based in Frankfurt, and was responsible for the transformation of several IT systems in his bank. Thomasz absolutely couldn't bear to hear that he needed to relax – he only knew how to push himself. And, implicitly, he was scared that if he relaxed, he wouldn't have the energy to work at the pace he wanted to. He didn't understand the need for relaxation. His brief self-examination, feeling into how he felt, gave him the sense he couldn't relax.

- **Phase one: curiosity:** Liane encouraged him to use a heart rate variability (HRV) device. She spoke of how high-performance athletes use them to maintain an optimal balance of performance. This caught Thomasz's attention, perhaps given his focus on performance. He started to wear one – and, frankly, was shocked at his data. He had very high stress levels and low recovery. The HRV device suggested he was at risk of some serious health dangers, including a heart attack. Liane and Thomasz also spoke about his sleep (woeful) and his mood (stressed or very stressed). He began to connect the dots.

- **Phase two: insight** (the 'aha' moment): Thomasz listened more intently in the next session. Liane told him about the science of resilience and tasked him with observing himself for two weeks – noting down his feeling state during meetings, or as he worked on his laptop, and how this correlated with the measurement data from the HRV device. Liane also asked him to observe his team, and how they behaved around him when he was in a high stress mode. His 'aha' moment was clear. He was highly stressed during meetings, and even when working on his laptop, and this also impacted his team, freezing them in a fixed mindset. Something needed to change, for himself and for his family, who he risked leaving without a father.

- **Phase three: exploration**: Thomasz softened. He'd realized the costs of his stress to himself, as well as to his team, for whom he cared a lot. He understood that recovery is essential to performance. He began his 'high-performance recovery journey', as we sold it to him – Liane's ingenious and tongue-in-cheek way of getting him even more interested in resting. He accepted it with humour. But he was still scared about fully relaxing. He worried he wouldn't be able to carry his workload with too much time resting.

- **Phase four: practice**: He began to practise recovery in the evenings. This involved not working after 8.30pm (late for some, but very early by Thomasz's normal working patterns). Liane encouraged him to sleep longer and to not push himself so much in sports, but instead actually to try to enjoy himself more. Liane didn't immediately try to get him to relax at work (she knew we'd be banging our heads against a brick wall). Thomasz noticed how his mood improved massively, and how he became a lot more curious about how his children were doing. He became quite serious about the three practices he discovered. It was slowly changing his life.

- **Phase five: habits**: Liane spoke again with Thomasz six months later, and he'd really stuck to his habits. He'd become more open. And when they chatted, he realized that he'd also begun to relax at work – a huge change. Liane did another HRV assessment and saw that there was now a lot more green (meaning the activation of the rest and digest nervous system) in his day in general. There were even a few green flashes in his workday (the moments when he was deep in the red previously). Reflecting, he realized that these green moments were when he had some of the best times at work, where he was able to think deeply, have a good conversation with someone or have flashes of creativity. He began to have confidence in extending his relaxation to work situations and didn't feel guilty. He enjoyed work more. He became closer with his family. His mortality risk declined. Relaxation was a much-needed, possibly life-saving, intervention.

So how long does this take?

After reading the past two case studies, you might be convinced. You might be thinking: 'I want these benefits, right now, as soon as possible.' But realism, as always, is important. There are no quick fixes.

Recent research has shown our brains are neuroplastic. This means that depending on the type of habits we engage in, brains build new neurons or strengthen new neural connections. While a lot of this research has been done with meditators, it's important to know that everything we do changes our brain, even when we are using unconscious processes. For example, addictive behaviour slowly decreases the connection to our prefrontal cortex, where decisions are made.[5] London taxi drivers have to learn 'the Knowledge' to gain their licence, requiring them to learn more than 25,000 street names by heart. As a result, they have larger hippocampi, the area of the brain responsible for long-term memory.[6] **If going to the gym builds muscle, using certain parts of our minds does the same for our brains.**

Mastering a mind–body skill such as relaxation or emotional regulation involves awareness, insight and then regular practice. And then this leads to actual neuroplastic changes in our brains. At this point, we can speak of a behaviour becoming a trait – it becomes part of who we are, as shown in Figure 6.2.

FIGURE 6.2 Practices as the basis of skill building and new behaviours

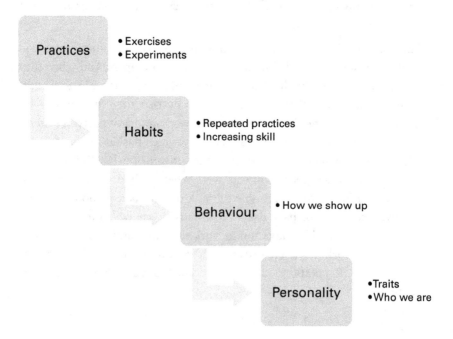

Practices
- Exercises
- Experiments

Habits
- Repeated practices
- Increasing skill

Behaviour
- How we show up

Personality
- Traits
- Who we are

We'll return to this concept later, as understanding and selecting practices are crucial for individual, team and organization-wide change. The time taken for this mastery to emerge can vary significantly from person to person and depends on several factors. This includes individual aptitude, dedication and the complexity of the skill. Mastery is a continuous process; we must practise the skill on an ongoing basis. In the TikTok, instant gratification generation, where attention spans are collapsing at an alarming rate, this might not be what some people want to hear.

But it's the truth. If we again use the gym analogy, no one can expect to be fit if they stop exercising. Their muscles will weaken without consistent usage. But, crucially, this becomes easier when we see it as a skill. If we continually apply the skill, it stays present and helps strengthen our resilience, rather than fading without use. It becomes part of us. There's a lot of evidence available on how quickly people can change their fitness level. So, for example, people who start to exercise can see gains related to several factors:

- **Initial improvements:** Untrained individuals or those who are relatively new to exercise often experience rapid improvements in the early stages of training. This phenomenon is known as 'beginner gains'. Within a few weeks of starting a structured exercise programme, beginners may notice significant increases in strength, cardiovascular endurance and overall fitness.

- **Specificity of training:** The type of exercise and the specific fitness component targeted will influence the rate of improvement. For example, cardiovascular improvements may be noticed earlier with regular aerobic exercise (eg running, cycling) compared to strength gains, which can take a bit longer to develop.

- **Duration and intensity:** The frequency, intensity and duration of the exercise programme play a crucial role in determining the rate of fitness improvement. Consistent and appropriately intense training is essential for achieving significant changes.

- **Age:** Younger individuals may experience faster improvements, due to their higher natural levels of growth hormones and general adaptability. However, older adults can still achieve substantial gains with appropriate exercise tailored to their abilities and needs.

- **Progress tracking:** Keeping track of fitness progress through metrics like endurance, strength or body composition changes can provide valuable feedback and motivation. Seeing a gradual upward curve on a chart can be enough to give you the motivation to keep on going.

We believe these same exercise principles apply to any skill development. The time it takes to establish a new habit or resilience skill can vary widely depending on various factors, including the complexity of the skill, individual differences, consistency of practice and the method of learning. For the impatient among you, we're talking weeks, months, years and onwards. Not days, sadly. While there's no one-size-fits-all answer, here are some general guidelines and examples of different types of skills:

- **Simple habits:** Simple habits like drinking a glass of water upon waking up or doing a short mindfulness exercise can take around 21 days to become automatic. This notion of 21 days was popularized by Dr Maxwell Maltz's book *Psycho-Cybernetics*.[7] More complex habit formation takes longer, but simple skills like learning to relax the nervous system or doing 7,000 steps a day might take this long.

- **Physical skills:** Developing physical skills, like playing a musical instrument, learning to cook a new dish or practising a new sport, typically takes more time. This is due to the need for muscle memory and coordination. Estimates vary, but it's commonly believed that it takes around 3,000 to 10,000 hours of deliberate practice to completely master a complex skill. However, resilience skills such as conscious breathing are simpler and can be learnt much more quickly. In our observations, we see that if people stick to it for at least two weeks, they'll find it increasingly easy to work with their breath.

- **Behavioural changes:** Establishing behavioural changes like improving attention management, practising better communication or adopting a healthier lifestyle can vary greatly. Some sources suggest that it can take around 66 days on average to establish a new behavioural change, but this can range from a few weeks to several months. Many lifestyle courses are over three to four weeks, as this is a sufficient period of time for people who practise with some diligence to establish some new lifestyle habits.

- **Mindfulness and meditation:** Developing a consistent mindfulness or meditation practice may take a few weeks to a few months to start experiencing significant benefits. Research indicates that after about eight weeks of consistent practice, individuals may notice improvements in attention, stress reduction and emotional regulation. When we work with businesses, we also usually witness notable improvements in these traits within six to 10 weeks.

- **Cognitive skills:** Developing cognitive skills such as learning a new language or mastering a complex software program can take several months to a few years, depending on the intensity of practice and prior knowledge. Research suggests that gaining proficiency in a new language might take anywhere from 600 to 2,200 hours of study.

What have we learnt by working with businesses?

We've also collected data from our interventions with businesses. We have seen several clear patterns when it comes to learning resilience skills. The first is that modular repeated interventions have a higher impact than one-off interventions. This aspect is well known in the field of wellbeing interventions and comes up again and again in all meta-studies reviewing the impact of wellbeing interventions. Further, in our data, collected over four years from over 2,000 individuals, the impact of these interventions is quite dramatic, as Figure 6.3 shows.

People must practise. Sitting in a longer training programme, with multiple modules over eight weeks, only leads to improved outcomes when people *actually practise*. In sport, we understand this deeply. It's the same for any

FIGURE 6.3 Wellbeing and compassion can be trained

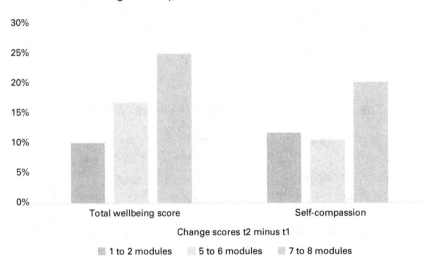

Improvements in skills based on a six- to eight-week Awaris training programme.

FIGURE 6.4 Practice frequency is related to greater impact

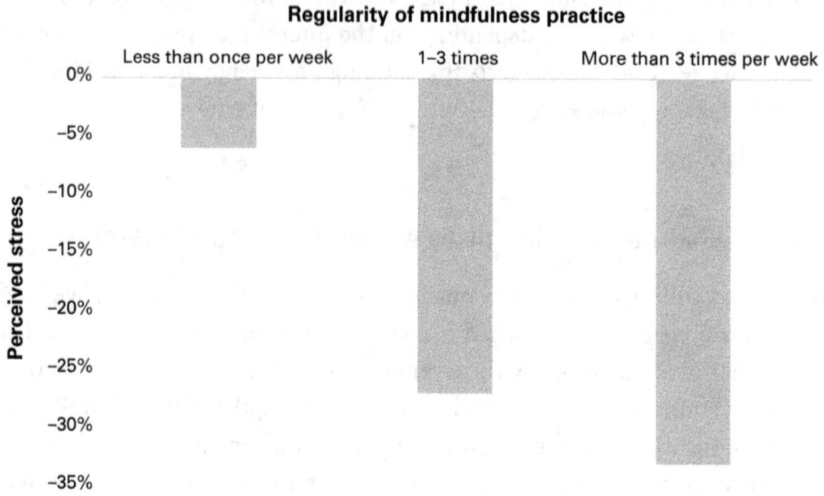

Regularity of mindfulness practice

When participants practise mindfulness at least once per week, they report significantly lower stress levels.

training of a mind–body skill, such as the resilience skills we teach. How committed you are with the practice makes the difference! Figure 6.4 shows this quite simply. The more frequently you practise mindfulness, for example, the lower your perceived stress. Practising once per week reduces perceived stress by 6 per cent on average – whereas with more than three times a week, perceived stress drops by a whopping 33 per cent. Need we say more? Hopefully not.

The secret hack: all the benefits without the effort?

People we work with often ask us for the cheat. The secret mental hack, the shortcut to all this cumbersome, long-term practice. 'What's the hack here, where I can get the immediate benefits, without the work?' 'There are no shortcuts' is always our answer. Just like men's fitness magazines, which promise 'rock-hard abs in no time' on the front cover – but then inside the magazine, it's explained that consistent, ongoing effort of calorific restriction and daily exercise is needed to get there. There are no cheats. When our clients look at us expectantly, hoping for the cheat code, we instead explain that the 'secret' is dedication. Consistency. Proven training methods. And above all, enjoyment.

They are usually disappointed by this answer, although they usually know it's true. This is life, after all.

This is important to clearly state in the context of improving people's wellbeing and resilience. Many wellbeing offerings are focused on acknowledging a problem or symptom, naming it, increasing awareness and giving a few good tips. While this is commendable, it does not in any realistic way address the actual effort and time it takes to learn a skill. It isn't realistic. We need to focus on the underlying skill, with courage, diligence and determination. Being reminded of its usefulness again and again, in the context of new challenges. It's only at this point that we can become resilient as individuals.

And this, of course, is the building block of making our teams and business cultures more resilient. We-silience, after all, is based upon the fundamental truth that we don't live in isolation. We're social beings. And we'll now turn to how we can make the move from looking at resilience from the 'I' to the 'we' level.

KEY CHAPTER TAKEAWAYS

- The coronavirus (Covid-19) pandemic has brought several workplace challenges into greater focus.
- These include loneliness, anxiety and poor mental health, physical inactivity, hybrid working, cost-of-living pressures and a greater push for diversity and inclusion.
- Although technology can take us some of the way, we view resilience skills as the most fundamental way of tackling these issues.
- Teaching people resilience skills can lead to empowerment and self-reliance, adaptability to adverse situations and positive business culture improvement. They represent a cost-effective, preventative approach to wellbeing challenges.
- Resilience skills are mastered in five phases:
  - Phase one: curiosity: Becoming aware of the skill.
  - Phase two: insight: The 'aha' moment where the person realizes they need to change.
  - Phase three: exploration: Experimenting with this insight and skill.
  - Phase four: practice: Regularly practising the skill.
  - Phase five: habits: The skill becomes an automatic and enjoyable part of life.
- There are no quick fixes. It takes time and regular practice over weeks, months and years, in most cases, to become truly proficient (although some resilience skills take less time than others).

Notes

1 See I Cacciatori, C Grossi, C D'Auria, A Bruneri and C Casella (2021) Resilience skills as a protective factor against burnout for health professionals: a cross-sectional study on new hires from the hospital of Lodi, *Journal of Italian Medicine*, **43** (2), pp. 131–6, https://pubmed.ncbi.nlm.nih.gov/34370923/ (archived at https://perma.cc/5RSV-GJB7); C Cohen, S Pignata, E Bezak, M Tie and J Childs (2023) Workplace interventions to improve well-being and reduce burnout for nurses, physicians and allied healthcare professionals: a systematic review, *BMJ Open*, **13** (6), https://pubmed.ncbi.nlm.nih.gov/37385740/ (archived at https://perma.cc/48YL-GDLZ)

2 P Warr and K Nielsen (2018) Wellbeing and work performance, in E Diener, S Oishi and L Tay, *Handbook of Well-Being*, Noba Scholar, Salt Lake City

3 Deloitte (2020) Mental health and employers: refreshing the case for investment, www2.deloitte.com/uk/en/pages/consulting/articles/mental-health-and-employers-refreshing-the-case-for-investment.html (archived at https://perma.cc/DJG9-RC3F)

4 D Goleman and R Davidson (2017) *Altered Traits: Science reveals how meditation changes your mind, brain, and body*, Avery Publishing, London

5 NIH News in Health (2015) Biology of addiction: drugs and alcohol can hijack your brain, https://newsinhealth.nih.gov/2015/10/biology-addiction (archived at https://perma.cc/VN6Y-8BEF)

6 F Jabr (2011) Cache cab: taxi drivers' brains grow to navigate London's streets, *Scientific American*, www.scientificamerican.com/article/london-taxi-memory/ (archived at https://perma.cc/2SSS-DYRB)

7 M Maltz (1960) *Psycho-Cybernetics*, Perigee Books, London

7

From 'I' to 'we': The importance of business culture

Humans are social beings. We grow up in families, get taught in schools surrounded by other children, and almost every product you consume was created by humans who cooperated. Businesses, as we've seen, are social units, fundamentally based on collaboration. But it's easy to forget this. After all, for many of us, we can now work from home, largely in isolation. If you want to 'hunt' for your food, you merely press a button on your smartphone, and 30 minutes later it'll be delivered to your door. Even shopping is no longer an excuse to leave the house. We think 'socializing' means looking at pictures of acquaintances on social media, while sitting alone on a sofa. In the West, more of us are living alone than ever before.

Despite these modern changes, humans are indeed primarily social beings. This is easily said, but what does this mean? From an evolutionary perspective, we've succeeded because we cooperate. Cooperation has always played a greater role in our survival and development as a species than competition (despite the persistent belief that we survive because we compete). Look at a human in isolation. They have puny physical abilities (gorillas are four to nine times as strong). We have thin skin, pitifully blunt teeth, fragile claws and a very dull sensory perception. Drop us in the jungle and we wouldn't survive long in any environment with snakes, gorillas, chimpanzees, lions, leopards or a plethora of other dangers. But drop 20 of us in the jungle and we'd stand a greater chance – and would probably empty the jungle of these animal threats in 10 years. Unfortunately, this seems to be what we're on course to do at the global level.

It's our ability to cooperate that has allowed us – a fragile species of ape – to build buildings as tall as mountains, dam rivers, change how the Earth looks from space and begin to unpeel the mysteries of the cosmos with our almost unbelievable technological advancements, particularly in the last 100 or so years. Because of the massive evolutionary advantages of cooperation, our brains are adapted and sculpted for cooperation, in far more ways than we realize. For example, let's have a look at some of the complex social processes that our brains must master:

- **Communication and language:** Humans have evolved sophisticated communication systems, including spoken language and non-verbal cues. Effective communication is vital for exchanging information, expressing emotions, coordinating actions and forming relationships.

- **Emotional regulation:** Social interactions depend on subtle emotional regulation. Observe the emotional regulation of a group of lions and you'll quickly notice how subtle our emotional regulation is compared to theirs. Even chimpanzees, which share 99 per cent of our DNA, are more likely to scream, fight and throw faeces at each other than settle a dispute calmly like a human (you'd really hope).

- **Social learning:** Humans can learn from others through observation, imitation and communication. Social learning requires the subtle perception of many cues and an ability to perceive how others feel.

- **Theory of mind:** Humans possess a unique cognitive ability called the 'theory of mind'. This allows us to attribute mental states, beliefs, desires and intentions to others. This capacity enables us to understand and predict the behaviour of others, which is crucial for successful social interactions.

- **Empathy and altruism:** Humans can experience empathy and understanding and share in the emotions of others, thanks to mirror neurons. This ability fosters pro-social behaviours, such as helping, cooperating and showing altruism towards others, which strengthen social bonds and contribute to the cohesion of communities.

- **Cooperative problem solving:** Human societies often face complex challenges that require cooperative problem solving. Having social brains enables us to work together, pool our resources and solve problems collectively, leading to innovations and advancements.

All these examples show how the brain is literally formed through and for social interaction. We even have regions of the brain with 'mirror neurons', which allow us to feel and subtly copy what others are doing. Feeling and observing, so we get a felt sense of what the other person's going through, to interpret, understand and learn from them.

CASE STUDY
An example of our social brain in working life

Think of this situation. You're navigating your way through the cafeteria of your office, while speaking to a colleague called Eleonora. You notice Juan across the cafeteria. You wave to him, smiling when he waves back.

Let's look inside the brain as something as seemingly simple as this is happening. Your brain is predicting the motion of 20 to 30 people in your field of view, figuring out how you can best walk without bumping into someone, while also respecting hundreds of implicit social movement hierarchies. For example, do you walk between two people having a close conversation? Do you walk on the left or right of someone with a tray in one hand and a cup in the other? You might be trying to project a sense of competence to your colleagues; how should you hold your posture and gait to do so?

While your brain is predicting the motion of all the people around you, you're also maintaining the conversation with Eleonora. You sense through her slight hesitation and pauses that, perhaps, she doesn't want to talk about how her husband is. Could it be they are having difficulties in their relationship?

At the same time, your brain's also been scanning the faces of everyone in the field of view (which takes an enormous amount of informational processing resource), and you recognize Juan – who you need to speak to. You wave to him, while still in conversation with Eleonora, signalling you've seen him, and you'll come to chat to him shortly. He waves back and you smile, to acknowledge your mutual recognition, and to signal your relief at having seen him. You explain to Eleonora that you need to chat to Juan and say 'bye'. You note she hesitates a little, as if she did want to say something. But you've already turned towards Juan. You make a mental note to reach out to Eleonora again tomorrow, and take more time for the conversation.

On the surface, this example seems so simple. So normal. This example shows that we don't really notice how much of our brain is occupied with social processing. It happens 'under the hood' as it were, unconsciously. And so, we don't realize the extent to which our brain is a social one.

Our nervous system is social too

Because our survival depends on cooperation, it's not just our brain which is social. Our entire nervous system is also primed for ensuring our survival in a social environment. While we previously wrote about our sympathetic and parasympathetic nervous systems, we now must dig a little deeper and talk about the three branches of our nervous system.

The interaction between our nervous system and our social environment is explained in **polyvagal theory**.[1] This theory, developed by Dr Stephen Porges, is a neurobiological framework that helps us understand the way our nervous system interacts with our social environment. We need to first understand this before we can look at how it relates to the workplace and to building resilient business cultures more generally.

The autonomic nervous system (ANS), which we've already spoken of, is responsible for regulating involuntary bodily functions. This includes heart rate, respiration, digestion and arousal levels. The ANS consists of three branches: the ventral vagal (social nervous) and the dorsal vagal systems (which together make up the parasympathetic nervous system), and the sympathetic nervous system:

- **Ventral vagal system** – This is associated with the rest and digest response to re-establish homeostasis. Crucially, it also promotes and regulates social engagement, feelings of safety and relaxation. When the ventral vagal system is active, it facilitates positive social interactions and emotional connection with others. The activation of the ventral vagal system also coincides with our window of tolerance – the window of our experience in which we're able to self-regulate.

- **Dorsal vagal system** – The dorsal vagal system is also a component of the parasympathetic nervous system. It's associated with the freeze or shutdown response in extreme situations of danger, helplessness or exhaustion. Activation of the dorsal vagal system can lead to feelings of disconnection, dissociation and social withdrawal. Here, we're outside our window of tolerance and not able to easily regulate attention and emotions.

- **Sympathetic nervous system** – This is separate from the ventral vagal and dorsal vagal systems (ie the combined parasympathetic nervous system). It's responsible for the fight or flight response when the body perceives stress or danger. Activation of the sympathetic system leads to increased heart rate, blood pressure and alertness, preparing the body for action. It also moves us out of our window of tolerance.

Our nervous system is thus extremely attuned to social context and signalling. We call this **neuroception**. This describes the way our nervous system detects safety or danger in our social environment, without conscious aware-ness. It influences our responses to social cues and interactions, shaping our social behaviours and emotional experiences. This is essential for our survival, especially as children. As children we're entirely helpless and dependent on adults around us, and so we become very good at reading them (mainly unconsciously). We adapt our behaviours to subtle emotional and social cues from our caregivers.

We also learn in this way. A lot of learning as children comes from mirror-ing others' experiences, and then resonating with them. We learn not from the spoken word, but from others' behaviours and emotional signals. And, in fact, this is also how we teach them as adults. We try to get into a positive resonance with children, listen to them, reflect their experiences, and empa-thetically suggest new courses of action. Many a time an overenthusiastic dad will find himself on all fours on the ground, barking like a dog. It's interesting to think about this. Why do we do this? And how did we learn how to bark like a dog anyway? Did we ever practise?

So, evolution has taught us that neuroception and mirroring are crucial for fitting in, learning and navigating the many unwritten social rules and hierarchies in our social environment. And in the modern world, perhaps the main social environment that most humans reside in is the workplace. Most people normally spend five out of seven days operating in a social working environment, which has all the complex hierarchies and power structures that a wandering tribe of our hunter-gather ancestors would have had.

How does neuroception work in the workplace?

How do the ventral vagal, dorsal vagal and sympathetic nervous systems relate to the modern workplace? As social beings, we're continually scan-ning the environment for cues for our behaviour. In a work setting, **safety cues** might include a positive and supportive work culture, respectful communication, clear expectations and a sense of belonging within the team. Even something as small as colleagues remembering your birthday might do the trick. When our nervous system detects these safety cues, it activates the ventral vagal system, prompting feelings of safety and relaxa-tion. Cues of safety can move us into a zone of self-regulation, unconsciously.

Conversely, neuroception is also vigilant for signs of danger in the work-place. These threats might include hostile interactions, perceived criticism, unfair treatment or a lack of psychological safety. You might have made a mistake and have been called into your boss's office. You know them, and you know you're about to have your head bitten off. If our nervous system detects these **danger cues**, it can trigger the sympathetic nervous system's fight or flight response, where you feel energized and would rather just run away from the office. Equally, these threats could activate the dorsal vagal system, leading to feelings of disconnection and withdrawal. You're immobilized in response to a threat. You could sit frozen, at your desk, in a state of shutdown.

The workplace, in many ways, is like our modern-day jungle. Our modern-day tribe. Social signals, resonance and communication all strongly impact our nervous system. They can move us quickly in and out of our window of tolerance. It's also important to note that we perceive cues differently. Someone who has experienced trauma, is exhausted or belongs to a minority group could be much more sensitive to cues of power imbalance or unfairness.

On the other hand, when we feel safe, supported or well rested, our ventral vagal system is engaged. This promotes positive social behaviours. This is why there's such a strong correlation between wellbeing and organizational citizenship behaviours. We're more likely to engage in open communication, collaboration and empathy with co-workers. We're much more able to practise resilience-building behaviours, which all include a form of self-regulation. The workplace will become a safer, happier and more creative place.

Perhaps, then, it won't surprise you that we believe creating such a psychologically safe workplace culture is a crucial component of building a truly resilient business. In fact, without it, we'd argue that resilience will remain elusive. No amount of individual resilience will be enough to overcome a psychologically unsafe and inharmonious social environment at work.

The social fabric of work: a crucial component of resilience

Once we understand that we're continually perceiving social signals, we can recognize the importance of the social fabric of our work environment, or its business culture. A workplace where people feel safe, get on with each other and feel respected will result in a virtuous cycle of positive outcomes, which reinforce themselves in a continuous process of improvement. This workplace doesn't need to be a place of merry sing-alongs and harmonious hand holding in team meetings, or flowers in everyone's hair. It merely needs to be a safe place where workers feel valued and respected. It is likely to be more focused and effective.

On the other hand, a dystopian workplace of tense or impatient bosses, office backstabbing and bitching and unrealistic workplace demands will do the opposite. It can lead to a vicious cycle of detrimental results reinforcing themselves. Sadly, the dystopian workplace seems to be a more common arrangement we see in the modern world, despite best efforts to create a positive workplace.

But many leaders are blind to the social signals they're continuously sending. These often signal irritation, or a lack of safety, respect and care for basic human needs. A working environment without basic respect for these needs will be a mess socially, no matter how well it may be performing on narrow financial measures. Despite the increasingly frequent talk of human-centric workplaces, we experience increasingly unsafe ones instead in our day-to-day work.

We need to realize that the social fabric of our work affects us deeply. Mirroring is a great example of this. People will unconsciously imitate each other in gestures, postures, mannerisms and other behaviours during social interactions, especially if they sympathize with each other. You can easily observe this in gestures, or postures. People will unconsciously adopt similar body postures, such as crossing their arms or leaning back, in response to the posture of the person they're interacting with. You can also see them imitating facial expressions, such as smiling, nodding or raising eyebrows, to show empathy and rapport. Given the truth of mirroring, it's easy to see how a negative social workplace culture can quickly spread among an organization and its workers, and vice versa.

Chris experienced this in an interesting way when someone invited him along to meet with the CEO of their company to pitch an idea. The CEO was heading a global chemicals company with over 10,000 employees, spread over 40 countries. Chris didn't realize it at first, but it soon became clear that the employee who had arranged the meeting didn't like the CEO or feel safe with him. This person was technical and slightly socially awkward, which included not really knowing how to hold their body. They sat in a somewhat rigid manner, continually leaning back from the table.

The CEO was very much used to the unconscious power dynamics of people mirroring his postures, voice and rate of speech. He became increasingly irritated during the meeting, despite agreement on the topic at hand. Even though there was a high cognitive agreement on the topic, which was clearly a good thing, there was no felt resonance around the topic. In the end, the idea didn't progress further. Chris found it interesting to observe that, despite the employee bringing a good idea to the CEO and the CEO essentially agreeing, the idea went nowhere because the emotional resonance and felt sense of agreement were missing. The CEO had no emotional buy-in to the idea, and was in fact irritated by the meeting. He was likely stuck in the stressed zone for too long, colouring the CEO's ability to connect with others.

Chris also observed that many employees feared the CEO. Most likely, this meant that they were moving into dorsal vagal or sympathetic arousal whenever they had to interact with him. Left in a state of wanting to flee or to freeze, they'd return to their desks demotivated and probably angry or upset. As we've previously discussed, this negativity can spread around an office in a negative feedback loop, or vicious cycle, as it was doing here. Even in meetings that Chris observed without the CEO, the atmosphere was often tense. Only a handful of people spoke in each meeting Chris attended, while junior employees or introverted people would rarely say a thing.

Fundamentally, this wasn't a psychologically safe place to work. It was making people dislike their managers, their fellow employees and their jobs. Chris could see it in the average worker's body language and posture. He could also see that it was impacting the performance and creativity of the business.

Leaders and managers play a crucial role in creating the business culture

The above example shows just how important social skills in leaders and managers are in a business. Emotional convergence is the idea that we mirror each other's body postures and speech. There's also an inner alignment which takes place, with people's emotions converging within two to three minutes when they're in the same space, even if they don't speak. Leaders have a higher emotional impact on others and cause more emotional convergence than they themselves receive. This is due to several factors:

- Leaders and managers often speak first. They set the tone of the conversation, giving meaning to topics.
- They speak more often than others, influencing the conversation more.
- When they speak, people listen to them more carefully, and tune in to their signals more precisely.

- Group members generally see the leader's or manager's emotional reaction as the most valid response. So they model their own emotions on it, particularly in an ambiguous situation where various group members react differently.

- Put simply, a shouty, angry boss will lead to a shouty, angry workplace.

Emotional contagion is real. Leader and managers, like the CEO in the example above, set the emotional standard for an organization. There have been several studies on this. One, 'The ripple effect: emotional contagion and its influence on group behaviour', by Sigal G Barsade, outlines the following.[2] In his study, he split business school students into four groups, led by a leader (an actor). Each fake leader conveyed different moods: cheerful enthusiasm, serene warmth, hostile irritability and depressed sluggishness. The results showed the impact of emotional contagion. The group with the positive leader had increased mood, displayed more cooperation and less conflict and felt they performed well on their tasks.

You can test this for yourself in your next meeting. See how you feel or how you cooperate after a meeting with a warm and positive leader, compared to an irritable or stressed one. Or, to gauge how you feel about your manager and business culture more broadly, consider these moments from your own experience.

You've just landed at (Frankfurt, Heathrow, JFK, Shanghai Pudong… insert your airport name here) at 6.30am from a fantastic two-week holiday with your family. By 7.45am you're on the train to get into town to go home. But you're surrounded by people commuting to work. How do you feel after 30 minutes on this train?

If anyone has travelled on the London Underground or the New York subway, you'll know what we mean. Deathly silence. Glazed eyes. A funeral-style atmosphere, particularly if it's a Monday. This really speaks volumes as to how many people feel about their workplace culture. And also consider how the feelings of others can impact your own state, as you start to dread your return to work the next day.

Or how about this moment?

> You've just come back to your desk after a very inspiring morning training session about positive emotions and gratitude. You feel a warm afterglow. Most of your colleagues are staring at their screens, some in calls. They're generally tense, and no one notices you. You're alone with your afterglow. How long does it last?

We can see how important emotional contagion can be. We've compiled the following list to show what can impact the social and emotional fabric of an organization or team:

- Work demands:
  - **Negative contagion:** An overwhelming workload or unrealistic expectations can lead to chronic stress and a feeling of being unable to cope, pushing individuals outside their window of tolerance.
  - **Positive contagion:** A manageable workload and adequate resources and skills can ensure that people remain inside their window of tolerance.
- Work–life balance:
  - **Negative contagion:** A poor work–life balance entails the intrusion of work into private life. It can include a lack of predictability of workload, shift work and long hours. With insufficient time for recovery, people struggle to regenerate or balance their nervous system. This can easily spread through an entire business.
  - **Positive contagion:** A more flexible work schedule, or policies that allow for work–life balance, can reduce stress and enhance wellbeing. Respecting personal boundaries and providing space for individuals to manage their emotions can also contribute to a sense of safety.
- Work autonomy:
  - **Negative contagion:** Low autonomy and degrees of freedom can include short, urgent deadlines, high perfectionism demanded by bosses and complex working systems. This often leads to a significantly heightened neuroception of stress and danger, spreading through the workplace culture.
  - **Positive contagion:** More individual choices and flexibility, and the ability to craft aspects of work ourselves, including timing, output, style of work etc, can give a sense of autonomy and self-efficacy.

- Emotional load:
  - **Negative contagion:** A work environment that lacks psychological safety can lead to feelings of being on guard and unsafe. Such a scenario arises when employees feel unable to express their opinions without fear of negative consequences. It includes work that requires high emotional labour, including dealing with sick or distressed people, or conflict, or jobs with a high degree of emotional suppression in order to appear 'professional' or 'tough'. Experiencing bullying or harassment can be highly threatening and lead to significant emotional distress.
  - **Positive contagion:** A workplace that embraces diversity and inclusivity fosters a sense of acceptance and belonging. A psychologically safe business culture arises when people are listened to, and their views are integrated into the business. This helps people feel more connection and greater safety, which can spread throughout the workplace.

- Uncertainty and change:
  - **Negative contagion:** Concerns about job security or job loss can trigger the fight or flight sympathetic nervous system response, leading to chronic stress spreading through a business.
  - **Positive contagion:** Job safety in times of change can have the opposite effect. People have feelings of safety about their work or involvement in large changes at work. They have high relational safety with their team in times of change, making them and the wider office less susceptible to stress.

- Role clarity:
  - **Negative contagion:** Feeling isolated or unsupported by colleagues or supervisors can contribute to feelings of disconnection, and emotional dysregulation can arise in teams.
  - **Positive contagion:** Having supportive relationships with colleagues and supervisors can foster a sense of belonging and security, contributing to wider emotional wellbeing and more ventral vagal system arousal across an organization.

- Leadership support:
  - **Negative contagion:** Receiving harsh or overly negative feedback from supervisors, colleagues or subordinates can be perceived as threatening. It can trigger feelings of inadequacy or fear of rejection.

- o **Positive contagion**: Receiving encouragement and supportive feedback can boost motivation and confidence, which then spreads around the wider team.
- Growth opportunities:
- o **Negative contagion**: A lack of opportunities for personal or professional growth will cut people off from a sense of connection to meaning, and also reduce positive outlook.
- o **Positive contagion**: Having opportunities for personal and professional growth can foster a sense of hope, optimism and connection to meaning, infusing the wider business culture.
- Social environment:
- o **Negative contagion**: Experiencing hostility, conflict or aggressive behaviour from co-workers or superiors can create a sense of danger and trigger sympathetic, fight or flight arousal. Subtle, often unintentional, derogatory microaggressions or actions based on race, gender or other personal characteristics can create a hostile working environment. A sense of feeling threatened can spread in a business.
- o **Positive contagion**: Receiving positive feedback or recognition for one's efforts can boost self-esteem and reinforce a sense of competence. Engaging in respectful and constructive communication can create a non-threatening environment. This is one where individuals feel comfortable expressing their thoughts and emotions. Sharing humour and laughter with others can create a positive and relaxed atmosphere. This can reduce stress and promote social bonding across and within teams. Small acts of kindness from colleagues, such as offering assistance or expressing appreciation, can create a positive emotional impact. Even the little things can count.

The power of the workplace culture

All the above factors impact and influence the social fabric of work. They define the business culture. As Peter Drucker, the famous management thinker, once wrote, 'Culture eats strategy for breakfast.'[3] We are deeply social beings. We have social brains more than logical brains. Thus, our social experiences at work, the social fabric of our work, will deeply impact how we and the whole organization function.

The power of our social connections plays a crucial role in our wellbeing. We've seen this time and time again. In places where remote and hybrid working has grown, without adequate attempts to develop a team culture, a sense of disconnection can grow within a business. Many business leaders we've spoken to have expressed their helplessness. They've sent wellbeing vouchers to people and invested in many digital offerings. But all these investments are like getting an annual present from an absent father. If he doesn't call, ask how you are, express his love and care, the presents are junk. Leaders who don't understand the deep web of social connection, who don't feel what others feel, will never get a handle on this.

Particularly for new starters and younger employees, who haven't had as much time getting to know other employees and managers in face-to-face environments, one culture is like the other – only the Microsoft Teams backgrounds are different. Businesses which fail to develop an effective and supportive workplace culture, which give employees the opportunity to become friends, or at least treasured acquaintances, and not just colleagues, can fail to reach their potential level of peak performance.

Numerous studies have backed up our own observations. For example, a commentary by Sonja Lyubomirsky in the *World Happiness Report 2022* said: 'Social support is by far one of the best ways to help people cope with any kind of adversity or stress or tragedy.'[4]

And the lead researcher of one of the world's longest running studies on wellbeing and happiness stated: 'Contrary to what you might think, it's not career achievement, money, exercise or a healthy diet. The most consistent thing we've learnt through 85 years of the study is: positive relationships keep us happier, healthier, and help us live longer. Period. The No. 1 key to a happy life: Social fitness.'[5]

The importance of social connections to our wellbeing is vastly underappreciated in the workplace. This is despite some leaders and managers increasingly recognizing how the culture of their organization matters. In a survey by Heidrick Consulting in 2023, 82 per cent of surveyed CEOs said they'd focused on business culture as a key priority over the past three years, much higher than for strategy or digitization.[6] However, even though culture is becoming a more important topic, leaders still likely underestimate just how important is it. A study by the MIT Sloan School of Management found a toxic workplace culture had a tenfold more powerful impact on employees' intent to quit than compensation did (see Figure 7.1).

FIGURE 7.1 Workplace culture is more important than strategy in retaining employees

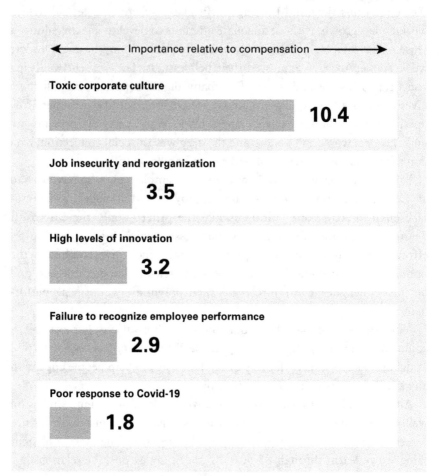

← —————— Importance relative to compensation —————— →

Toxic corporate culture

10.4

Job insecurity and reorganization

3.5

High levels of innovation

3.2

Failure to recognize employee performance

2.9

Poor response to Covid-19

1.8

SOURCE *MIT Sloan Management Review*[7]
Importance relative to compensation, in multiples.

Most businesses, however, don't understand how important workplace culture and care are. They might do everything in their power to shave 1 per cent off business expenditures. But at the same time, they do not realize their own toxic culture is costing them an enormous amount – both in terms of employee attrition and in needing to throw pay rises at unhappy, over-worked employees (who'll nevertheless leave one day anyway). They believe higher pay packets will automatically lead to higher performance. But the data says this simply isn't true. A much more nuanced interplay of factors contributes to performance, with, perhaps, none being as important as the culture.

We collated data from 110 teams in 2022. It showed that **psychological safety was the single biggest factor that correlated with team performance** (see Figure 7.2). It had a correlation of 0.7 with team performance. This means that 70 per cent of the variance of team performance could be explained by the degree of psychological safety in the team. Having feelings of psychological safety is one of the key hallmarks of a positive workplace culture. And, as Daniel Goleman argues, workplace culture is overlooked at an organization's peril, since '[e]motions are contagious, team members take their emotional cues from each other, for better or for worse. If a team is unable to acknowledge an angry member's feelings, that emotion can set off a chain reaction of negativity.'[8]

Business culture is a crucial aspect of resilience

At this point it's useful to briefly summarize what we've covered so far. We feel what others feel. How others feel impacts how we feel. The workplace culture of an organization affects how we feel – and our resilience. How leaders feel impacts how resilient their employees are. If I want to feel better, it'll be harder to do so if everyone else feels rubbish. When we get caught in our thinking brains, we're blind to this. Many leaders and organizations can become one big social wound, which everyone feels but few can name. This social wound has a deep negative impact on both resilience and on performance.

FIGURE 7.2 There's never too much psychological safety

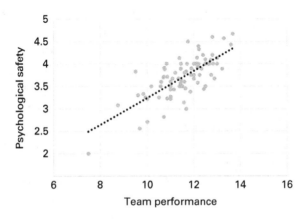

We can't try to address resilience or performance without addressing the social fabric and business culture of an organization. It's that simple.

In other words, we're deeply connected. We can't fundamentally shift our resilience without thinking of others and considering the social 'we' aspects of businesses. Even if we're doing well generally, others' states will affect us. And if we're not doing well, business culture can impact us even more. We get stuck in sympathetic (flight) or dorsal vagal system (freeze) arousal. With a smaller window of tolerance, and the lack of self-regulation we find when outside this window, we rely on others more. We need help from friends, colleagues, bosses, HR staff or coaches to get us back into our own window of tolerance, where we can regulate ourselves.

Chris has experienced this on a personal level. He remembers one Sunday afternoon. He'd been working at Boston Consulting Group (BCG) for about six months in Munich. He'd worked for about six weeks, six days a week (or sometimes seven), for at least 12 hours a day. Chris was really struggling, to put it lightly.

He remembers thinking it wasn't just BCG – it was him. He was poor at self-regulation and boundaries, and at this time he found himself completely out of energy. On this particular Sunday, he had to go into the office for a very simple task. A partner whom he worked for had to submit an article to a magazine the next day. It simply needed writing. Two pages maximum, and Chris knew all the content well. It was not a difficult task. Or so he thought. But Chris was simply out of his window of tolerance. He couldn't think straight (let alone type coherently). He was stuck in dorsal vagal activation and had, in effect, shut down.

In the end, Chris called his office mate and dear friend Veronika, and she came to the office to sit with him. She didn't do much – but her presence helped Chris a lot. They talked through the logic together, they drafted the article in 45 minutes, and then Chris was able to finish it in another 45 minutes. The task was simple, but at that point it was still beyond his abilities alone. As Chris grew older, he had children and a family. He also realized deeply how their support and his time with them helped him cope with the stresses of work. It helped him move back into ventral vagal system arousal, the rest and digest mode which allowed him to recover, and then meet the challenges that working life would throw at him.

Since then, working with Awaris, Chris and Liane have both recognized that 'I' alone isn't enough. That businesses must tackle resilience at the social, 'we' level. They've developed interventions aimed at tapping into the many benefits that social support can give us, to help develop a positive business culture.

Building a positive, psychologically safe business culture is a crucial aspect of resilience for any business. It really is important not to underplay how key the social fabric is here for individuals and the wider organization. In fact, we'd say that unless employees feel safe, unless they feel supported socially at work, you can throw any chance of your business becoming resilient out of the window.

We've now looked at what resilience is and the importance of understanding our inner landscape. We've examined key individual resilience skills, competencies and profiles, and highlighted the importance of mindfulness in stitching this all together. Now we'll try to use these building blocks to see how we can start looking to build resilience skills at the business-wide level, where resilient cultures are built. This is where things start to get really interesting.

KEY CHAPTER TAKEAWAYS

- Humans are fundamentally hardwired to be social.
- The interaction between our nervous system and our social environment is explained in 'polyvagal theory'. This posits that the autonomic nervous system (ANS) is comprised of:
  - the ventral vagal system: rest and digest response, associated with social comfort
  - the dorsal vagal system: freeze or shutdown response to social disconnection, among others
  - the sympathetic nervous system: fight or flight response
- Our nervous system is thus extremely attuned to social context and signalling; we call this neuroception.
- A lack of psychological safety at work can activate the sympathetic nervous system's fight or flight response or the dorsal vagal system's freeze response.
- This is why creating a psychologically safe workplace culture is crucial to building We-silient businesses.
- Leaders and managers set the tone and play a particularly important role in creating the business culture.
- Positive or negative social contagion can spread through a workplace culture.
- A positive business culture is the key factor influencing employee retention.
- We can't address resilience or performance without addressing the social fabric of a business.

Notes

1 S W Porges (2011) *The Polyvagal Theory: Neurophysiological foundations of emotions attachment, communication, and self-regulation*, W W Norton, London

2 S G Barsade (2022) The ripple effect: emotional contagion and its influence on group behaviour, *Administrative Science Quarterly*, 47 (4), https://journals.sagepub.com/doi/abs/10.2307/3094912 (archived at https://perma.cc/56AP-9PKJ)

3 J Engel (2018) Why does 'culture eat strategy for breakfast'?, *Forbes*, www.forbes.com/sites/forbescoachescouncil/2018/11/20/why-does-culture-eat-strategy-for-breakfast/?sh=63d0688c1e09 (archived at https://perma.cc/QA8U-4F5M)

4 J F Helliwell, R Layard, J D Sachs, J E De Neve, L Aknin and S Wang (2022) *World Happiness Report 2022*, https://happiness-report.s3.amazonaws.com/2022/WHR+22.pdf (archived at https://perma.cc/BGP4-92UE)

5 R Waldinger and M Schulz (2023) An 85-year Harvard study found the no. 1 thing that makes us happy in life: it helps us live longer, NBC, www.cnbc.com/2023/02/10/85-year-harvard-study-found-the-secret-to-a-long-happy-and-successful-life.html#:~:text=Contrary%20to%20what%20you%20might,Period (archived at https://perma.cc/R5UT-UGUK)

6 R Gailey, I Johnston and A LeSueur (2021) Aligning culture with the bottom line: how companies can accelerate progress, Heidrick and Struggles, www.heidrick.com/-/media/heidrickcom/publications-and-reports/aligning-culture-with-the-bottom-line.pdf (archived at https://perma.cc/LZ7L-AM8T)

7 D Sull, C Sull and B Zweig (2022) Toxic culture is driving the Great Resignation, *MIT Sloan Management Review*, https://sloanreview.mit.edu/article/toxic-culture-is-driving-the-great-resignation/ (archived at https://perma.cc/VG4L-SAEA)

8 D Goleman, R Boyatzis and A Mckee (2002) The emotional reality of teams, *Journal of Organization Excellence*, 21 (2), pp. 55–65, https://doi.org/10.1002/npr.10020 (archived at https://perma.cc/7H95-DCY7)

8

How to build resilience skills at the business-wide level

'Stress is in the mind.'

'I understand you feel like your workload is high. But everyone else is in the same boat, it's about managing your workload more effectively.'

'We have deadlines to hit, that's the reality of working in a business like this.'

'Just put your foot on the gas a little more, just for the next few months, then things will calm down. Probably.'

If you're reading this book and you've worked in a business, you'll probably have experienced bosses or managers saying something like this to you. No doubt about it. The workload is ratcheting up, deadlines are fast approaching and you feel like there literally aren't enough hours in the day to complete the workload set for you. The complexity of getting everyone onboard, the endless meetings, the continually shifting targets all contribute to the pace and load. Even when you get home, you wolf your dinner down while checking emails, get back to work and then go to sleep (with difficulty, as your mind whirs about your impossible and growing workload for the next day, and the one after that).

Your alarm buzzes you awake and, immediately, your heart rate pumps worriedly, as the panic of what you need to do sets in. You head to work, do it all over again, and this process repeats itself. You work on weekends and you don't have time to socialize. Your work–life balance becomes an imbalance; you lose your social connections. And if you're honest with yourself, you have moments where you think 'Is this it? Is this really what life is about?' There doesn't seem to be an end in sight to you ploughing onwards, suffering really. And you can't remember that last time you had 'fun', or did something, anything, just for the sheer joy of it. A bleak way to live.

But then, as you get called into your boss's office, after months of this non-existence, you get told that you're 'doing brilliantly'. 'Well done for really pushing yourself and making this happen for the team and the business.' 'I can see that you've been stressed, but you've dealt with it excellently… This will be noted on your performance review and renumeration package next year.' And as you sit there, feeling a bit numb, and confused as to why your bleak existence of 65-hour weeks is something to be celebrated, your boss adds for good measure: 'One final thing. I know it's been a lot for the last few months, but we've organized a weekly yoga session on Thursdays. So, if you feel stressed again, you could always do that.'

You internally doubt whether 45 minutes of Vinyasa will compensate for 12-hour working days, seven days a week. Somewhat speechless, you can only mumble, 'Oh, that's a brilliant idea,' and head back to your desk.

Personal resilience skills have a limit

The misunderstanding of resilience as endurance is the starting point for this negative approach to resilience, still taken by many businesses across the world. If resilience is like endurance, and rocks endure, then you should be more like a rock. Cold and unmoving in the face of hardship. But we've shown that resilience is a skill which crucially has to be practised and applied daily, weekly, monthly, and that, as individuals, yes, we do have an individual responsibility to become more resilient.

The thing is, there are limits to personal resilience. You could be the most resilient person in the world – but if you face a 'tipping point' of stressors in the workplace, we argue that your resilience skills will fall short. After all, they only work when you exercise them, as Figure 8.1 explains, based upon data we collated from 1,200 respondents. It shows the proportion of people who define themselves as in a state of 'resilience' or 'low resilience', depending on how many stressors they're exposed to.

In simple terms, as the number of workplace stressors increases, the number of people reporting 'high resilience' drops and, at the same time, the number of people reporting 'low resilience' increases. These trends are most noticeable once a toxic 'tipping point' of workplace stress is breached (interestingly enough, this number varies by the type of the stressors and the population).

FIGURE 8.1 Limits to individual resilience

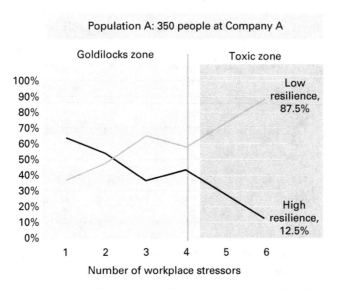

Percentage of people who class themselves as resilient compared to the number of stress factors at work.

Not too surprising, really. When faced with more stressors, employees' ability to engage in resilience behaviours declines. If facing constant work stress, people can't walk the dog as often, cook healthy meals, spend evenings with their friends, put their children to bed or play tennis with their friends as often. It's hard to find time to meditate when you're on call from 7am until bedtime. Thus, workers are less able engage in the resilience skills and behaviours that help them regulate their internal state – because of a lack of either energy or time.

Let's delve a little further into the data, which connects to our earlier explanations of the resilience skills. Look at the 'Goldilocks zone', the zone of normal work–life stress. Not too much, not too little, just right. In this zone, when people face up to three strong workplace stressors, the impact of resilience skills is more effective and notable. Here, there's a strong correlation between individuals' resilience skills and their perceived stress levels. There's also a weaker correlation between the number of stressors and their levels of resilience or stress. Simply put, resilience skills help more than stressors harm.

In the Goldilocks zone, for most people, it's most effective to try to support them in developing their own personal resilience skills. But in the toxic zone (above three or four workplace stressors), there's a quicker decline in resilience, and a stronger correlation between stressors and perceived stress. Thus, in the toxic zone, resilience skills become less effective. There needs to be an intervention from outside. And the responsibility falls upon the workplace to do this.

Organizations and individuals are mutually responsible for resilience

Work will always be stressful. It's its nature that it requires an expenditure of energy, and that we'll be challenged by work. If organizations create more supportive work environments and are successful in reducing toxic environments, but individuals still have no resilience skills, then they'll struggle. Conversely, if individuals become good at their resilience skills and are surrounded by others who struggle, or are in toxic environments, they'll still empty their resilience batteries. And fast. Resilience depends on the individual and their environment because we're interconnected.

In other words, for a business to become resilient, it does mean individuals have to become more resilient. But, equally, the responsibility falls on employers not to overload their workers with too many stressors. Resilience is also an organizational responsibility, especially in the toxic zones to build resilience, where individual resilience skills become less effective.

Just as individuals need skills to regulate their stressors and internal states, so organizations need them. Businesses have a lot of skills already – for example, financial planning or recruiting. However, there's also a need for organization-wide skills in building resilience, which will be the key thrust of this chapter. We'll explain the view of organizational resilience skills shortly. Put simply, from what we've seen, most organizations are generally poor at building human-centric organizational resilience skills. There's a lot of work to do here, to build skills and to shift toxic environments.

When we work with businesses, a first step is to help answer a few key questions. How many stressors can our employees bear? What's the cut-off level for a toxic environment? How big is the Goldilocks zone of stressors? To help these businesses answer these questions, we normally begin by showing them a few figures, which we'll talk you through below.

Figure 8.2 shows data from two of our clients, let's call them Company A and Company B. Company A had a more resilient population of employees than Company B. It had 40 per cent reporting high resilience at four stress

FIGURE 8.2 Different stress factor resilience profiles exist

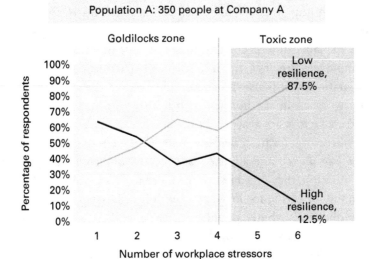

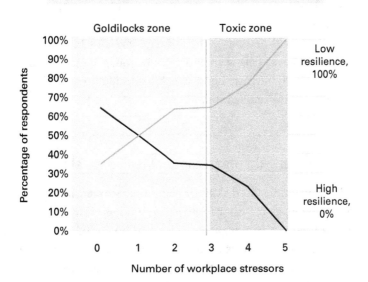

factors, 20 per cent at five stress factors and 12.5 per cent at six stress factors. By comparison, Company B's self-reported high resilience was just 20 per cent at four stressors and 0 per cent at five. Clearly, trying to apply the same policy prescriptions to both companies wouldn't make sense.

What explains differences like these? It will in part depend on how many employees are engaging in resilience behaviours, and how resilient they are naturally. It'll also depend on the average age and demographics of those working in the businesses. It'll also be a function of what the major stress factors are at work. In the above example, Company A was a more resilient organization because many of the employees were expatriates who had moved and adjusted to new environments throughout their lives. In addition, they faced less of the more toxic stressors, such as a lack of autonomy or caring for loved ones with health issues. Company B was a more globally distributed population. Their workers were younger. They faced more rapid changes at work, less autonomy and thus more challenging stressors. There was also less engagement with resilience behaviours on average in Company B.

Before we work to build truly resilient working cultures, each organization needs to look at its wider employee stress and resilience profiles. Only then can they discuss what levels of stress they believe their employees can cope with, which will determine the ultimate levels of business-wide resilience they can achieve. This is an entirely new journey for most businesses, which have normally just used guesswork to decide how much stress they should allow in their organization.

Building up organizational resilience skills

Successful organizations need skills of planning, resource, allocation, review mechanisms and resource allocation plans, among many others. Each of these skills is learnt over time, and needs to be anchored into the fabric of work. Much like other aspects of any business: for example, financial planning. This skill has a core monthly accounts reconciliation practice. But, again, this skill needs to be learnt. And we speak from experience here. Leading a small start-up, with 30 staff and 70 trainers worldwide, we had to learn the hard way how to build up our organization's financial management skills. This includes department budgets, plans and quarterly reviews. We are, like many growing organizations, in the midst of that learning journey.

We'd also argue that to build resilience as an overall organizational skill – for businesses to become truly resilient – organizations need to cultivate several resilience-related sub-skills. We call them **human-centric resilience skills**. Organizations need to agree on a framework and habits that create the foundation for their staff to be able to practise more resilience skills. While this may seem unusual in the business context, when humans can appear at times as mere cogs in a profit-making enterprise, we feel this underscores a key point – that these skills must be mastered to help humans, and not systems, become more resilient. To help employees master some of the challenges we face as humans at work, which, if done correctly, will then benefit the business system as a whole.

Let's run through some examples of such resilience skills and see how modern businesses stack up in achieving them in our experience.

Physical health

Description: The ability of an organization to protect and positively impact the physical health and movement of their employees.

Examples: Organizations have made fantastic progress on protecting their employees from physical harm and work-related accidents. Many companies have in-house fitness centres, offer subscriptions for fitness clubs, do step challenges and offer physical health screenings. They have sports teams, support sports and have ergonomic facilities.

Healthy nutrition

Description: The ability of an organization to support their employees with healthy nutrition.

Examples: Organizations have made reasonable progress here, with company cafeterias having a wide variety of healthy offerings including salads, fruit and low fat and low sugar meals. The meeting culture (cookies, coffee, etc) has improved. Alcohol isn't available in most business premises.

Rest and recovery

Description: The ability of an organization to support their employees in getting enough rest and recovery.

Examples: This is mixed. There's been an overall reduction in work hours in the last 50 years. People work less on average in the West and more flexible work models are available. Maximum work times and rest times are subscribed to and enforced in manufacturing plants, and in a number of other industries. Knowledge work, however, has struggled with this. Here, there's a poor understanding of and support for rest and downtime, and a high likelihood of continual interruption of off-work time. Some companies have cultures which glorify lack of rest and are appropriately sick as a result.

Resilience awareness

Description: The ability of an organization to be aware of the level of employee wellbeing, in enough detail to act on this appropriately.

Examples: This has improved, but there's still a long way to go. Most businesses have some form of annual wellbeing surveys. Some go deeper and offer health screenings, with a high level of detail on mind and body health. But most of this data is limited, slow and not actionable, nor does it really relate to how people feel.

Relaxation

Description: The ability of an organization to regulate its collective nervous system, and to respond appropriately to situations.

Examples: This is one of the weakest areas for many organizations. High frequency of emails marked 'urgent', regular changes of company direction and overreaction, a tense tone of communication and an emphasis on unrealistic response times are common. Businesses think everything's urgent, although this isn't so in reality. As a result, many companies and their employees in our view have dysregulated nervous systems.

Attentional regulation

Description: The ability of an organization to support good attention regulation. Helping employees deploy their attention on the right matters, with the right amount of effort and non-distraction.

Examples: Another weak area for many organizations. A lot of multitasking, too many ongoing projects and emails, frequent interruptions, multiple goals, too many KPIs and poor resource planning are hallmarks of companies with poor attention regulation – which is most companies, from what we've seen. Many companies are descending into attention disorder frenzies, at an increasing rate over the past decade. Some software development organizations have made significant progress in supporting focus and deep work, with positive outcomes.

Emotional regulation

Description: The ability of an organization to be aware and manage the emotional load of its employees appropriately.

Examples: This is a challenge for many organizations, especially technical, financial or administrative ones. Signs of poor emotional regulation include unresolved conflicts, a lack of interest in emotions (it being considered not professional to be 'emotional'), high emotional load in staff, poor morale, high turnover, frequent tolerated toxic behaviour and poor employee reputation. Some companies have begun to address this, but there's a long way to go.

Positive outlook

Description: Organizations ensuring a positive work environment, and appreciating the successes and the contributions of all.

Examples: This is also difficult for some organizations, although some are working to address this. Signs of a lack of positive outlook include negative communication styles, lack of team spirit, unhealthy competition, blame culture, lack of appreciation and a lack of growth mindset, among others.

Sense of meaning

Description: An organization being clear about its purpose, and the ability to support employees in remaining connected to that purpose.

Examples: Some progress has been made. There's been a lot of work on purpose statements and communicating purpose. Organizations that struggle with this tend to experience lack of clarity in goals and purpose, conflicting goals, disengagement, decline in reputation in the market, cynicism, burnout in staff and possibly innovation stagnation.

Social connection

Description: Organizations being aware of and maintaining a positive social fabric at work and supporting social connection in their employees.

Examples: This is an area where some companies have made a lot of progress, especially since the pandemic. But, in our eyes, just as many have regressed. Companies with poor social connection skills struggle with low engagement and belonging, a transactional nature of relationships, poor employee loyalty, low innovation and adaptability, more intense silos, lack of team building and even physical spaces which discourage communication.

Compassion and care

Description: The ability of an organization to extend compassion and care to its employees and other stakeholders.

Examples: Organizations have progressed here in the last 20 years, with multiple forms of care that they express towards their employees. Many engage in volunteering to help others. But, still, there's a gap for many companies and leaders. This is evident in cold or insensitive communication, a lack of leadership support, authoritarian cultures, customer or environmental disregard and a lack of employee support.

Synchronization

Description: The ability of an organization to synchronize its human resources, so there's a felt sense of energy and connection.

Examples: This has only recently emerged as an important skill. Many organizations function with dispersed teams but struggle to get the felt sense of forward motion. This is because it requires cognitive alignment and feeling alignment to make change or innovation happen. Emotional synchronization happens naturally in shared meetings, tasks and projects. But with the dispersal of people, virtual meetings and micro-tasks devoid of clear outcomes, it's much harder to get the felt synchronization companies need. Companies that lack synchronization have difficulty making progress and adapting to change, often act in disconnected ways and have a lack of trust and engagement.

Integration

Description: The ability of an organization to integrate diverse people, styles or work locations.

Examples: There's been an improvement in this area over the past decade, particularly on creating more ethnically and gender-balanced workplaces. However, much more work is needed, especially regarding psychological safety, which helps integrate diversity. Further, in some companies diverse thinking is not encouraged, with top-down decision-making structures dominating.

At first, the idea of organizational skills for resilience might seem strange. But, we hope, you read the above and felt a stirring in your heart. An inner agreement, as you recognize these features in companies you've worked for.

A crucial component of this is organization-wide **practices**, which help build the skills. Practices are rituals or exercises which teams or organizations engage in regularly, and which build a skill over time. A familiar example is Agile working. When teams or organizational units want to work in an Agile manner, they begin to anchor practices into their work. These includes practices such as daily standups, scrums (a project management framework), retrospectives and sprints (a time-limited period to complete a task). If they stick to these practices, then the team will become more skilled at Agile working.

It's important to approach skill building in this manner. If someone wants to become skilled at tennis, then they must practise forehands, backhands, serving, volleying and lobbing. Only when they master a series of practices can they then bring them together to become skilled at the game of tennis.

With this process in mind, we've reviewed the above 13 skill areas and identified the five practices which are the crucial ones for each skill.

Building business-wide attention management

Let's look at the skill of organization-wide attention management, a key component of building resilient working cultures. This goal of the skill is to help employees work in focused ways, without too many interruptions. This is a sorely needed skill in modern workplaces. One which both individual employees and organizations struggle with. In our experience working with organizations, there are five practices for individuals, teams and departments which have the biggest impact.

- **Meeting-free days or times:** Agreements about meeting-free times or even days are crucial for employees to work in a concentrated manner. Research published in the *MIT Sloan Management Review* showed that companies introducing meeting-free days observed a profound positive impact on business outcomes. When one or two no-meeting days were introduced per week, autonomy, communication, engagement and satisfaction all improved. This resulted in decreased micromanagement and stress, which caused self-reported productivity to rise by up to 70 per cent.[1]

- **Individual or shared focus time:** Individual or shared focus times are also key. Focus times go further than meeting-free times. They support the teams in setting up non-distraction boundaries with devices and emails. This helps them with deep work on important projects, sometimes collaboratively, in a specific time window. Microsoft has published data from their own employees showing that people who set up two-hour blocks of focus time had a 30 per cent higher perception of work–life balance, because they were able to get their work done and didn't have to work in the evenings.[2]

- **Limiting device unlocks:** We're increasingly disturbed by our devices. Employees who want to work in a focused manner need to put their devices on standby. They also need to limit their device usage to a certain number of minutes per day and switch off notifications for some time. Given that we unlock our devices between 80 and 110 times per day,[3] employees will need help in implementing these changes, with guidance from management. In some safety-critical environments, companies already limit smartphone usage. This practice of encouraging us to put aside our devices, to focus and think deeply, will become more important (and hopefully widespread) over time.

- **Email agreements:** Agreeing email response times and email checking frequencies is key. Most people believe they must check their emails continually. It leads to higher anxiety and difficulty relaxing. It's also not effective. Research shows email checking increases the amount of time we spend on emails by over 15 per cent.[4] And, in fact, only in a few instances do senders expect such quick response times. The reality is, people check their emails often because they're addicted to it, or are anxious as they believe they have to do it.

- **Workplace quiet zones:** Supporting the above are workspace designs that assist in quiet or focused working. These are also popular and beneficial for those wanting to do deep work.

These five practices, when anchored in an organization, can build up the skill of organizational attention management.

Another example is positive outlook. Here are some core practices which we've observed make a real difference:

- **Positive tone in meetings and starting with the positive**: A lot of meetings are time pressured. Thus, they end up focusing on problems, critical issues and conflicts – things that bring forth a negative state of mind. However, there's much that happens at work which is positive. In reality, more things go well than go poorly at work, and people contribute in many ways to these positive outcomes. Beginning meetings with positive comments sets a constructive tone. It fosters an environment of trust and openness. It shifts people's perspective from a problem-oriented mindset to noticing what's going well. Positive emotions broaden individuals' perception and thinking styles, encouraging exploratory thoughts and actions. When meetings start positively, team members are likely to be more creative and cooperative, contributing to a better working culture.

- **Positive feedback**: Providing regular positive feedback – during meetings or at the end of the working day or week – significantly boosts employee morale and job satisfaction. Research by Gallup found that employees who receive regular positive feedback are more engaged, indicating that such feedback can lead to a more positive work environment.[5]

- **Celebrating achievements**: Regularly recognizing and appreciating positive outcomes and behaviours in the workplace can lead to a more positive work climate. It might sound obvious, but actually taking time to celebrate events, such as an employee becoming a parent, birthdays, the seasons or annual social events, also contributes to a positive climate.

- **Appreciating people and their contributions**: Acknowledging individual contributions is crucial for fostering a sense of belonging among employees. Companies that take time to honour positive organization-wide behaviours or recognize employees' contributions are more likely to have a positive working culture. Indeed, recognizing and rewarding employees for their achievements can significantly boost morale, motivation and outcomes. One report found that employee recognition was associated with a 29 per cent increase in profitability and a 22 per cent increase in productivity.[6]

- **No blame culture**: Cultivating a no-blame culture encourages open communication and learning from mistakes, without fear of retribution.

In a no-blame culture, employees are more likely to engage in creative problem solving and innovation, fostering a positive and productive work environment.

Taken together, these practices, rooted in psychological and organizational research, collectively contribute to creating a positive, supportive and productive work climate.

Like all skills, however, these business-wide resilience skills have to be planned, practised and measured before they can become real organization-wide resilience skills:

- **Planning:** This is important and often forgotten. What kind of work do different people do? How much time are they in meetings? How many emails do they get? What are realistic goals for focus time, meeting-free times or the frequency of email checking?

- **Practising:** For a period, for example four weeks, the team or department has to now practise these skills. They must see how they work and adjust them based on outcomes. Many people we work with think that talking about the positive is unrealistic. But once they try it, and regularly practise giving positive feedback, they notice that it makes a big difference.

- **Measuring:** This is often a crucial missing piece. For example, if a team decides on one meeting-free day per week, 12 hours' focus time and limiting email checking to four times daily, they must measure whether it worked. They must ask: how did we do? How are people adapting? What has the impact been on business outcomes?

Driving this change can be hard. We've experienced mature employees and managers, who manage complex processes, budgets or technologies behave more like teenagers when it comes to adjusting their behaviour in the workplace. We've had conversations like the one below too many times to mention:

Liane [cheerfully]: 'So how did focus times work last week?'

Employee one: 'Oh, I forgot to plan them in the preceding week, and then by the time I got to Monday, my day was too full.'

Liane: [Silence].

Employee two: 'I did implement the changes, but it didn't work. People just placed meetings into my calendar. They didn't respect meeting-free times.'

Liane [patiently]: 'How many hours of focus time did you plan?'

Employee two: '12 hours, like we discussed.'

Liane: 'That's great. So how many did you manage?'

Employee two: 'In one week eight hours, in the other nine hours.'

Liane: 'Okay. So how did that work out?'

Employee two: 'Well, it was great when we adhered to the focus time. But like I said, I got meetings placed in my calendar by senior people, so it kind of went out of the window.'

Liane [somewhat less patiently]: 'So let me understand. In two weeks, you had eight and nine hours of focus time, and were able to stick to it? You got a lot of work done. And you're saying it didn't work because you only fulfilled around 70 per cent of the total planned focus time?'

Employee one: 'Yep.'

Liane: 'This is a massive improvement on what you had before we implemented this focus time … ?'

Employee two: 'Yes, I guess so. Er, sorry.'

It's important to measure the implementation of the practices. To stick to them. And if necessary, do root cause analyses, asking questions like: who placed the meetings in my agenda? How could we avoid making the same mistakes next week? How can we each be reminded to schedule focus time? Like we'd do with any business problem. It requires management support and discussion at the team or organization-wide level, helping to set goals, agree priorities and follow up on these business-wide skill-building initiatives. It takes time and dedication to make these practices work.

But when businesses do make them work, it really pays off. In our experience, businesses that manage to do this are taking a crucial step in becoming more resilient organizations. By adhering to these team and business-wide practices, they're reducing the risk of their staff being stuck in the stressed state for too long. They're supporting their ability to personally practise resilience skills, by not exposing them to too many stressors. And in doing so, they are helping staff recharge their resilience battery profiles when they work. With happier, less stressed staff, better placed to shift their state according to the challenges they face, it's not hard to see why such business cultures become fundamentally more resilient.

See the Resilient Culture website for the five to eight practices per skill which help build organization-wide resilience skills.[7]

Targeted interventions are needed

Numerous sources point to the fact that toxic work practices, or, in our language, a lack of human-centric skills, in a few departments, business areas or locations drive the greatest amount of burnout, disengagement, attrition and other signs of lack of wellbeing.

Our data also confirms the importance of focusing on departments compared to general organization-wide interventions. Our data shows that departmental factors have more than twice the impact on wellbeing and engagement of organization-wide factors. Departmental factors include inter-actions with colleagues, team dynamics, communication and leadership styles within a team or department. They are crucial for wellbeing. A supportive team, with positive relationships, can contribute to a sense of belonging and reduce stress. Conversely, a toxic or unsupportive team environment can lead to increased stress and conflict and decreased job satisfaction.

Organization-wide factors such as the company's culture, management practices, policies, work–life balance initiatives and overall organizational structure and strategy can also impact wellbeing, but usually less strongly than departmental factors (see Figure 8.3).

FIGURE 8.3 Organizational factors also impact engagement and wellbeing

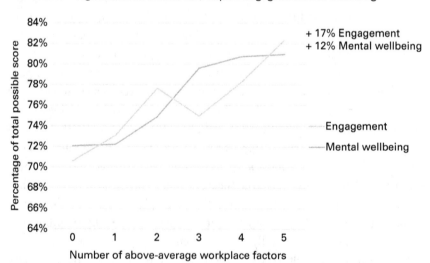

Organizational factors such as reward or strategy have a measurable, but lower, average impact on wellbeing.

Organizations must take responsibility for building skills and healthy behaviours

Organizational skills require not only organizational responsibility, but the willingness to impact employees' behaviour. Both leaders and the employees who exhibit poor resilience behaviours are often multitasking a lot and constantly checking their phones. This willingness to address behaviour at the workplace level is crucial – and there's often resistance to this. Chris remembers one particularly telling conversation with the global HR director of a chemicals company, when he suggested that a more comprehensive approach to wellbeing and resilience was required:

Patrick (HR director): 'Chris, are you suggesting we begin dictating how people should behave?'

Chris: 'No, training isn't dictating. Its aim is to help them cultivate the right behaviours.'

Patrick: 'But, seriously, telling them what's good behaviour with their phone, with answering their emails late at night or not, seems childish. They're adults.'

Patrick reflected for a moment and leaned back. He was uncomfortable. He thought of his leadership team and felt they'd have no appetite for these policies. After some reflection, he spoke.

Patrick: 'No, Chris, that's not something we can really think about. Fundamentally, you're suggesting we treat people like kids. We don't do that. We treat people like adults.'

Chris: 'Patrick, I'm slightly puzzled by your response. You treat people like children all the time.'

Patrick: 'What do you mean? We'd never do that. We give people goals, budgets, and then expect them to get on with it!'

Chris: 'So why do you get them to report on their goals weekly? On their budgets monthly? Why do you give them 20 KPIs to measure up to? Why do you bombard them with reporting? If you had this unerring faith in how adult your people were, you wouldn't do that. And what about in the manufacturing plant? You force them to wear helmets, specific shoes, you get them to walk around certain lines and do specific rituals all the time.'

Patrick: 'Well that's different, that's core business… That's what they have to deliver on.'

Chris: 'So because it's important, you can treat people like children? So, is wellbeing not important? We don't want to treat your staff like children. We're helping them build skills for resilience and anchoring them into your working culture. In the same manner as you build skills for financial management, and anchor them in weekly, monthly, quarterly and annual reviews, you have to anchor skills into the fabric of work.'

In the next chapter, we'll show how this can be done at the team level.

KEY CHAPTER TAKEAWAYS

- Personal resilience skills are only a part of building resilient working cultures.

- When a 'toxic' level of workplace stressors is surpassed, then resilience skills become less effective, and resilience drops. This is even true for normally highly resilient people.

- This means We-silience is both a personal and organization-wide responsibility; they're equally important.

- Most businesses we work with lack human-centric resilience skills. They fail to understand the resilience profiles of their staff, including how much stress they can cope with.

- Successful businesses need skills not just in planning, reviewing and resource allocation; they need to implement human-centric resilience skills.

- A resilience skills approach is much more likely to succeed than a narrow focus on wellbeing.

- Such an approach requires a fundamental shift in focus, response styles, intervention types, stress responses, employee participation, recruiting, employee coverage, leadership, long-term targets, business culture, employee empowerment, preventative focus and overall goals.

- These interventions should be implemented at the department level, rather than just at the organization-wide level, to have maximum impact on engagement and employee mental wellbeing.

Notes

1   B Laker, V Pereira, P Budhwar and A Malik (2022) The surprising impact of meeting-free days, *MIT Sloan Management Review*, https://sloanreview.mit.edu/article/the-surprising-impact-of-meeting-free-days/ (archived at https://perma.cc/AB6A-KYBW)

2   D Klinghoffer (2021) Hybrid tanked work–life balance. Here's how Microsoft is trying to fix it, *Harvard Business Review*, https://hbr.org/2021/12/hybrid-tanked-work-life-balance-heres-how-microsoft-is-trying-to-fix-it (archived at https://perma.cc/8ZNC-EF4S)

3   T Ranosa (2016) How many times do you unlock your iPhone per day? Here's the answer from Apple, *Tech Times*, www.techtimes.com/articles/151633/20160420/how-many-times-do-you-unlock-your-iphone-per-day-heres-the-answer-from-apple.htm (archived at https://perma.cc/3GZ6-9DM9)

4   M Plummer (2019) How to spend way less time on email every day, *Harvard Business Review*, https://hbr.org/2019/01/how-to-spend-way-less-time-on-email-every-day (archived at https://perma.cc/E5UN-4LSD)

5   C Porath (2016) Give your team more-effective positive feedback, *Harvard Business Review*, https://hbr.org/2016/10/give-your-team-more-effective-positive-feedback (archived at https://perma.cc/RB3N-FRWP)

6   O C Tanner (2018) *2018 Global Culture Report*, www.octanner.com/press/2018-global-culture-report (archived at https://perma.cc/KL5D-8FPH)

7   Resilient Culture (nd) www.resilientculture.info (archived at https://perma.cc/JN6G-H726)

9

Team resilience skills

It's always interesting to notice what goes on in the moments before a meeting starts. In some companies, everyone remains solitary. They stare, eyes glazed, into their devices or phones. Finishing up some work, or perhaps pretending to (while instead scrolling to avoid feeling bored or having to have inane small talk with Tom from finance). In these teams, people can seem tense and somewhat solitary, even if they've known each other for quite some time. Chit-chat doesn't flow. The sound of coffee slurps and ruffling papers is all that's audible above the awkward silence. The agenda is the first order of business. When the meeting is over, people leave quickly. In these businesses, we know quickly that a lot of work lies ahead of us in helping these teams connect at a deeper level.

In other teams we work with, however, things are different. People choose to engage in actual, real-life conversations, with warmth – either in small groups or, more tellingly, in the whole group as they settle in. In teams like these, there's often some time to establish human connection, even if it's just three minutes. From what we've seen, these teams often operate in a more collaborative manner, supporting the performance of their business as well as the wellbeing and connection of their staff.

The above examples show how teams have widely varying cultures, and how this is directly observable through their habits of connection at the team level. These habits of connection, and other interaction habits, are more important than people commonly realize, given that modern knowledge work occurs primarily in teams. We've seen for ourselves how more modern work requires collaboration, in a variety of team forms and structures. This ranges from departmental teams to project-based teams to cross-functional teams, among many others.

Even what we used to call classic 'blue-collar' work is increasingly skill based. For this reason, the share of work that requires social skills is growing

FIGURE 9.1 Work is becoming more collaborative: change in tasks performed by US workers relative to 1980

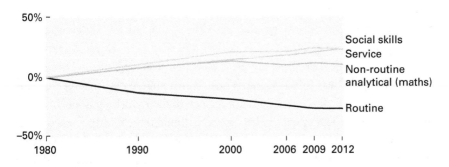

SOURCE Deming (2015)[1]
The US economy has seen a rise in jobs requiring social skills, while growth in jobs requiring maths skills has slowed.

(see Figure 9.1). Equally, the share of work that's collaborative is also growing, and with it the importance of teamwork. For example, the 2019 Gensler US Workplace Survey found that the share of time spent doing teamwork in the US had doubled between 2013 and 2019.[2] With this in mind, understanding team dynamics has never been so important.

Successful teams are defined by their skills and habits

Most teams we've worked with assumed that if they had clarity of goals, roles and processes, then effectiveness would emerge in teamwork, like magic. However, developments in teams in the last two decades have shown that this view doesn't bear up to scrutiny. Many teams have clarity of goals, roles and processes, but are still ineffective. Several studies have found that most teams are lacking core skills like shared attention, emotional awareness and a learning orientation,[3] and that 45 per cent of meeting time is wasted unproductively because of non-inclusive patterns of communication.[4]

There have been many responses to this, one of them being the Agile transformation of teams. The **Agile Teams Manifesto**, launched in 2001, started a far-reaching Agile revolution and a deep shift in team mindsets. For our discussion, it's important to point out that a core part of working in an Agile manner is specific Agile practices. Agile practices include daily standups, scrums, sprints, extreme programming, weekly demos, sits together, root cause analyses, retrospectives and backlog management. Taken together, these are applied to bring an Agile skillset and way of working to teams.

Agile teamwork uses these practices to cultivate Agile skills in teams, and an overall Agile way of working. Thus, teams that work together in this manner utilize specific practices that intersect all their working hours, not just in team meetings. The practices they use contribute to the effectiveness of their teamwork, and usually have an impact on cohesion. In our work we've seen, for example, that Agile teams tend to have better attention regulation than a lot of teams (through practices such as clear requirements management, sprints and regular customer demos). They also seem to have better meta-awareness, through practices such as retrospectives and backlog management.

We have also experienced many Agile teams struggling. And in our experience, these teams that struggle often lacked the right habits of inter-action – in terms of positivity, emotional awareness and connection – something we address later. But the success of Agile teams highlights the importance of how practices can build skills, and also lead to improve-ments in interactions between team members.

Building team emotional intelligence and psychological safety: through regular practices and habits of interaction

In a similar manner, in the world of so-called 'normal' teams which don't work in an Agile manner, there's also been a growing understanding of the importance of team resilience and collaboration practices. Research on teams shows that simply setting up teams and clarifying roles, tasks and processes or ensuring the right mix of people doesn't lead to high performance.

It's not just these measurable concrete factors that drive team success. A research project by Google found that habits of interaction were crucial for building trust and psychological safety in teams:

> The project, known as Project Aristotle, took several years, and included interviews with hundreds of employees and analysis of data about the people on more than 170 active teams at the company. The Googlers looked hard to find a magic formula – the perfect mix of individuals necessary to form a stellar team – but it wasn't that simple. 'We were dead wrong,' the company said. Google's

data-driven approach ended up highlighting what leaders in the business world have known for a while; the best teams respect one another's emotions and are mindful that all members should contribute to the conversation equally. It has less to do with who is in a team, and more with how a team's members interact with one another.[5]

A separate MIT research project used objective markers like equality of turn taking in meetings. They then linked these insights to team performance, as measured by the ability of teams to solve shared problems. They called this ability the 'collective intelligence' of teams. They found that the highest predictors of team performance were based on how team members interact with each other (see Figure 9.2).[6] In highly innovative teams, team members contributed equally to conversations and solutions, they connected outside of meetings, and they scored higher on a measure of social-emotional intelligence.

We have seen this again and again with our work with teams – that **soft factors, and particularly psychological safety, are the best predictors of team**

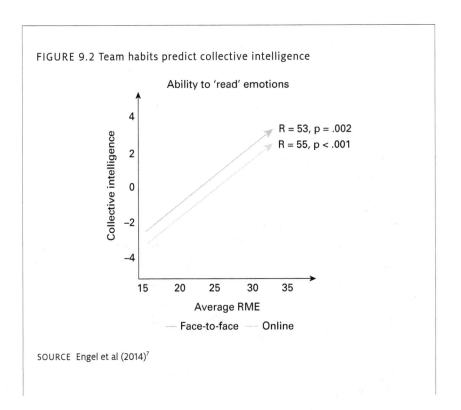

FIGURE 9.2 Team habits predict collective intelligence

SOURCE Engel et al (2014)[7]

Collective intelligence is not strongly correlated with the individual intelligence of group members. It is simply teams where the sum of individuals creates better outcomes than just the work of individuals.

Collectively intelligent teams have the following habits:

- they contribute equally to team conversations
- they have a higher average emotional intelligence, measured in the Reading the Mind in the Eyes (RME) test of the individual team members

This was true for both online and face-to-face settings.

performance. These can be hard to measure but are observable as behaviours and show up in teams that master them as skills.

Just as we're creatures of habit individually, we have seen how much of teamwork is driven by observable but often not noticed habits. And, as we mentioned earlier, persistent practice of specific rituals and practices leads to skills. These things can seem trivial, like:

- how employees arrive at a team meeting
- how they take their seats, whether in a room or in front of a camera
- how meetings start (with the problems and all the critical issues we have to address immediately or a discussion of what's gone well recently)
- how team members listen to each other (or don't)
- how they resolve differences
- how they manage agenda items
- and so much more

All of these add up to an expression of our team habits – and they're much more important than one might think.

When we worked with teams in the automotive industry dealing with the aftermath of the diesel scandal, or with teams in the semiconductor industry trying to sort through the repercussions of the semiconductor crisis of 2021 to 2023, we found the same pattern. These were individuals and teams that were quite effective. They were focused, and clear about the challenges they faced. But they were also stressed, solitary, anxious and in danger of burnout. So, while they were effective in the short term, it wasn't clear if they'd still be effective in the long run, or if they'd be able to master the transformational challenges they faced.

Working with these teams, we focused on their interactions: how they spoke and how they listened. We took time for them to share how they felt. This raised the hackles of some of the senior engineers at first, as if we were asking them to talk about fairies or something else bizarre. But as we continued to work with them, they noticed that they felt better, that they were more positive – and, in fact, increasingly proud of what they were mastering. Recently we met a member of the automotive team, and he greeted us with a hug. He said that the diesel crisis, perhaps the darkest point in his life, had become a source of pride and wisdom. How they'd navigated this time had deeply affected him.

In our work with teams and organizations, we thus differentiate between habits of effectiveness and interaction habits. **Habits of effectiveness** are what we do to get our work done. These might include necessary (but slightly boring) protocols for managing goals, agendas and tasks for team members. These are processes teams have for getting work done, for coordinating tasks and for giving each other updates. It could also include checking resource utilization and progress control. **Habits of interaction**, on the other hand, are things we do that define how people and teams interact. This includes whether we take time for each other to chat, listen well, or have a roughly equal share of talking time (there's usually one team member who loves the sound of their own voice), among others. From what we've seen, habits of interaction are those that many teams simply forget about or don't notice. They assume that team interactions will somehow magically align optimally, all by themselves.

It's the habits of interaction that define the sense of connection, trust and psychological safety that exists in teams. Ultimately, this will play a massive role in determining whether a team is resilient or not. This is an increasingly important consideration in modern work. And as we shall see below, our interaction habits are the ones that also contribute substantially to teams being resilient. Put simply, teams become resilient because of the sum of their interaction habits.

A team might have a good focus on processes, but in a manner that is judgemental, impatient and highly stressful. This might mean team members don't feel connected or safe. Think of a boss checking in with everyone at the start of each meeting, asking 'Let me know how you're all feeling,' before quickly caveating this with 'But please God don't waffle on as we have much more important issues to get stuck into.'

Conversely, a team might have decent habits of interaction without good habits of effectiveness. This means they're a nice team, but not necessarily an

FIGURE 9.3 Interaction habits are becoming increasingly important: psychological safety is necessary for high-performing teams

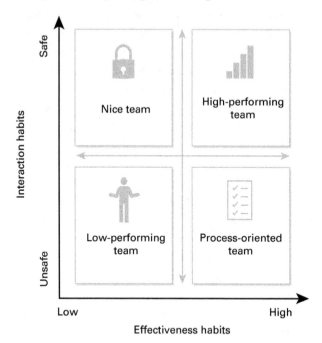

effective one. Here, we can imagine a team spending an hour checking in with each other, expressing their feelings openly and freely, holding hands, in an image of utopian, heartfelt team unity, but forgetting to actually do any work.

Crucially, there's a balance to be sought (see Figure 9.3). Teams with both habits of effectiveness and habits of interaction are high-performing teams. They learn and grow, and, in doing so, become resilient teams.

In our work with teams, we've identified eight habit areas, some closely matching our resilience skills. These are shown below.

Team resilience habit areas

CONNECTION

Description: Ensuring there's a felt sense of connection between team members. Allowing sufficient time and opportunities for this to deepen.

Examples of relevant practices:

- making time for social connection in team meetings (or before meetings)
- end of week social or team building events

SYNCHRONIZATION

Description: Ensuring sufficient synchronization of team members' collaborative time, shared emotions and mindsets.

Examples of relevant practices:

- agreeing on collaborative hours for shared teamwork

- having specific forms of team meeting that are collaborative or creative

- shared calendars for collaborative work

REST AND RECOVERY

Description: Allowing real rest and recovery in the team. Not explicitly or implicitly expecting each other to work beyond healthy workplace boundaries.

Examples of relevant practices:

- agreeing on clear workplace boundaries

- agreeing on how to deal with emergencies and out of hours messages

- sharing personal obligations

ATTENTION REGULATION

Description: Ensuring there's shared attention in the team and that members can be collectively present, listen to each other and address problems with sufficient depth of concentration.

Examples of relevant practices:

- mandating whether cameras should be on or off in virtual meetings

- agreeing on how to deal with multitasking in meetings

- jump-on or jump-off practices – agreeing to partial participation in meetings, but with full attention

- team focus times, where they aren't expected to answer emails

- meeting-free times

EMOTIONAL REGULATION

Description: Having emotional awareness of each other in teams. Emotions being regularly given the space needed for a healthy workplace culture.

Examples of relevant practices:

- check-ins at the start of meetings
- check-outs at the end of meetings
- emotional mapping in the team

POSITIVE OUTLOOK

Description: Ensuring there's enough appreciation, celebration and positivity in the team to create a positive working culture.

Examples of relevant practices:

- starting meetings with the positive
- end of week celebrations
- weekly positive feedback

INTEGRATION

Description: Allowing for diverse cognitive and emotional styles and personalities in the team. Integrating various forms of hybrid or remote team members.

Examples of relevant practices:

- equality of turn taking
- rotating timings of meetings
- rotating roles in meetings

REFLECTION

Description: Allocating time for reflection on the nature of team collaboration, processes and emotional culture. Enabling teams to learn and adapt.

Examples of relevant practices:

- team retrospectives
- team feedback processes

For each habit area we've identified specific practices that teams can establish. Regular practices (or rituals) will make these habits. As they are mastered, they can become a strength, or a 'real team skill', in our language. We've assessed these habits in over 100 teams and found some important insights and their associated implications for resilience, which we'll discuss below.

Mastered practices make a difference

First, we found huge differences in the prevalence of team skills. This often reflects team types, maturity levels and experience in teamwork. Crucially, we also found that team skills had a big impact on team stress levels and performance. Put simply, more team interaction practices and skills equal less stress and better performance. Teams with a resilient team culture are significantly less likely to suffer from team exhaustion. The skills and habits they regularly engage in support the team's health significantly (see Figure 9.4).

FIGURE 9.4 Teams with resilience skills have lower burnout

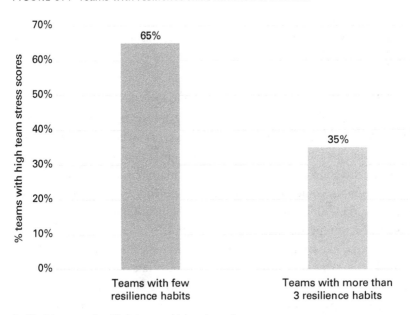

Resilient teams are less likely to score high on team stress.
N=104 teams.

FIGURE 9.5 Collaborative teams are twice as innovative

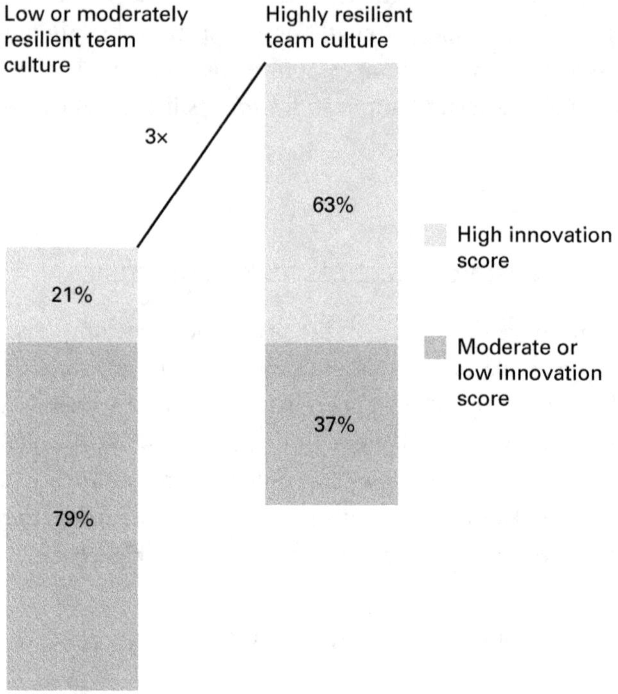

Highly resilient teams, defined as highly engaged in three or more habit areas, are three times more likely to be highly innovative.
N=104 teams.

Figure 9.4 can be interpreted in two ways. First, resilience skills protect team members from stress. Second, when teams get too stressed, their shared skills break down. This coheres with what we saw when looking at individuals' resilience scores earlier: at normal stress loads, individuals' engagement in resilience-boosting behaviour mattered most. At high stress loads, individuals couldn't maintain their resilience-boosting behaviours. Interestingly, these skills of collaboration, or habits of interaction, also have a strong impact on performance (see Figure 9.5).

Teams with collaborative and resilience skills were three times more likely to be highly innovative teams according to our data, a remarkable result (see Figure 9.6). Investing and upholding resilience habits on a team level is an investment in psychological safety. About 53 per cent of teams score high on psychological safety in these teams compared to 11 per cent in teams that do not focus on resilience-boosting team skills. So, it's clear that these skills of collaboration strongly impact both performance and wellbeing.

FIGURE 9.6 Resilient teams are significantly more psychologically safe, more motivated and highly effective

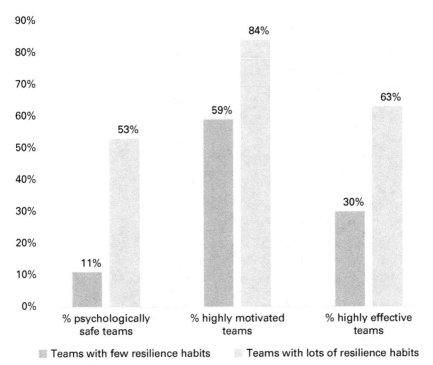

Teams with few resilience habits   Teams with lots of resilience habits

N=104 teams.

Some team skills matter more than others

Almost all the specific team habit areas we tested had an impact on aspects of team performance. But some team habits mattered more than others. Having the skill of positivity played a particularly important role. Around 55 per cent of teams that regularly practised some of the positivity practices scored above average in team effectiveness and innovation – compared to just 3 per cent of teams without skills of positivity. The skill of positivity included practices such as giving each other positive feedback, sharing appreciation, having a positive outlook, using positive language and noticing and sharing successes.

Another key practice is the ability to listen attentively. When team members feel listened to, the performance score goes up. The third key practice is feedback: in teams where feedback contributed to an improved quality at work, team effectiveness scores were higher. Leaders who want to boost

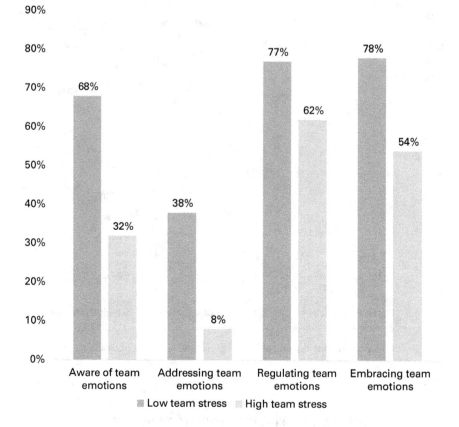

FIGURE 9.7 Teams that process emotions well are five times less likely to suffer burnout

Low team stress   High team stress

team resilience quickly should invest in a good feedback culture, a positive working climate free of bickering and good listening skills in the team.

How about the key team habits that boost team wellbeing? While habits that boost performance are often also likely to boost team wellbeing, there was one habit area that stood out strongly: team emotional intelligence. Overall, 62 per cent of teams with high emotional intelligence also scored high on team wellbeing, compared to 38 per cent of teams with low emotional intelligence.

The starkest difference was in the team's ability to address emotions in the team. Only 27 per cent of all teams surveyed scored high in this habit. When teams processed emotions well, they were **five times less likely to experience team burnout** (see Figure 9.7). As a result, 70 per cent of teams with high team wellbeing also experience a lot of positive emotions, creating an upward loop of team wellbeing and performance.

So, we can see how important the skill of emotional regulation in the team is to its wellbeing, and, thus, its wider resilience. This view's also been supported by numerous other researchers, such as Druskat and Wolff (2001), who stressed that teams being able to name and deal with team emotions is crucial for efficacy, trust and identity:

> Trust, a sense of identity, and a feeling of efficacy arise in environments where emotion is well handled, so groups stand to benefit by building their emotional intelligence... Group emotional intelligence isn't a question of dealing with a necessary evil – catching emotions as they bubble up and promptly suppressing them. Far from it. It's about bringing emotions deliberately to the surface and understanding how they affect the team's work. It's also about behaving in ways that build relationships both inside and outside the team and that strengthen the team's ability to face challenges... Emotional intelligence means exploring, embracing and ultimately relying on emotion in work that is, at the end of the day, deeply human. This requires a team atmosphere in which the norms build emotional capacity (the ability to respond constructively in emotionally uncomfortable situations) and influence emotions in constructive ways.[8]

Positive outlook also has a major impact on a team's wellbeing, performance and innovation. In our work with the teams trying to master significant, almost company-critical challenges (the diesel teams and the semiconductor teams), we found that positive outlook was one of the facets most missing, but which also had the highest impact. At one point, we asked the teams involved to pause and list all the things that they'd mastered in the last 12 months. As they made the list, they went through a profound transformation. They realized that they'd solved business challenges which had seemed unsolvable for years. While they still had important challenges facing them, the list of challenges was far lower than the list of solved challenges.

This really affected them. It not only made them feel proud, but also reminded them they could cope with any new challenge they faced.

A five-step process towards improved team resilience

Anchoring team discrete resilience and collaboration practices builds resilience skills. These make it possible to shift the wellbeing scores of teams, as our data has highlighted. This is especially true for highly interdependent teams. The more teams work together and depend on each other, the more time they spend with each other, and thus the more important habits become. We work with teams to build these team resilience habit areas in large scale ResilientTeam Labs, where 10 teams come together at the same time.

Modern teams need to build team-specific practices and skills into their work to be resilient. Our experience is that anchoring these practices and building skills takes time, but that it can be achieved if the following sequence is followed. First, it's important to ensure **human connection and synchronization**. Make sure team members have time to socialize, connect, chat and just be human together (sometimes we can forget this when we spend 12 hours per day staring at screens). Second, it's important that people are **present in meetings**. To do this, addressing issues of videos being on or off, multitasking and listening is crucial here. **Anchoring positive practices** is the third step. This is often met with cynicism, particularly if there's not sufficient human connection and shared attention. Positive practices build the skill of positivity, which is the basis for step four: team members being willing to **address emotions and give feedback**. This in turn leads to step five: having a **psychologically safe and resilient team**.

Our data shows the importance of this five-step approach. For starters, humans tend to like and understand things that progress in a logical order (we are wise animals, but like simplicity). And you can't have the benefits of the later steps before your team completes the first steps.

For example, teams that don't invest the time in building social connection as a starting point are unlikely to start sharing emotions with each other. 'I've never even spoken to Liz from IT, and now I'm supposed to tell her how I'm feeling... fat chance! I'll just say I'm fine,' might be an example of the common internal resistance you'd encounter. Further, if teams fail to agree how to be present in team meetings, good luck having sufficient psychological safety for diverse views and creativity. People will be reluctant to prepare a 10-minute pitch for an online meeting if, deep down, they know half the team will be secretly checking their devices and reading emails.

We've built this five-step process into our ResilientTeam Labs approach. Here, we bring up to 10 teams together at the same time. We help them reflect on their habits, share insights and anchor new practices into their work and build skills using the five-step process mentioned above. In this approach to large-scale team development, we ensure teams share responsibility for building and maintaining habits across the team, not just leaving them with the team leader. We also make sure that individuals in the team take responsibility for establishing, maintaining and tracking each team habit for the team for three months.

FIGURE 9.8 The training impact on habit change

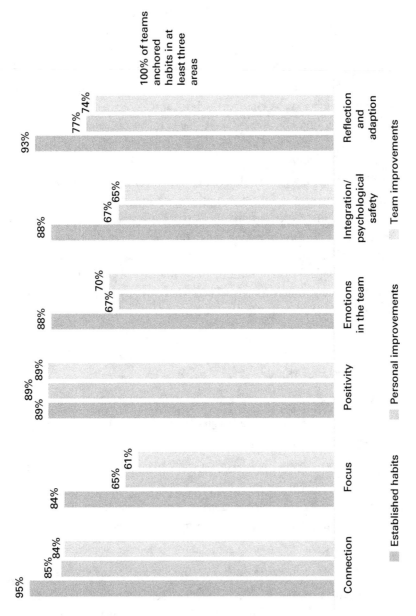

% respondents agreed

Connection · Focus · Positivity · Emotions in the team · Integration/psychological safety · Reflection and adaption

Connection: 95%, 85%, 84%
Focus: 84%, 65%, 61%
Positivity: 89%, 89%, 89%
Emotions in the team: 88%, 67%, 70%
Integration/psychological safety: 88%, 67%, 65%
Reflection and adaption: 93%, 77%, 74%

100% of teams anchored habits in at least three areas

Established habits   Personal improvements   Team improvements

Focusing on definable team practice and building skills, and taking responsibility for them, takes team development out of the realm of the vague and into something actionable. We've seen strong habit adoption using this approach (see Figure 9.8), laying the foundation for improved team resilience. Crucially, we've seen that team members experienced improvements both in team outcomes and also in personal outcomes using this approach. Although our approach allows team members to take more responsibility, the role of the manager or leader does remain of crucial importance, as we'll discuss more in the next chapter.

We tend to find that teams welcome a focus on interaction habits. We worked with a senior global leader of a software development firm. He was responsible for Agile software development at a large technology firm with over 200,000 people. He said that this approach gave him words for something that everyone in his team had already felt, but no one knew how to name. In fact, our experience has been that Agile teams in some ways are the most receptive to this approach, since they already understand the value of habits of effectiveness. They find that habits of interactions are what cause them to struggle in their Agile transformations. People remain too fragmented, too negative, too unsynchronized, too psychologically unsafe, to really enter the Agile mindset and Agile ways of working.

KEY CHAPTER TAKEAWAYS

- Modern knowledge work is becoming increasingly collaborative.
- Team skills and practices have a greater impact on team performance and wellbeing than clarity of goals.
- Soft factors like trust, psychological safety and team identity are strong predictors of team performance.
- Both invisible and visible habits in teams might seem trivial, but they play a greater role than most realize in team performance and resilience.
- Team habits of effectiveness are what teams do to get work done.
- Team habits of interaction are how teams and their members interact.
- Habits of interaction more closely define a sense of trust, connection and safety in a team, and, in doing so, will partially determine how resilient a team is.

- Teams that apply more team resilience skills have lower burnout scores, are less stressed and have improved performance.

- Teams with collaborative habits are more than twice as likely to be innovative, and half as likely to suffer from burnout.

- Emotional regulation is particularly important in protecting teams against burnout and supporting their resilience.

- Awaris's TeamMind programme has a five-step approach to team resilience:

  o build connection

  o ensure people are present in meetings

  o anchor habits of positivity in the team

  o allow team members to express emotions

  o a psychologically safe and resilient team emerges

Notes

1 D J Deming (2015) *The growing importance of social skills in the labor market*, NBER Working Paper 21473, www.nber.org/papers/w21473 (archived at https://perma.cc/S2L8-5P3N)

2 Gensler Research Institute (2019) US Workplace Survey 2019, www.gensler. com/doc/u-s-workplace-survey-2019.pdf (archived at https://perma.cc/N2QB-T4YT)

3 D Day and L Dragoni (2015) Leadership development: an outcome-oriented review based on time and levels of analyses, *Annual Review of Organizational Psychology and Organizational Behaviour*, 2 (1), pp. 133–56, https://doi. org/10.1146/annurev-orgpsych-032414-111328 (archived at https://perma.cc/N4EU-NKRB)

4 M J Eppler and S Kernbach (2021) *Meet Up! Better meetings through nudging*, Cambridge University Press, Cambridge

5 A Mohdin (2016) After years of intensive analysis, Google found the key to good teamwork is being nice, *Quartz*, https://qz.com/work/625870/after-years-of-intensive-analysis-google-discovers-the-key-to-good-teamwork-is-being-nice (archived at https://perma.cc/A68Q-DMZL)

6 A Williams Woolley, C F Chabris, A Pentland, N Hashmi and T W Malone (2010) Evidence for a collective intelligence factor in the performance of human groups, *Science*, 29 (330), pp. 686–88, https://pubmed.ncbi.nlm.nih.gov/20929725/ (archived at https://perma.cc/M8WQ-4MMR)

7 D Engel, A W Woolley L X Jing, CF Chabris and T W Malone (2014) Reading the mind in the eyes or reading between the lines? Theory of mind predicts collective intelligence equally well online and face-to-face, *PLoS ONE*, **9** (12), e115212, https://doi.org/10.1371/journal.pone.0115212 (archived at https://perma.cc/6JYQ-VBVJ)

8 V U Druskat and S B Wolff (2001) Building the emotional intelligence of groups, *Harvard Business Review*, https://hbr.org/2001/03/building-the-emotional-intelligence-of-groups (archived at https://perma.cc/T3NF-ARBM)

10

The importance of having resilient leaders

Liane recalls being in a meeting once. It was with HR and the business leaders of a German automotive business she'd been working with for a few years. At one point, the discussion turned to the new CEO of the company and his incoming performance improvement programme. Rather worryingly, it was to be called the English equivalent of 'Pedal to the Metal' (ie time to work even faster and harder). The new CEO felt that the company was slow and backwards. It needed to accelerate its output, so it could respond to the challenges it faced. The new programme aimed to communicate his urgency. But it also implicitly shared his view that everyone had been idling for a few years before his arrival.

Liane raised her hand. She suggested that 'Pedal to the Metal' might not be the most inspiring programme name. She felt there'd be resistance to it. The HR staff in the room agreed, nodding almost urgently. However, none of them said anything. They perhaps were too afraid of the CEO to speak up, which is never a great sign.

The other business leaders in the room felt quite differently. They were close to the CEO, or so they'd like to claim. More likely, the CEO was responsible for their renumeration and career prospects. So, they didn't hesitate when it came to simply accepting his point of view. They agreed with the CEO's logic and the need for change. They too wanted the transformation to be quick and impactful – so, the name 'Pedal to the Metal' seemed perfect to them. Or, at least, it seemed like a perfect chance to agree with their CEO.

Liane paused. She felt exhausted listening to them so brazenly focus on performance, with no consideration for the wellbeing of the wider staff in the business. And she said as much. 'I'm not sure this is a great idea,' she said. She added that she didn't 'truthfully believe a word of what you've all being saying.' And that she 'doubted any of you in the room do either, if you're really being honest with yourselves.'

There was a moment of stunned silence. Everyone looked at Liane, mouths slightly agape. Several of the executives defended what they'd said. But she again asked each one of them if they really believed that merely making everyone work harder would be effective. After three of them fumbled through a few justifications, the meeting time was up. Or, at least, the senior leaders decided that the time for discussion was over. There was a feeling that Liane had been unhelpful, or even obstructive.

But, truthfully, Liane had done nothing of the sort. She'd merely tried to connect these performance-focused concepts to the reality of people's experience. Employees were already tired. There was a lack of psychological safety, as evidenced by the HR staff being afraid to speak up in the meeting. Innovation had declined in recent years. There was a lot of uncertainty. This was an equal part of the reality, as she experienced it. The solutions to these complex issues were not as simple as: 'Everyone needs to just accelerate the pace and work harder and be more like me!' But she'd seen this many times before, where the gravitas of a CEO and team members not feeling like they could disagree led to suboptimal outcomes for a variety of businesses.

Resilience is on the radar, but putting it into practice isn't

Liane and Chris have both had many conversations like this, with ambitious but also exhausted leaders who were focused on performance, but who had no felt sense of what was happening down below deck. In our dataset of 250 leaders, 37 per cent of them were in the burnout category prior to our training programme (compared to 46 per cent of non-leaders). Many of these leaders lacked their own conscious resilience skills. This translated into them taking poor business decisions, which in turn undermined any hope of their businesses becoming resilient as a whole. Crucially, we found that after our programmes, the rate of burnout dropped to 16 per cent and 18 per cent respectively for leaders and staff, based on their individual and shared resilience skills.

We find many of the leaders we speak to are aware of the importance of resilience for their staff and organizations. Sustainable performance, wellbeing and resilience often come high on the list of priorities in leadership surveys. In theory, and in conversations with us, they say they'd like to build human-centric businesses, with organization-wide resilience. But alas, concrete actions are harder than words. Leaders often fail to put these ideas into practice, for several reasons:

- Leaders don't realize how much they impact organization-wide resilience.
- Many leaders don't feel as stressed as their staff.
- Leaders don't know how to consciously address resilience skills.
- Performance often takes priority in busy times.

Leaders don't realize how much they impact organization-wide resilience

We all know leaders make a difference to a business. What's also becoming more apparent is how they impact the stress and burnout levels of their teams. Many organizations are rife with anecdotal stories of how certain managers might leave a trail of stress and burnout in their wake. And there is research that shows the detrimental effect of bad leadership.

To illustrate, a Mayo Clinic study showed that a composite leadership score was significantly negatively associated with the burnout rate and positively with job satisfaction (see Figure 10.1).

Indeed, employee burnout scores are closely related to leadership style, with an r score of 0.33 – a strong value for a topic as multifaceted as burnout is. The relationship with satisfaction is even stronger, with an r score of

FIGURE 10.1 Leadership style is related to employee burnout and job satisfaction

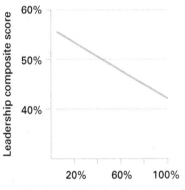 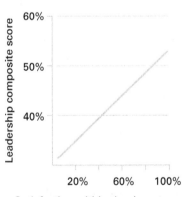

SOURCE Shanafelt et al (2015)[1]
A higher leadership score is negatively related to employee burnout (r=-0.33) and positively related to job satisfaction (r=0.68).

0.68, meaning that 46 per cent (which is derived from r2) of the variation in unit satisfaction can be explained by leadership style. Put simply, a good leadership style is related to higher unit satisfaction scores and lower unit burnout scores. Thus, a useful starting point for leading for resilience is understanding the impact of leadership styles on resilience – and, in turn, on wellbeing and retention in organizations. In this way, it becomes much more than a personal matter – leaders' resilience is important for business.

Many leaders don't feel as stressed as their staff

A second obstacle to building resilient cultures is that leaders lack the felt experience of stress in their organizations. Our in-house data shows that leaders overall have significantly lower perceived stress levels than employees and middle managers, even if the ones we speak to often confess they feel stressed. The percentage of leaders with elevated stress (37 per cent) is about 10 per cent lower than employees without management or leadership responsibilities (46 per cent).

This may be linked to several factors. Managers often have more control over their schedule. They may have more experience with stress management. Some leaders suppress or hide stress when they feel it, like the CEO in the case study who became more demanding as he felt more stressed. And there's likely a selection bias in management roles, towards those better equipped to deal with stress. To illustrate, 33 per cent of leaders in our dataset can be viewed as highly resilient, compared to 21 per cent of non-leaders.

Business leaders also navigated the Covid-19 pandemic more easily than junior employees. The 2021 Microsoft Work Trends report showed leaders were twice as likely to be flourishing than young single employees during the pandemic.[2] In our own dataset with over 2,500 individuals, we found 35 per cent of leaders were flourishing, while only 25 per cent of non-leaders were flourishing. A 2022 report by *The Economist* showed that 61 per cent of managers felt the pandemic improved their work–life balance, compared to 21 per cent who felt it worsened it.[3] For other employee groups, the changes were less welcomed – just 25 per cent felt their work–life balance improved, while 41 per cent felt it worsened.

This makes sense. Many managers might have been sitting in their quiet home office, with children at university, looking out at their garden thinking: 'Ah, this is the life.' They simply had a different experience compared to more junior employees. These employees may have been perched at a kitchen table, a child on their lap, trying to get work done while keeping an eye on what was in the oven. At the same time, they may have also been deeply questioning the wisdom of getting a dog at the start of the pandemic too.

A manager's resilience is also supported by their purpose, which is largely absent for junior employees. A McKinsey study showed that 85 per cent of senior leaders strongly agree that they're connected to their purpose in their day-to-day work, compared to just 15 per cent of other employee groups.[4] Leaders and managers are nourished and energized by purpose. It can contribute to their resilience, whereas more junior employees may simply not thrive on work in the same way. Taken together, many managers simply don't feel stress in their bodies in the same way their teams do. So perhaps it's no surprise that they don't give burnout the importance it deserves.

Leaders don't know how to consciously address resilience skills

Time and again we've met with leaders who weren't conscious of what they were doing that contributed to their resilience, as we did in Chapter 1. We've met many leaders with a strong connection to sport, others to healthy eating, and others who prioritize rest and recovery. A number have learnt to be positive. Some of the most senior executives have strong attention regulation skills. They don't get distracted easily and maintain calm and steady attention throughout the day. This is a typical sign we see when conducting heart rate variability (HRV) assessments with senior staff; they exhibit steady but low stress levels throughout the day, with no real peaks. And just as consistently as we've seen these skills, we've noticed that most leaders haven't been conscious about these skills and their resilience. They haven't been aware that the lack of these habits in others might be contributing to their lack of resilience.

So many leaders have built up regular resilience behaviours. Many managers' resilience skills have become so automatic they're not conscious of them. Our data suggests these skills and behaviours explain why managers tend to be more resilient than average employees, rather than them simply being tougher (see Figure 10.2).

Since some managers don't understand that their resilience behaviours are skills, they fail to see that they can be nurtured over time. Much like the skills of project management or leadership, building resilience skills takes time, attention, training and measurement. Some programmes suggest that resilience can be learnt in a couple of hours, and appear merely as a 'box ticking' exercise for HR. But in truth, there are no quick fixes. Resilience is

FIGURE 10.2 Managers demonstrate higher resilience skills, which may influence their stress management ability

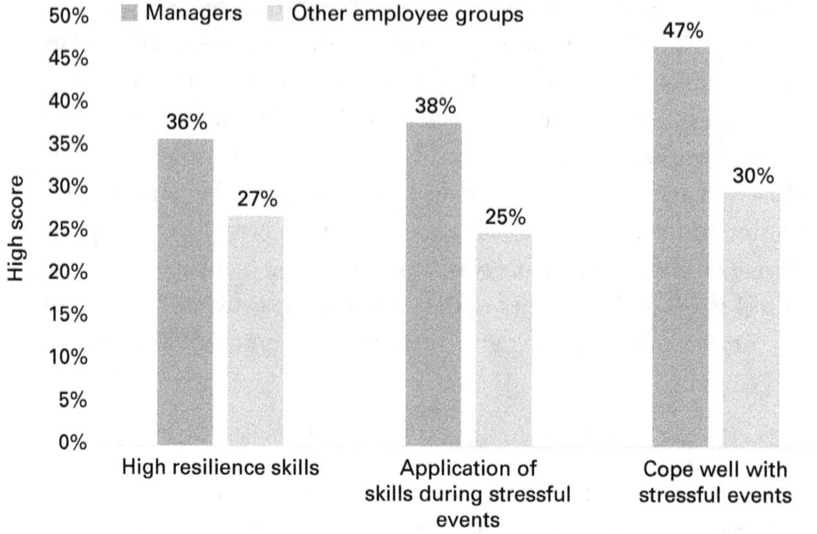

SOURCE Data from 436 participants of Awaris resilience screening.

a long-term journey of skill development, which requires effort over time. Sorry, everyone, we're not going to promise a silver bullet here.

Performance often takes priority in busy times

In busy times, such as the end of month or when working on specific client projects, we've noticed that any existing focus on resilience can fall away, and almost all attention shifts back towards work output. This implies leaders believe there's a conflict between performance and care. In fact, they are inextricably linked. Indeed, by focusing relentlessly on performance during tough times, some managers are undermining their team's resilience and performance in the long run.

The deep links between performance and care are more important than ever, because the working world has changed enormously over the past 20 years. The rise of digital communication tools, often designed to hijack our attention, leads to increased busyness and negatively impacts the ability to focus. Chronically fragmented attention can in turn lead to chronic stress. And this is associated with many health risks, such as hypertension, heart disease and depression. All these factors negatively impact productivity, innovation, collaboration and focus (and, probably a bit more importantly, can kill you). Perhaps it used to be enough to go on holiday. But, today, it isn't. We need to embed our practices of resilience into the fabric of our work, especially when things get tough, and not let them go out of the window.

Many leaders, however, don't realize the agency they have. For example, when we worked with engineers and leaders tasked with clearing up a scandal in an automotive company, they didn't feel their resilience would make a difference. The sums involved were mind-boggling; the pressures on staff crushing. Senior executives, while concerned that their employees were exhausted, couldn't do more than simply shrug their shoulders. 'What can we do? The issue simply must be fixed.' Interestingly, it was a medical doctor who eventually managed to get ongoing resilience support for those involved.

We worked with mindfulness and dialogue practices, as well as using HRV devices, helping staff acknowledge the stress and pressures they faced, and sharing experiences and discussing emotional regulation and focus strategies. They were given time and ongoing support in skill development and processing their stress. Ultimately, the care they received helped them perform. And, indeed, they felt that they emerged stronger, more resilient and conscious, from this challenging time.

Despite their initial resistance, the leaders of this firm realized that, paradoxically, prioritizing care was the best way to improve performance. Years later, they confessed they wished they'd realized this truth much earlier.

Cultivating resilience intelligence in leaders

Research shows the importance of leaders' stress mindsets, of having an awareness of their own mental state in the face of work pressures. It can impact a leader's perception of stress in their team and how they support the unit. A study by Kaluza and colleagues posits that a 'leader's stress mindset' impacts the 'degree to which leaders intend to show health-promoting support'.[5] In other words, managers aware of their own stress are more likely to lead for resilience in their teams. Our experience at Awaris shows that it's effective to take leaders on a resilience journey which includes 24/7 measurement of their HRV. This helps them reflect on the percentage of time they're stressed, and how it impacts their sleep and recovery. It also shows leaders which activities help them regulate their stress levels. In doing so, it helps them understand the importance of building resilience skills into their working life. And also, it helps them understand that this takes time and effort.

From taking over 500 leaders on resilience journeys over the past three years, we've found that leaders tend to have both different stress and resilience profiles to their employees. In terms of their exposure to stressors, they typically have a higher workload. They often see more of what has to be done, work coming down the pipeline towards them (with horror, perhaps), and are aware of the balance of workload and resources across the team. Therefore, we often see a higher perception of workload as a stress factor for leaders, and a lower prevalence of private factors. Managers also tend to be older, have fewer personal life stressors, fewer interpersonal conflicts, and cope better with change.

When we dig into the resilience skill profiles of leaders, we see they also have slightly higher resilience skill levels compared to non-leaders and engage in more resilience skills. They score moderately higher in self-regulation skills, specifically in self-compassion and care. Some 42 per cent of leaders reach high self-compassion scores. Overall, leaders in the Healthy Habits competency (diet, sleep and exercise) tend to engage most frequently in sports (37 per cent). However, leaders' sleep quality is on average lower compared to non-leaders, and they score lower in breathing scores than non-leaders. All of this combines to give them a slightly different battery profile than we described in the earlier chapters.

Leaders score significantly higher in connection to purpose, positivity and emotional regulation. This helps them endure high workloads and stress, supported by their self-regulation and body management skills. But this connection to purpose can be so strong in comparison to that of frontline workers that they fail to understand that others don't have the same experience. A boss might get cross that a junior worker isn't willing to work until midnight on a project, not realizing that the junior worker simply doesn't care as much as they do; they aren't as invested as they are.

Around 59 per cent of leaders feel highly connected to others and their purpose, and 38 per cent score highly in emotional regulation skills. This doesn't necessarily mean they're good at working with their emotions; it might well be that they're good at suppressing them. After all, this is often leaders' definition of emotional regulation. Research highlights the enormous impact of effective emotional regulation as a core leadership quality, especially in terms of their ability to invoke positive emotions in their teams.[6]

Given that our dataset shows that leaders don't seem to be exceptionally well trained in this skillset, this should be a potential area of focus for leaders hoping to drive resilience changes in their teams and businesses.

Leading for resilience

When there's a readiness and emerging skills in resilience leadership, only then can resilience behaviours take root in an organization. Awaris sees five areas that managers and leaders need to focus on to help resilience emerge at the organization-wide level:

- living resilience
- making the time for management
- leading well
- supporting employees
- anchoring business-wide habits

Living resilience

Leaders need to live resilience. Living with a positive mindset, as well as having healthy social connections and healthy habits of movement and diet, can extend a life on average by 10 years![7] Living resilience benefits not only leaders themselves, but also their teams and organizations. Evidence from organization-wide wellbeing interventions shows leaders' behaviour impacts the quality of company-wide wellbeing initiatives. So, it pays for leaders to engage in a lifelong journey of learning the habits of resilience – and, then, share their experiences with their teams.

Given the challenges leaders face, there are areas they need help with. Those that don't move enough, or struggle with sleep or attention management, will need support here. These are foundationally important to help handle workload (and to be less prone to grumpiness at work). While leaders are often good at dealing with high workloads, they struggle with the competency of Social Integration. Improvements in this competency would help their teams adapt well to change. Working with emotions (and not just suppressing them), being positive, expressing care and improving their social connections within their team and in their private lives would have a strong impact in their organizations.

Concretely, we recommend they should practise mindfulness daily (even for 10 minutes) and take time for their friends and teams on a weekly basis. They need to notice, name and express their emotions more, even if it makes them cringe initially, in team situations. Doing so can help the whole team. Contrary to the view of the hero boss, leaders sharing their vulnerability helps leaders to connect with their terms. In doing so, it sets those in the team on a path to being able to connect with their own emotions and inner landscapes. This will increase the chances of them becoming resilient too, in a virtuous cycle.

Making the time for management

Recent surveys point to surprising data. Many leaders spend less than 5 per cent of their time managing people – that is, having one-to-ones, reviewing progress and giving feedback.[8] This is perhaps not surprising. Managing isn't sexy. It's not the most exciting part of a business. But surveys by Gallup and others have demonstrated that when leaders spend more time engaging with their teams – prioritizing management – team happiness and productivity increase.[9]

Leaders need to prioritize managing; helping their employees, who face endless demands on their time, to say 'no' to certain tasks. Research shows managers have a positive impact on employee resilience when they:

- **Organize well:** This has a strong impact on the workload of team members, the amount of time they need to work outside of normal work hours and their degree of clarity of tasks. Designating email-free time and focus time and setting boundaries for working outside work hours is key here, reducing the scope for employee burnout.

- **Communicate frequently:** Communicating frequently with teams helps ensure all remain connected and that tasks are coordinated, both of which contribute to resilience. Regular sharing of emotions in meetings, an 'open door' policy to feedback and making sure team members all get the chance to contribute in meetings would help here.

- **Pay attention to their workload:** Leaders need to take workload pressures seriously. Saying 'no' sometimes and delegating tasks, perversely, can support the wellbeing and resilience of their employees. A stressed, overworked boss can lead to 'top-down' negative contagion through the working culture, as we've mentioned previously.

- **Are reachable:** Being reachable not only helps resolve problems and resource conflicts, but also gives an ongoing sense of support to team members. Taking time for one-on-one meetings, encouraging honest feedback and taking staff wellbeing concerns seriously are all important.

- **Provide staff with necessary resources:** Financial resources, training, contact, skills and additional person power can help team members manage their workload and minimize their stress load.

- **Manage conflicts:** Conflicts can be particularly stressful, because of the emotional intensity that comes with them. They can block resources and cause friction in collaboration.

Leading well

Leaders can have a positive impact on wellbeing and resilience through their leadership style – in particular, if they demonstrate some of the following specific leadership behaviours:

- **Provide a compelling vision of the future and a wider purpose:** This helps employees connect to purpose, which, as we've seen, is a strong source of resilience.
- **Act as positive role models:** Driving a positive business culture and appearing as authentic human beings helps employees connect to positivity. It can also help them notice and share emotions, rather than suppressing them. In addition, a leader modelling good rest, recovery and sleep habits also has an impact on the teams.
- **Coach and listen well:** Being open and empathetic, not always talking first.
- **Encourage people to solve problems themselves:** This empowerment helps employees in multiple ways – above all, in regulating their stress, being more positive, connecting to purpose and managing their own boundaries, rather than always being 'on', or relying on direction from more senior employees.

In other words, you don't need to be a scary or fierce boss. Authentic, open and compassionate leadership will lead to better results than autocratic and despotic leadership. These empowering styles of leadership help employees feel emotionally safe, have more agency and manage their own resilience.

Supporting employees

Leaders also act as gatekeepers, helping to signpost employees in particular directions, giving them access to wider resources across the organization. Taking this role seriously is important. This doesn't mean leaders should become employees' therapists. But it does mean they actively check in and see what the employee needs and what resources are available to help.

Specifically, leaders can educate themselves and their teams about mental health, including recognizing the signs of stress and mental health struggles. By providing training sessions or resources, they can create an environment where wellbeing and resilience are understood and valued. Leaders can also help ensure that their teams have access to mental health resources. These could include counselling services, employee assistance programmes or wellness initiatives (even though we believe that resilience initiatives are more effective). Providing information and guidance on how to utilize these resources effectively is also important.

Anchoring business-wide habits

Finally, leaders can lead for resilience when they anchor habits in their teams and business units which further resilience. As decision makers, leaders and managers can drive change within the wider organization.

For this reason, perhaps few others in the organization can take more crucial steps towards building truly resilient firms. And it is to this topic – acknowledging the important role a business must play in resilience – that we'll now turn.

KEY CHAPTER TAKEAWAYS

- Although leaders are increasingly aware of the importance of the resilience and wellbeing of their staff, they fail to take steps to address these issues in practice.

- This happens because:
    - leaders don't realize how much they impact organization-wide We-silience
    - many leaders don't feel as stressed as their staff
    - leaders don't know how to boost We-silience
    - performance often takes priority in busy times

- A crucial first step for leaders is to become resilient themselves, as a leader's mindset impacts wider resilience in their teams. Stressed leaders beget stressed teams. Stressed teams bring about stressed businesses.

- Our resilience profiling finds that managers have good self-regulation and mind–body skills.

- But they fall short when it comes to social, emotional and connection skills, in particular failing to realize they have a higher connection to purpose at work than junior staff.

- A boss will be in a better position to drive resilience in the wider business if they focus on five things:

  o living resilience

  o making the time for management

  o leading well

  o supporting employees

  o anchoring business-wide habits

Notes

1 T D Shanafelt, G Gorringe, R Menaker, K A Storz, D Reeves, S J Buskirk, J A Sloan and S J Swensen (2015) Impact of organizational leadership on physician burnout and satisfaction, *Mayo Clinic Proceedings*, **90** (4), pp. 432–20, https://doi.org/10.1016/j.mayocp.2015.01.012 (archived at https://perma.cc/T4VQ-PJNZ)

2 J Spataro (2020) A pulse on employees' wellbeing, six months into the pandemic, Microsoft Work Trends Index, www.microsoft.com/en-us/microsoft-365/blog/2020/09/22/pulse-employees-wellbeing-six-months-pandemic/ (archived at https://perma.cc/885F-ZVG5)

3 The Economist Impact (2022) The great rebalancing: priorities and work–life balance in a hybrid working environment, https://impact.economist.com/projects/nextpectations/executive-summary/ (archived at https://perma.cc/9ZVT-BRU5)

4 N Dhingra, A Samo, B Schaninger and M Schrimper (2021) Help your employees find purpose – or watch them leave, McKinsey, www.mckinsey.com/capabilities/people-and-organizational-performance/our-insights/help-your-employees-find-purpose-or-watch-them-leave (archived at https://perma.cc/82D6-4MHU)

5 A J Kaluza, N M Junker, S C Schuh, P Raesch, K von Rooy and R van Dick (2021) A leader in need is a leader indeed? The influence of leaders' stress mindset on their perception of employee well-being and their intended leadership behaviour, *Applied Psychology*, **71** (4), pp. 1347–84, https://iaap-journals.onlinelibrary.wiley.com/doi/full/10.1111/apps.12359 (archived at https://perma.cc/Q3JL-DPFV)

6 D L Joseph, L Y Dhanani, W Shen, B C McHugh and M A McCord (2015) Is a happy leader a good leader? A meta-analytic investigation of leader trait affect and leadership, *The Leadership Quarterly*, **26** (4), 557–76, https://doi.org/10.1016/j.leaqua.2015.04.001 (archived at https://perma.cc/87LN-462C)

7 PA Media (2020) Healthy habits extend disease-free life 'by up to a decade', *The Guardian*, 8 January, www.theguardian.com/society/2020/jan/08/healthy-habits-extend-disease-free-life-by-up-to-a-decade (archived at https://perma.cc/XGL5-SRMP)

8 I Ilke, G Thomas, C Chu, D Plans and A Gerbasi (2019) Leadership behaviour and employee well-being: an integrated review and a future research agenda, *The Leadership Quarterly*, **29** (1), www.sciencedirect.com/science/article/abs/pii/S1048984317301418 (archived at https://perma.cc/4SZ2-ZMEE)

9 The Global Council for Happiness and Wellbeing (2019) *Global Happiness and Wellbeing Policy Report 2019*, Sustainable Development Solutions Network, https://s3.amazonaws.com/ghwbpr-2019/UAE/GHWPR19.pdf (archived at https://perma.cc/MZA4-QA9N)

11

Why resilience is a business responsibility

Organizations (and societies) often fail at human resilience. Stress is getting worse, negative affect is growing, and individuals' felt sense of engagement is declining in many companies. Sadly, many companies have to some degree given up on solving this problem. After the pandemic boom – where companies were inadvertently forced to increase their focus on staff wellbeing – wellbeing investments in many companies have started to decline again. A global wellbeing lead for an 80,000-person business based in Asia recently told Chris, 'We're simply back to where we started out almost 10 years ago… It's such a shame. It's now performance, performance, performance. Our wellbeing team's been reduced. Many leaders or managers just don't get it. Or maybe, they don't really care. It sometimes feels that way, at least.'

This wellbeing officer exhibited something we've seen often in wellbeing teams: a sense of defeat or fatigue. All the wellbeing and healthcare leaders we've met care deeply about the issue. But sadly, they're usually underfunded or underequipped to make a real dent on the enormity of the challenge. All they have is a number of Band-aids for everyone. Perhaps these will suffice, for a lucky few. But there's rarely enough attention or funding to solve the overarching problems of stress and burnout, and an absence of resilience across their business.

To address the fact that wellbeing and resilience aren't yet taken seriously enough, we believe business leaders need to fully understand three mindset shifts:

- Resilience is a business responsibility, not just a wellbeing officer's responsibility.

- Resilience requires building resilience skills, not a symptom-treatment approach.
- Resilience is a shared responsibility – it's neither an individual's nor an organization's responsibility alone.

Let's now look at these mindset shifts in more detail.

Resilience is a business responsibility, not just a wellbeing officer's responsibility

The proportion of workers who flourish – defined as having high social, psychological and emotional wellbeing levels – declines rapidly as perceived stress increases. This is shown if we look at our data. It shows the percentage of employees who are flourishing (who score highly in psychological, emotional and social wellbeing) against perceived stress scores (see Figure 11.1). Normal data on perceived stress shows that those scoring above seven are associated with increases in incidence of mental distress.[1] Interestingly, the boundary where flourishing declines is actually much lower, at a score of four. To illustrate, to get a score of four, a person needs to experience difficulties that they couldn't overcome 'sometimes' during the last month.[2]

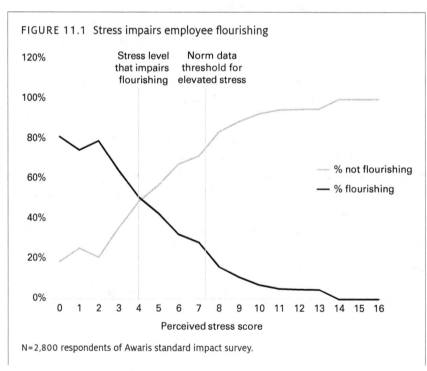

FIGURE 11.1 Stress impairs employee flourishing

N=2,800 respondents of Awaris standard impact survey.

- Only 30 per cent of respondents are flourishing.

- 41 per cent have elevated stress scores.

- When stress reaches the elevated stress threshold, only 17 per cent are flourishing.

Given that most companies we work with have an average perceived stress score of six and a half, this isn't good news. Perceived stress is at levels here which massively impair flourishing. The main category in the flourishing scale is called 'moderately mentally healthy', and there's a smaller (but rising) group of 'languishing' individuals. In our dataset of 2,500 employees, 8 per cent were languishing, 62 per cent moderately mentally healthy and 31 per cent flourishing.

This is why wellbeing or human resource teams are fighting a losing battle. They're working from a starting point where perceived stress has already pushed most of the employees into the only 'moderately mentally healthy' category, where there's a heightened chance of mental distress, while almost 1 in 10 were already in distress. Businesses attempts to take 'preventative' action, when so many employees are already at risk of distress, is like closing the stable door after the horse has already bolted. Too many staff members are already above this boundary.

Let's take another look at perceived stress scores. Our resilience data shows another powerful insight – namely that self-reported work performance is significantly lower when perceived stress is high (see Figure 11.2). Naturally, the underlying cause could be linked to the stressors experienced at work: unrealistic demands, poor processes, lack of supportive leadership, tight deadlines, and many more. Our data shows that when employees experience a high stressor load and elevated stress levels, performance deteriorates dramatically. However, Figure 11.2 shows that the important factor is not the number of stressors, but perceived stress. Performance is impaired in highly stressed people more so than in people with a high stressor load.

The first line, at a stressor load of 5, marks a 10 per cent drop-off in self-reported performance (see Figure 11.3). This line is clearly before the line of mental distress, and close to the line where 60 per cent of workers are still flourishing. So, making sure employees aren't suffering too much stress isn't a wellbeing issue. It is a business and performance issue first. It's in a business's best interests to keep their workers within the zone of ideally perceived

FIGURE 11.2 Performance declines as perceived stress increases

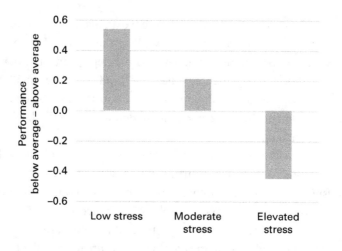

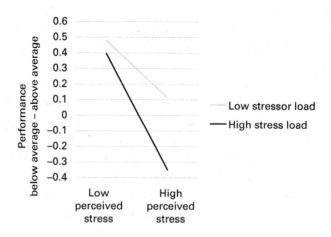

N=460 participants of the Resilience 3.0 screening.
The average self-rated performance is 7 out of 10 in our sample.

stress, below a score of four and, at most, reaching a maximum of six. Interestingly, many executives start to change their tune on the importance of staff wellbeing when we show them charts like this.

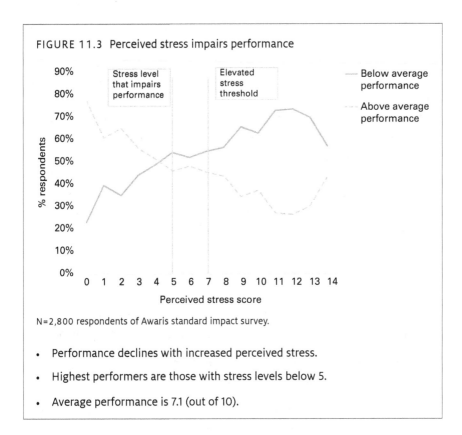

FIGURE 11.3 Perceived stress impairs performance

N=2,800 respondents of Awaris standard impact survey.

- Performance declines with increased perceived stress.
- Highest performers are those with stress levels below 5.
- Average performance is 7.1 (out of 10).

Resilience requires building resilience skills, not a symptom-treatment approach

A lot of the work wellbeing departments do is based on helping people who are struggling. Significant shares of wellbeing budgets are spent on rehabilitation, or on offering courses and interventions for new challenges staff are facing. In addition, they offer a sensible range of preventative solutions for people. But the language is key here. These departments focus on helping, treating or preventing, but not on *managing* these issues.

This distinction is crucial. Managers tend not to feel responsible for helping, treating or preventing, believing wellbeing or HR have this covered.

Instead, managers and leaders feel responsible for what they see as business-relevant outcomes, like performance, which are measures associated with organizational skills. This is why wellbeing teams often fight in vain to get management to feel responsible for symptoms or states. It's a vicious cycle. A manager's focus on performance is making staff too stressed. In turn, these stressed staff complain to HR they can't perform, because they're too stressed. Then managers, worried about performance dropping, adopt measures to make their staff work even harder! And the downward spiral continues.

We need to make the link between performance and wellbeing clearer for managers. When resilience is packaged like an Agile rollout, rather than a traditional wellbeing approach, this can be empowering for business leaders. To do this, managers need to take responsibility for individual and organization-wide skill building – establishing healthy practices, which build human-centric resilience skills, and measuring compliance with certain practices. When these steps are taken, We-silience, resilient working cultures and improved performance are likely to follow.

Resilience is a shared responsibility – it's neither an individual's nor an organization's responsibility alone

Using our approach of building resilience skills, we also see things differently here to most, as the following points outline:

- There are 12 underlying resilience skills and three resilience competencies which all individuals can have or develop. They are applicable for all challenges we face in life, even those outside the workplace. If someone is a member of a minority group, faces special care responsibilities at home, has low psychological safety and suffers microaggressions from colleagues, they stand to benefit from learning resilience skills (particularly if they have a high workload too). It won't make the problems disappear, but it might help them relax more, sleep better or nurture their social connections, supporting their resilience in trying circumstances.

- At the same time, the data clearly shows that we can't expect people to build these skills completely alone. Burdening employees with a high stress load and, after limited help or treatment, putting them back into the same stress load situations is problematic. There's a clear responsibility for businesses to build the resilience skills that help manage pressure, emotional burnout or a lack of connection at the business-wide 'we' level. So it's both an individual and business-wide responsibility. If management is excellent at ensuring positive attention management practices in organizations, but individuals still check their emails and smartphones 100 times daily, there won't be much felt sense of improvement. The balance between the two is what makes We-silience a challenge for many businesses.

• Both individual and organizational-wide resilience skill building must be managed like all skill building. It must be managed across the entire workforce. This should be a role not just for learning and development or HR. Resilience skill building must be managed like any business skill, by the responsible managers. Based on our work with businesses, we see that 60 per cent of individuals have already built a resilience competency, and thus also feel responsible for their own resilience and engage in significant measures to build their resilience. We'd estimate that just 10 per cent to 30 per cent of managers feel responsible for building resilience in their organizations, and probably less than 5 per cent know what to do about it. Clearly, work needs to be done by both individuals and businesses. But it's business management structures that need to go through the largest amount of change.

Making businesses responsible for resilience

Once business leaders feel responsible for human-centric resilience, then there can be a fundamentally different approach. It's one which can be based on business units and, indeed, this is how we at Awaris work. We talk to business leaders about staff resilience and wellbeing issues. We share the data from the resilience screenings we do. And we then agree joint priorities for resilience skill building at the individual and business-wide level.

The approach must be based on mutual agreement, so we can then share this data and the approach in town halls with the whole population of the business unit. This allows businesses to share and even vote on which resilience skills people want to cultivate individually, and which they think their organization should help cultivate. Resilience then becomes a shared, visible project of individual and organization-wide responsibility. There's no more finger-pointing. Individuals and decision makers have a clear path for resilience mapped out.

This approach is measurable. Skills, perceived stress scores and resilience can be measured. This allows us to identify targets for check-ins, focus time, email boundaries and many more measures that we'll cover in the next chapter, and measure them. This means management can take responsibility for their part of skill development, as can the individuals. In the next chapter, we'll outline how exactly this can be done.

KEY CHAPTER TAKEAWAYS

- After a boom during the pandemic, care and investment in staff wellbeing is declining again.

- Businesses still don't take enough responsibility for creating resilient working cultures, failing to see how too much perceived stress inhibits employee performance and flourishing.

- To change this attitude and to help their businesses become We-silient, businesses need to realize three key truths:

  o resilience is a business responsibility, not just a wellbeing officer's responsibility

  o resilience requires building resilience skills, not a symptom-treatment approach

  o resilience is a shared responsibility – it's neither an individual's nor an organization's responsibility alone

- Businesses need to agree joint priorities for learning resilience skills at both the individual and organization-wide level, mapping a clear path towards We-silience.

- The success of this approach can be measured, by monitoring skill development, perceived stress scores and changes in resilience.

Notes

1 S Warttig, M Forshaw, J South and A White (2013) New, normative, English-sample data for the Short Form Perceived Stress Scale (PSS-4), *Journal of Health Psychology*, **18** (12), pp. 1617–28, https://doi.org/10.1177/1359105313508346 (archived at https://perma.cc/VQX3-UAEC)

2 S Cohen, T Kamarck and R Mermelstein (1983) A global measure of perceived stress, *Journal of Health and Social Behaviour*, **24** (4), pp. 385–96, https://doi.org/10.2307/2136404 (archived at https://perma.cc/GWR3-VTGZ)

12

Anchoring resilience in organizations

When we work with organizations on building resilience skills, we seek to integrate our best practice learnings from the world of wellbeing with the unique approach of building individual and organizational skills (see Appendix III for more details). Below, we'll outline our typical step-by-step approach that we'd take to anchor resilience firmly in the organizations and businesses that we work with.

Step one: working with an appropriate group size

We've found it's best to work with discrete organizational units, ranging in size from 150 people to around 1,000 people at a time. This fits with Robin Dunbar's anthropological observation of 150 as a limit to meaningful relationships.[1] Several organizations have taken this as a serious organizing principle. Smaller groups are possible, but groups well beyond 1,000 don't work as well. For a resilience intervention to work, it's crucial in our eyes that at least 30 per cent of a population take an active part in the process, so there's a feeling of a shared journey and resonance.

As organizational units get larger, there tends to be a lower participation rate. Against this backdrop, we make sure we work with businesses that are willing to work in appropriate group sizes. Groups that are too small don't make enough of a dent on the wider business. Groups that are too large can dissipate the quality of the shared experience. So, even if a company of 5,000 people approaches us, we find it helpful to break it down into smaller groups, focusing on the parts of the business where the leadership is truly on board.

We are the co-contract holders for the resilience programmes for the 51 institutions that make up the European Union (EU), a body which has 50,000 employees. We've worked with many of these institutions or the directorates within them. We split these institutions into groups ranging in size from 150 to 1,000, and this has given us a feeling for the right size. Another aspect of the size of the groups we work with is getting the relevant management team involved, as we'll discuss below. Once an organization gets much beyond 1,000 people, the personal connection from staff to senior management becomes tenuous. This also works the other way around. When most of the people in an organization are personally known to at least one person in a management team, there's a different level of connection and human resonance.

Step two: getting management on board

For any resilience intervention to work, you must convince management that the resilience intervention is actually needed. As we've discussed previously, this isn't always easy. It first requires us to convince managers that staff wellbeing is crucial for performance; that flourishing declines as perceived stress increases. That by focusing only on performance, they as managers are hurting their staff and their output.

So, as part of the process of getting management on board, we share our approach with them. We explain that it's an approach which involves gathering population-wide data, discussing priorities, communicating these priorities to all in the organization and then setting up resilience journeys for all to take part in.

Our experience is that this approach gets management approval fairly easily, for several reasons. First, we show the managers and executives that our approach is resonant with best practice learnings, by explaining it via the information included in Appendix III. Second, our approach offers interventions to everyone in the organization who wants to take part, thus making it inclusive. Third, our resilience journey focuses on data-driven patterns and priorities found in the population, which appeals to leaders' sense of effectiveness and general trust of data-backed decision making. Fourth, the approach we outline addresses skill building rather than problem identification, which we find tends to resonate with leaders.

Fifth, we clearly map out where there's individual responsibility and where there's responsibility at the business-wide level. This tends to satisfy those in management who think the individual should do more to boost their resilience, and, also, some leaders or HR leaders who often feel that the organization must take more responsibility.

Sixth, we target specific business units where workload or other factors pose too many challenges for employees to be expected to remain resilient. Intervening here is closely aligned with our repeated findings that parts of the organization where stressor loads are too high (sometimes called 'toxic work environments', a term we prefer to avoid) are the source of more than 70 per cent of burnout and retention challenges. Here, resilience needs to be anchored into shared work practices, and this is crucial in these challenging settings. Finally, we guarantee we can always protect the anonymity of all involved, thus ensuring there are no concerns with confidentiality.

Once management are on board, we then plan a town hall with all company staff. We outline our approach to resilience. We make it clear that **all are invited to take part in the resilience journey of their businesses**, starting with the self-assessments that we offer. Our experience is that, depending on the size of the organization and the degree of support from management, we tend to get 30 per cent to 70 per cent enrolling in the self-assessments and then taking part in the resilience journey following the town hall.

Step three: starting with individual resilience screening

A key part of our approach is individual resilience skills screening, as we touched upon in Chapter 4. Here, staff fill out and receive an individual resilience report, and then receive their resilience battery profiles. Normally, stress and resilience related-data isn't extensive in organizations. We have been surprised time and again how little actual usable data is present. Many organizations only realize the scale of their problems or their causes too late, when one of their staff members is wheeled out of the office following a panic attack, or an employee suddenly quits because they've simply 'had it' with the workload.

This lack of data is puzzling, although the cause is easily found. There's only a limited number of questions one can ask on annual staff assessments, especially to do with resilience or wellbeing. And this is why it is important to have specific wellbeing and resilience-focused assessments at certain times to get a deeper source of data.

Some leaders argue that people don't like filling out assessments trying to measure their stress. The head-in-the-sand approach might also win here for some, rather than having to acknowledge they're struggling. But in our experience, people *do* enjoy filling out resilience screening assessments, which gives them individual feedback on their challenges and skills. So, the crucial point is that the process of assessment has a direct benefit for the person providing the data – in the form of their individual report and positive feedback on their skills.

In doing this for one global technology company, with staff all over the world, we were surprised how many spontaneous and unscripted messages of appreciation we received for the survey itself. Many said they'd never been asked these kinds of questions or reflected on these issues before. They appreciated the process of the assessment itself. They felt heard. The resilience screening and its individual report also help convey important messages to those who take part. And, as you might realize if you've been paying attention, these are some of the key messages we've tried to convey in this book:

- Resilience isn't about endurance. It's not about being naturally resilient (or not). Resilience is about being able to shift our state from stressed to growing to regenerating to letting go.

- Each of us has a unique collection of resilience skills, which we engage in knowingly or unknowingly. Thus, our resilience profiles are unique. We don't have to try to compare ourselves to others, particularly the annoying colleague who never seems to get stressed. We simply need to understand our own strengths and weaknesses and our own unique resilience profile.

- We help participants understand how their resilience skill profile matches, or doesn't match, their stress profile. We explain their resilience battery profile, so they better understand what drains and what recharges their battery.

- Participants benefit from understanding when they can do something about their resilience, or when a 'tipping point' of stressors has been breached and resilience skills alone will become ineffective. By pointing out the aspects of resilience which depend on the individual or the wider business, staff and management are less likely to point the finger at the other. This clarity is welcomed.

- This knowledge helps participants identify what might be helpful for them. It encourages them to take part in the aspects of the resilience journey that best suit their resilience profile, and to work on their resilience 'blind spots'.

Knowledge is power, and arming staff with an understanding of their own resilience and what can be done about it is an important step. It lays the foundation for individual needs assessments. It gives individuals motivation and responsibility for the journey ahead.

Step four: looking at staff-wide data

We use aggregated data from the resilience screening to generate population trends from the workforce. This is novel, surprisingly. We'd estimate that around 80 per cent of health, wellbeing or HR departments we've interacted with had no such data and couldn't answer some simple questions, such as:

- Can you define the population you're serving?
- How many staff are you responsible for?
- What are their demographics?
- What does their stress load look like?
- What are their issues?

When we ask these questions, we usually get a helpless shoulder shrug. Chris and Liane have spent weeks working with wellbeing teams trying to get such data in a usable manner. And even when they have the data, teams often fail to run a sophisticated analysis of it. They often fail to have answers to more of our questions, such as:

- What are your targets for the reach and impact of our interventions?
- How many people have we reached with our interventions thus far?
- What outcomes did you want to change?
- What percentage of the staff achieved positive outcomes on the programme?
- What interventions were the most effective in terms of outcome?
- What interventions had the best cost–benefit ratio?

Again, it's concerning how long it usually takes for most to give an answer to these questions. In our eyes, it's not due to the incompetence of wellbeing teams (and they certainly agree with this analysis when we mention it to them). Usually, it's a lack of resources, data gathering and management capabilities.

Luckily, we can step in to help them with these points. Once we've gathered the data, based on the resilience individual assessments, we can look at the population and understand crucial pieces of information:

- We learn the stress level of the staff and how many are in danger of mental distress. We see how many people are in the zone of flourishing, are burning out or are at least functioning well. Together, this data helps us identify goals for the business's shared resilience journey.

- We gain an understanding of the stress load of the population, and in particular departments or units. This helps us understand how many people are in the zone of self-regulation and how many people aren't, and where business interventions are necessary instead of individual ones.

- We learn which resilience skills are strong and which are weak among staff. We pinpoint the proportion of staff with resilience competencies, and those who have none. Crucially, this helps us see which skills have the highest correlation with resilience. It's interesting for us that this isn't always the same, depending on the business.

Overall, this approach allows us to identify specific groups that face higher stress loads than others, or who might face unique resilience challenges. For

FIGURE 12.1 Chronic stress decreases for both genders over their lifetime

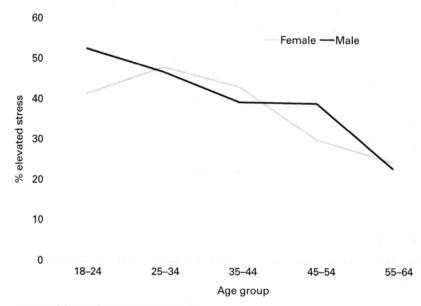

2,000 participants of Awaris standard survey.
Female stress peaks at 25–34, male at 18–24.

example, our data shows that the number of stressors stressors decreases with age for men and women, with men peaking at 18–24 and women at 25–34, and spiking again for men in the over-55 category (see Figure 12.1). Women tend to experience more personal stressors, which come from juggling multiple responsibilities compared to men (42 per cent vs 35 per cent), while men in our dataset suffer significantly more from a lack of predictability (44 per cent vs 25 per cent) and from work demands in general. This is also true for specific minority groups.

This knowledge allows us to quantify these challenges, and design appropriate resilience interventions.

Step five: selecting shared priorities with management

The purpose and meaning of businesses vary widely. Knowing these differences can be crucial in the business becoming We-silient. In the context of working with EU institutions, for example, we've seen that connection to purpose can be more important than in many for-profit institutions. This suggests to us that people working for EU institutions are purpose-driven, and this should be a priority during its resilience journey.

We've also seen in numerous HR departments that social connection was a strong predictor of staff resilience. People working in HR, not surprisingly, care about others (they aren't there simply to make your life more difficult, as some people like to argue). Those in HR want to nurture their felt sense of connection as a priority, which can be a big driver of resilience.

We've also seen for staff populations with high workloads that their ability to manage attention and remain focused was one of the biggest drivers of resilience. So, for them, this would be an appropriate priority. Equally, in environments with a high emotional burden, emotional regulation skills are predictive of resilience outcomes and would be an appropriate priority – either because staff have to deal with customers or patients who visibly suffer, or because the emotional atmosphere in the organization is toxic.

We review information and data like this with management. And, armed with this knowledge, we can identify shared priorities moving forward. These will include which resilience skills should be focused on at the level of the entire staff population, and which ones need to be matched at the organization-wide level. Typically, we agree on a maximum of three to four resilience skill areas to focus on. These must be areas that management resonates with, so they can personally work on them and can try to demonstrate themselves leading in these resilience skill areas.

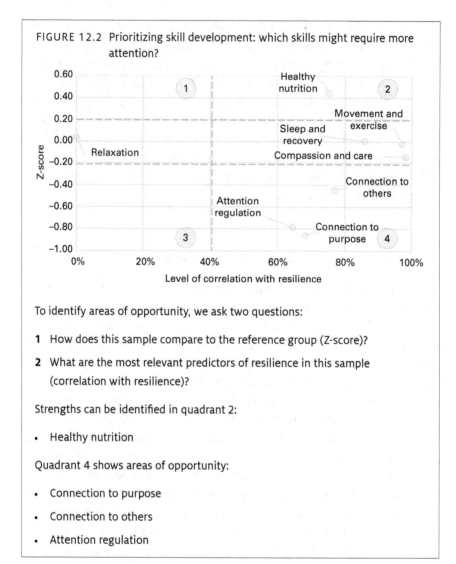

FIGURE 12.2 Prioritizing skill development: which skills might require more attention?

To identify areas of opportunity, we ask two questions:

1   How does this sample compare to the reference group (Z-score)?

2   What are the most relevant predictors of resilience in this sample (correlation with resilience)?

Strengths can be identified in quadrant 2:

•   Healthy nutrition

Quadrant 4 shows areas of opportunity:

•   Connection to purpose

•   Connection to others

•   Attention regulation

Step six: consistent individual resilience skill building

Most organizations we work with don't initially have a robust wellbeing model, let alone a clear set of resilience skills they want to build. Thus, they neither have a consistent set of interventions they offer, nor do these interventions relate to skills or causal mechanisms that improve outcomes. All these factors reduce the effectiveness of their interventions.

This is why, in our resilience journeys, we make consistent resilience skill building a central pillar of our programmes. We usually strengthen skills with several important measures:

- A **deepening workshop**, in person or virtual, to focus on the specific skill – for example, focusing on positive outlook or nervous system regulation. If it's virtual, then it can encompass more than 100 people at a time. This workshop provides some of the science and the rationale for the skill and then begins to introduce some of the specific practices that can build the skill.

- We then offer a **10-day sprint, of 25 minutes daily**. Here, we focus on specific practices, and, in turn, everyone gets to try the new skill. The following day, we ask them how the skill went, and share another practice. For example, if we're working on attention regulation, we might focus in the first week on individual strategies for improving attention regulation and focus. In the second week, we might then focus on group-level practices, working with leaders to ensure these habits are anchored. These sprints are crucial. They help break a resilience skill down into a single practice that should be tried out in the next one to two days. For this, there's both shared experimentation and immediate feedback. This felt feedback strengthens skill building.

- We use the **Awaris app and peer group exercises** that work on strengthening these practices. The app allows the participants to continue building the skill, even when we've finished working with the businesses. They can then continue building this skill in the long term using the practices they've learnt.

Step seven: building business-wide resilience skills in parallel

In parallel, we identify several organization-wide practices, which help units or teams to anchor that skill in their business. This is often aimed at the parts of the organization with high stress loads. So, for example, if we're working on attention regulation, we might share individual-level practices like:

- working with our devices and minimizing interruptions
- working with our emails and limiting email checking
- working with our calendar to strengthen focus time and deep work

At the business-wide level we'd work on:

- shared focus time and meeting-free times
- shared agreements on email processing
- how to protect focus time as a team
- how to reduce multitasking demands in individuals

We'd then use a period of three to six weeks to implement these changes. We follow a clear process with the teams, departments or business units involved. We meet with the relevant leaders to review the data regarding stressor loads, decide which priorities can be addressed and map out a rough plan to do so. We then kick off a simple process with all in the department. In a series of four to five sessions of around an hour, we delve into the most pressing issues and reach shared agreements on how they can be addressed. This might include shared practices, for example on emotional regulation, or agreeing on how to protect each other's work boundaries and recovery times. It often includes strengthening the social connections between employees or frequently talking about the things that are going well.

In this process, the participants would work on anchoring these skills in their personal work and in their teams. We'd then measure both outcomes and compliance with the practices (for details of the practices connected to each individual and organizational skill, see the Resilient Culture website[2]). This approach has a tremendous advantage. All in a particular business unit know they're working on this skill for these six weeks. Thus, it's a topic of conversation. There are organizational practices that support this. And it's a shared effort, ideally reflected in management behaviour.

After a period of three to six weeks working on one skill and anchoring habits into the organizational unit, we'd begin working on the next skill that was prioritized. Once the resilience skills to be focused on have been identified and practised, then even if there are one-off interventions in the future, staff can always refer to these underlying skills they've learnt. For example, if an organization notices a specific population in their staff are facing challenges to their financial wellbeing, then it can organize a specific workshop for that. It could include some necessary financial education. But it would also refer to underlying skills of emotional regulation (to work with some of the potential anxiety) and social connection (to ensure one has a good network of supportive friends and family). Thus, such a one-off workshop fits into the existing resilience skills profile and strengthens this.

Step eight: measuring outcomes

It's possible to improve outcomes in a reasonably short period of time using this approach, and for a significant share of the population. In doing so, it's possible to begin truly anchoring resilience skills at the business-wide level. But to do this, these outcomes need to be measured. We measure the same perceived stress and flourishing scores that we've previously measured. We tend to see strong improvements when we measure them at t2, at the end of the intervention period. We measure with a shorter survey to minimize the survey load on the participants. We also report on compliance with some of the practices, and employees' engagement in resilience skills.

Towards resilient business cultures

With these eight steps, some of the outcomes we've seen have been significant. Overall, with our programmes, in our dataset we see average reductions in perceived stress of between 30 per cent and 35 per cent. Those stuck in the high stress category normally drop from over 45 per cent to around 15 per cent. This is a reduction of those in danger of mental distress or burnout of more than 60 per cent. And due to this, we see improvements in resilience (using the Connor-Davidson resilience scale[3]) of over 25 per cent. The proportion of employees flourishing rises by 30 per cent on average.

We'd hope that allowing your staff to flourish and improve their mental wellbeing should alone be enough to convince businesses to engage in programmes like this. However, we do appreciate the performance pressures many are under. Thus, we highlight the importance of linking performance and care. For this reason, we also measure self-reported productivity and self-efficacy, and see positive changes of 3 per cent to 8 per cent in these categories. This is at the high end of comparable wellbeing interventions. It's also the aspect of resilience skills which has the highest impact on firms' bottom lines. And so, our interventions often lead to a significant increase in creativity, productivity and business outcomes.

Beyond this, there is a new shared language around resilience and wellbeing which everyone – management, HR and staff – can agree on. There is a shared sense of learning and going on a journey together, and a clear understanding that resilient staff are the foundation of resilient businesses. You can't have the latter without the former. Period.

One of our clients is a well-known Formula 1 team. It has a strong focus on wellbeing and psychological safety. They deeply believe that these two are crucial for sustainable performance. We've worked together on focused resilience skill-building interventions with some of their teams. It's interesting to see that in such a relentlessly high-performance environment – one of the most competitive industries on Earth – they didn't see a perceived clash between resilience and performance. They accepted that the two concepts are deeply linked. And given that they succeed in one of the most high-pressure environments in the world, they highlight how a focus on care can and should exist alongside performance.

Overall, we deeply believe that building a human-centric business makes a positive difference in people's lives, as well as business performance. It's deeply pleasing to see the impact of our resilience programmes on people's lives. Some estimates suggest we spend a third of our lives on average at work.[4] So being happy at work, flourishing at work, will contribute significantly to one's overall life satisfaction. If you are miserable at work – and far too many people still are – good luck trying to compartmentalize that away at the end of the day. Wishing away the time you spend at work is simply wishing away the one life you have. Which is not ideal, to say the least.

Even better is to view our working challenges as opportunities to learn and grow. A chance for each of us to become more resilient, compassionate and wise, and go on a shared journey of building human-centric practices into the fabric of work. Making work more human will make us more resilient.

It is the personal stories, the human feedback, which make us most pleased to be doing what we do. One particularly poignant moment was when a senior leader said, in front of her whole global team in a town hall: 'You have helped improve my life as a leader. You have helped improve my life as a parent. And you have helped improve the lives of most of us who have taken part in this journey. We will all remember this shared time.'

These are lives transformed for the better, and this feedback is something that (thankfully) is quite common following our resilience journeys. Indeed, it isn't too much of a stretch to say that our resilience interventions have actually saved lives. A number of people, based on data that came up in our HRV assessments, visited their doctors and then went on to receive life-saving interventions. This was mirrored back to the leadership of the company that made these interventions available to their staff. Lives really have been saved. For these stories alone, we both feel privileged to do the work we do.

Taking staff and businesses on a journey from individual resilience to collective resilience is, more than anything, a journey of self-discovery, allowing individuals to use their work as a vehicle for personal development and self-optimization. All humans deserve to thrive and flourish. And such efforts shouldn't stop every time you set foot in your office.

KEY CHAPTER TAKEAWAYS

- A targeted, skill-based approach is needed to build We-silience across businesses.
- The most successful interventions have multiple components, sustained over time, and with individual assessments.
- We typically follow an eight-step programme to anchor We-silience in organizations:
    1. working and selecting appropriate group sizes
    2. getting management on board
    3. starting the programme with individual resilience screening
    4. analysing staff-wide resilience data
    5. selecting shared priorities with management
    6. ensuring consistent individual resilience building
    7. building business-wide resilience skills in parallel
    8. measuring outcomes
- These steps often result in lower staff burnout and stress levels, enabling human flourishing at work.
- In turn, this can lead to increased creativity, productivity and outcomes at work.
- Human flourishing shouldn't be inhibited by work. As more business cultures become resilient, we hope work can be the catalyst for personal development and change.

Notes

1 R Dunbar (2021) *Friends: Understanding the power of our most important relationships*, Little Brown, London

2 Resilient Culture (nd) www.resilientculture.info (archived at https://perma.cc/66B7-GM3S)

3 Connor-Davidson Resilience Scale (nd) www.connordavidson-resiliencescale.com/ (archived at https://perma.cc/G3JR-5JZQ)

4 Gettysburg College (nd) One third of your life is spent at work, www.gettysburg.edu/news/stories?id=79db7b34-630c-4f49-ad32-4ab9ea48e72b (archived at https://perma.cc/N89Y-JZGJ)

Epilogue: A letter to a business leader

Dear Sir or Madam,

Many people in your organization think you are responsible for current high stress levels and that you are not doing enough to prevent burnout.

Reducing work stress and preventing burnout isn't your responsibility alone. There are 12 resilience skills and three resilience competencies. Your employees can choose to engage in them (or not). These skills, or being resilient, are not necessarily inherent. They must be practised, like any skills. As a business leader, you probably practise at least four of these skills and have some mastery of at least one or two of the competencies, even if you are not conscious of it.

As a manager, you can lead by example. You can make it clear that anyone can cultivate these resilience skills, because they aren't traits. Nor is resilience simply endurance. If your staff practise these skills, they're sure to become more resilient. An individual practising resilience skills makes a bigger difference on their perceived stress and wellbeing than the actual number of stressors they face – but only up to a point.

However, it is also highly likely that most of your employees, unfortunately, are at that point already, where their stress load is too high to reliably engage in the things that make them resilient. Many of them are thus unable to effectively regulate stress themselves. This highlights how resilience is both a personal and a business-wide responsibility.

What can you and your organization do? You need to have a clear understanding of the resilience skills and competencies that you want to develop among your employees. You then need to help them develop these resilience skills, as you would with any relevant business skill. You'll need to ensure this is consistently built upon over the next five years. Responsibility for this multi-year resilience journey should probably be held by HR or leadership

and development, rather than wellbeing departments. These two departments are responsible for systematic skill building. Wellbeing departments
are responsible for prevention, treatment and rehabilitation.

Crucially, you'll need to build organization-wide resilience skills. These
skills must be human-centric, focusing on fostering a positive outlook or
social connection by rolling out habits and practices which help these traits
become embedded across your organization. This is a responsibility of
managers. Resilience needs to be clearly understood and measured, and
managed to targets. These targets should be as important as KPIs.

While individuals are responsible for their own resilience skills (but not
their own resilience), your organization is responsible for helping them
develop such skills and embedding them in the work fabric. So far, our data
shows us that individuals have done more to build their resilience skills than
most businesses have done to build their organization-wide resilience skills.
So you'll probably have to make the first move here.

There'll be challenges. Your organization might be skilled at marketing,
or supply chain management. But, generally, when it comes to the human-
centric skills needed to promote We-silience, organizations tend to be
lacking. The good news: resilience skills themselves aren't complex. Your
team will manage them after some experimentation, as long as your organization honestly measures outcomes. And, interestingly enough, embedding
resilience skills will finally help you shift the dial on stress levels and burnout. Taking your company on a resilience journey will lead to better business
outcomes, like improved engagement and retention, innovation and sustainable performance. And this will have a positive impact on the bottom line.

Best wishes,
Chris and Liane

APPENDIX I

Why wellbeing approaches fall short compared to skill-building approaches

In the introduction, we talked about why wellbeing interventions alone don't work effectively. We don't need to repeat ourselves too much here, other than to say that stress levels have grown significantly in recent years, even as wellbeing initiatives have grown. We consistently encounter organizations where 30–45 per cent of the employees have high stress loads and are in danger of mental distress or ill health. Personally, we see this as an issue of a lack of skills, rather than any ill intent on anyone's part. We strongly feel that a wellbeing approach falls short.

Below, we compare typical wellbeing approaches in the workplace to real skill building at the business-wide level, to highlight why resilience skills are more effective.

Wellbeing vs resilience skills

Primary focus

Wellbeing approach:	Resilience skills approach:
Addressing immediate stressors and providing support when issues arise.	Proactively equipping employees with core skills to manage stress and challenges.

Response style

Wellbeing approach:	Resilience skills approach:
Reactive. Responds to problems as they occur, with short awareness-focused interventions.	Proactive. Prepares employees to handle challenges before they become overwhelming. Responds with a combination of new skills for the specific issue at hand, but builds original core skills.

Intervention types

Wellbeing approach:	Resilience skills approach:
Emphasis on restorative interventions and external interventions, such as employee assistance programmes (EAPs) and mental health resources.	Emphasis on internal resources, skill building and training, and empowering employees to cope effectively with realistic challenges they can master.

Nature of interventions

Wellbeing approach:	Resilience skills approach:
Short, awareness-building interventions, minimizing cost, with no follow-up.	Longer modular interventions as part of skill-building plans, and annual skill-building goals. All interventions must map to each organization's core resilience skills and be measured against these skills.

Approach to stress and resilience

Wellbeing approach:	Resilience skills approach:
Stress seen as a problem. Offers basic stress management tools and coping mechanisms after stress is experienced.	Stress is expected as a normal part of working life. Uses individualized resilience levels and skills profiles, ongoing development of resilience skills and personal journeys.

Employee involvement

Wellbeing approach:	Resilience skills approach:
Employees may reach out for support, but participation is often passive.	Targeting 100% employee penetration on resilience skill development.

Measurement

Wellbeing approach:	Resilience skills approach:
Minimal measurement of wellbeing, with a limited focus on causes and no root cause understanding.	Frequent measurement as part of employees' ongoing learning. Their own responsibility.

If we compare how wellbeing approaches show up at the organization-wide level to organization-wide resilience skill-building approaches, we'd also likely see the following shifts in different parts of businesses.

Recruiting

Wellbeing approach:	Resilience skills approach:
No involvement of wellbeing in recruiting.	Helping people match their resilience skills with the stress factors of the role and identifying resilience competencies required for roles.

Employee coverage

Wellbeing approach:	Resilience skills approach:
No targets. Typically reach only 5–10% of employees with interventions.	Coverage of close to 100% with general resilience skills approach. Targeted intervention for 100% of toxic areas.

Targets

Wellbeing approach:	Resilience skills approach:
Targets only at the level of sick days or wellbeing scores.	Organizations have a complete range of outcome targets, including stress levels and factors, resilience scores, resilience skill development and competency levels.

Leadership role

Wellbeing approach:	Resilience skills approach:
Leadership may promote available resources, but may not actively model wellbeing behaviours.	Leaders actively assess their own resilience skills, model them and take responsibility for organizational resilience skills.

Long-term impact

Wellbeing approach:	Resilience skills approach:
May provide short-term relief, but lacks sustained benefits if underlying skills aren't developed.	Builds a foundation for long-term resilience and wellbeing, leading to a human-centric, truly We-silient organization.

Organizational culture

Wellbeing approach:	Resilience skills approach:
May not be integrated into the core values and culture of the organization.	Becomes an integral part of the business culture, influencing policies, practices and interactions. Employee empowerment.

Wellbeing approach:	Resilience skills approach:
Limited focus on empowering employees to manage their own wellbeing.	Shared responsibility between employees and the organization to manage resilience and improve outcomes.

Preventative focus

Wellbeing approach:	Resilience skills approach:
Primarily reactive, addressing issues once they impact productivity or mental health.	Focuses on prevention, helping employees develop skills to minimize the impact of stressors.

Overall goal

Wellbeing approach:	Resilience skills approach:
Aims to alleviate immediate distress and reduce absenteeism.	Aims to create a human-centric, resilient workforce capable of thriving in the face of challenges.

The physiological, psychological and behavioural outcomes of our three resilience competencies

1. Mindful Self-Regulation

Description

The ability to regulate our inner and outer state through the skills of conscious breathing, relaxation, interoceptive awareness, attention, emotional regulation and positive outlook.

Outcomes

- **Physiological:** Knowing and shifting our inner state from high arousal and negative valence to neutral arousal and positive valence.
- **Psychological:** Knowing ourselves and accepting ourselves. Awareness of our own thinking and emotional styles. Knowing our weaknesses and what works for us. Coherence and self-confidence. Ability to self-regulate.
- **Behavioural:** Saying 'no' and taking care of ourselves. Keeping good mental and emotional hygiene.

Connections to resilience

Self-regulation skills are built on self-monitoring, self-evaluation and self-intervention. This competency is closely connected to having a clear and coherent self-concept and the feeling of self-efficacy or autonomy and competency – two core psychological needs.

2. Healthy Habits

Description

Engaging in positive body-related behaviours such as exercise, sleep and healthy nutrition, even in challenging circumstances. This correlates strongly with the competence of energy management.

Outcomes

- **Physiological:** Healthy cardio, digestive and immune system function, high energy levels and vitality. Physiological intervention leads to shifts in emotional valence and nervous system arousal.

- **Psychological:** Exercise, good sleep and good nutrition give one an embodied feeling of wellbeing, which contributes to self-esteem and self-confidence.

- **Behavioural:** Knowing how to take care of our physiological needs and sticking to this even in difficult times.

Connections to resilience

Good physical habits give us a bodily feeling of wellbeing, which in turn positively influences self-confidence. Engaging in this behaviour and feeling the outcomes (such as achievement in sport) contribute to self-efficacy.

3. Social Integration

Description

The ability to maintain good connections to the positive things in life, our purpose and others (rather than ourselves and our own problems).

Outcomes

- **Physiological:** Shifting of our internal state to positive valence, lower arousal and activation of the social engagement network.

- **Psychological:** Living with a sense of meaning and connection, being part of a whole. Feeling seen and integrated. Having a feeling of efficacy in the world.

- **Behavioural:** Maintaining a positive social fabric and network, helping others, regularly trying new things and learning new skills.

Connections to resilience

Positive connections to others lead to positive self-esteem and self-confidence. Feeling connected fulfils deep needs for relatedness.

Our approach to implementing organization-wide resilience interventions

There are numerous reviews of wellbeing and resilience, and we've categorized the evidence into six categories: approach, commitment, leadership, communication, intervention and measurement. We give each category a score of between 5 and 15, where there's evidence that this intervention has an impact on resilience outcomes.

For our discussion here, we'll focus on the 'approach' and the 'intervention' categories. In the approach category, there are seven points for which there's evidence that intervention leads to improved outcomes for workplace wellbeing.

Our approach to anchoring We-silience in organizations:

- **Holistic:** A broad approach, which is holistic. Including performance and social wellbeing, rather than a narrow cost-based approach.
- **Tiered:** Adopt a tiered approach to mental wellbeing in the workplace, by using organization-wide approaches as the foundation for mental wellbeing. The bottom (first) tier should be followed by individual approaches (the second tier) and targeted approaches (the third tier).
- **Targeted:** Targeting specific parts of the population and specific needs to ensure impact.
- **Individualized:** Based on individualized assessment and individual needs.
- **Skill-based and prevention-based:** Building skills for wellbeing and prevention, not recovery-focused.
- **Experimental:** Experimenting and assessing interventions.
- **Organization-wide:** Individual-level approaches must be matched with organization-wide strategies for reducing work stressors.

All these factors suggests that a targeted, skill-based approach is needed to build We-silience across a business – one which includes the individual and the workplace.

The list below summarizes how we typically implement resilience interventions at the business-wide level, based on best practices and our effectiveness reviews.

Key components of our We-silience interventions:

- **Multiple components:** A series of connected interventions generally have higher efficacy. All the successful cases reviewed featured several workshops or activities. One-off interventions or single sessions usually have limited impact.

- **Social components:** Training for wellbeing has a much higher chance of being effective if it includes social components like dialogues, peer group work and discussion.

- **Skills-based:** Personal resilience-based skill training is more applicable in multiple settings, including in private ones. This means they're more sustainable.

- **Fun and novelty:** Novel interventions that are fun get higher buy-in from staff.

- **Convenience:** Interventions must be easily accessible, and not too burdensome.

- **Mobile access:** Wellbeing interventions should have mobile access for ongoing use, either online or via smartphones.

- **Quality:** High-quality programmes have an impact on the outcomes.

- **Activate mechanisms:** It's important for the intervention to activate intended resilience mechanisms. There must be a clear understanding of the causal mechanism the intervention seeks to impact. If the intervention isn't clear about the mechanism it seeks to impact, then there's less chance it will be effective.

- **Sequencing:** A planned sequence of activities, including needs and risk assessments, leads to more successful interventions. This should be followed by workshops, peer group learning and more.

- **Continuity in learning:** A critical success factor for resilience interventions is continuity in implementing, adapting or sustaining the intervention.

- **Delivery innovation:** Innovation in delivery forms is necessary for wellbeing interventions.

- **Portfolio of interventions:** Organizations need a mix of interventions to address the challenges faced by their employees.

- **Good organizers:** Strong organization is needed from occupational health or HR professionals.

- **Group effects:** Group health initiatives have better outcomes.

- **Group and social learning as part of e-learning:** E-learning interventions should have a group learning component, otherwise they tend not to be effective for resilience.

- **Evidence-informed programmes:** Programmes must be evidence-informed.

- **Multiple programme delivery options and modalities:** Organizations should use multiple programme delivery options and modalities for reach and depth.

Thus, the most successful interventions are likely to be skill-building interventions with multiple components, sustained over time and with individual assessments. They should have a clear causal understanding of the mechanisms by which they work, and group components too.

INDEX

adaptability
  benefit of resilience skills 109
  nature of humans 2–3
  resilience as 43–45
  shifting between the four internal
    states 35–37
addiction to stimulation 40–42
adrenaline 29, 95
Agile teams 176
Agile Teams Manifesto 161–62
Agile working 151
alcohol consumption, unhealthy stress
    response 40–41, 52, 53
allostasis 29
altruism, role of mirror neurons 124 *see
    also* mirroring
American Psychological Association, 10
    ways to build resilience 24–25
anchoring resilience in organizations 201–13
  appropriate size of groups 201–02
  business-wide resilience skills
    building 209–10
  consistent individual skill
    building 208–09
  getting management on board 202–03
  implementing interventions 224–26
  individual resilience screening 203–05
  looking at staff-wide data 205–07
  measuring outcomes 211
  selecting shared priorities with
    management 207–08
  towards resilient business
    cultures 211–13
anxiety
  emotional regulation resilience skill 54,
    56
  influential factors 31–32
  workplace 3–5
apathy 37
arousal, influence on emotional
    response 31–35
artificial intelligence (AI) technologies,
    challenges and opportunities 1–2
attention deficit disorder (ADD) 18
attention management
  email agreements 152
  five practices for 151–53

focus time (individual or shared) 152
  limiting device unlocks 152
  meeting-free days or times 152
  workplace quiet zones 152
attention regulation resilience skill 54, 56
automatic responses to situations 28
automotive industry 6–8
autonomic nervous system (ANS)
  stress response 28–29
  three branches 126–27
Awaris
  app 209
  resilience model 25–26
  TeamMind programme 177

Bacon, Francis 17
Barsade, Sigal G 131
BDNF (brain-derived neurotrophic factor)
    gene 22
behavioural changes, time required to
    establish 118
behavioural level resilience skills 50–53
belonging crisis 106, 107, 108
brain
  complexity of 86
  disconnect between thinking and
    feeling 87–88
  feeling brain (emotional processes) 87
  mirror neurons 124 *see also* mirroring
  social processing (case study) 125
  thinking brain (cognitive processes) 87
  unconscious processing 86–87
brain development, neuroplasticity 2–3
breathing
  conscious breathing resilience skill 54,
    55
  effects of lengthening the outbreath 95
  importance in mindfulness practice 95
British Association of Mindfulness-Based
    Approaches 102
burnout 5, 8, 18, 37, 82–83
  global levels of 107
  impact of style of leadership 181–82
  in teams 169, 170, 172
  preventative approach 109
  rates among leaders and staff 180
business crises, U process 45

business culture
    ability to move through different
        states 44–45
    advantages of cooperation 123–25
    building resilient cultures 44–45
    component of resilience 128–30
    crucial aspect of resilience 137–39
    effects of a dystopian workplace 129–30
    emotional contagion (positive and
        negative) 130–34
    from 'I' to 'We' 123–39
    importance of social support 134–39
    influence of leaders and
        managers 130–34
    influence on resilience 22
    neuroception in the workplace 127–28
    positive effect of resilience training 109
    power of workplace culture 134–37
    psychological safety at work 127–30
    resilient working cultures 13
    social bias of the nervous system 125–28
    social nature of humans 123–25
business-level resilience building 141–58
    attention management 151–53
    departmental focus 156
    implementation challenges 154–55
    increasing pressures on
        employees 141–42
    limits to personal resilience 142–44
    organizational resilience skills 146–51
    planning, practising and measuring 154
    positive outlook 153–54
    responsibility for employee
        behaviours 157–58
    responsibility for resilience 144–46
    targeted interventions for toxic work
        practices 156
business performance, effects of the four
    internal states 35–37
business responsibility for
    resilience 193–200
    building resilience skills
        197–98
    focus moving away from
        wellbeing 193–94
    link between performance and
        wellbeing 194–98
    making businesses responsible for
        resilience 199–200
    mindset shift required 193–98
    moving away from symptom-treatment
        approach 197–98
    not just the wellbeing officer 193–98
    shared responsibility for
        resilience 198–99

Calm app 89
change
    challenges to resilience 1–2
    impacts on people 5
children
    capacity to adapt and learn 3
    effects of stress and trauma 3
chilled state, positive and negative
        aspects 42
China
    'lie flat' movement 42–43
    worker responses to stress 40–42
circumplex model of emotions 32–35
cognitive skills, time required to become
        proficient 119
collaboration 6–8
    nature of humans 2–3
    shifting from 'I' to 'we' 13
communication skills, role in social
        interactions 124
compassion and care resilience skill 54, 57
competition, misplaced focus on 6–8
connection to purpose resilience skill 54, 57
Connor-Davidson resilience scale 211
conscious breathing resilience skill 54, 55
cooperation, advantages of 123–25
cortisol 29, 95
cost-of-living crisis 106, 107
Covid-19 pandemic
    adaptation of working habits 2
    leaders less disrupted than their
        staff 182–83
    workplace wellbeing crises 105–08
culture see business culture

danger cues in the workplace 127–28
Deloitte 110
depression 37
digestion
    effects of the stress response 29
    rest and digest response 29
distress 30, 33
diversity and inclusion 107
    organizational integration efforts 151
dopamine 95
dopaminergic pathways in the brain 32
dorsal vagal system 126–27
Drucker, Peter 134
Dunbar, Robin 201

emotional contagion, positive and negative
        aspects 130–34
emotional convergence 130
emotional regulation
    example (Mark) 51–53

resilience skill 54, 56
role in social interactions 124
through mindfulness practices 95–96
emotions 30–35
circumplex model 32–35
degree of arousal 31–35
influence of physiological energy
levels 31–32
influence on mind and body 31–32
valence of 30–35
empathy, role of mirror neurons 124
employees
disengagement from work 105–08
effects of increasing stress at
work 141–42
individual resilience screening 203–05
limits to personal resilience 142–44
role in developing resilience 23–24
costs of being stuck in the stressed
zone 38–40
increasing levels of stress 3–5
workplace wellbeing crises 105–08
empowerment, benefit of resilience
skills 109
endurance, misunderstanding of
resilience 19, 20
energy levels, influence on 31–32
energy management, Healthy Habits
competency 72–73, 74–75, 77–79,
222–23
environment
influence on brain functioning 88
influence on resilience 22–23
European Union (EU) 202
eustress 30, 33
exercise, movement and exercise resilience
skill 54

fight, flight or freeze response 3, 29, 126
financial challenges 108
Firstbeat 38–39, 97
flow states 96
focus, attention regulation resilience skill 54,
56
freeze or shutdown response 3, 126

global workforce stress 3–5
Goleman, Daniel 137
Google, Project Aristotle 162
Grant, Adam 75–76
gratitude, positive outlook resilience
skill 54, 56
Great Resignation 106
growing state 34, 35
effects on business performance 36
growth mindset 37

habits 111, 112, 118
Headspace app 89
Healthy Habits (energy management)
competency 72–73, 74–75, 77–79,
222–23
healthy nutrition resilience skill 54, 55
heart rate variability (HRV)
performance data 114–15
window to neurophysiological
regulation 97
Hell Joseon concept (South Korea) 43
hikikomori phenomenon (Japan) 43
homeostasis 29, 126
four internal states and 34–35
hormonal systems
'approach' and 'avoid' states 95–96
influences on hormone levels 50, 58
HSBC mindfulness training programme 102
human resources (HR), role in staff
resilience 23–24
human-centric business 212–13
human-centric resilience skills 147
hybrid working
sense of disconnection 135
wellbeing issues 106–08

immune system
effects of the stress response 29
parasympathetic nervous response 29
inclusion and diversity 107
organizational integration efforts 151
individual resilience screening 203–05
inner landscape 28–46
automatic responses 28
balance of stress 30
circumplex model 32–35
emotions 30–35
nervous system and arousal 28–29
innovation in teams 170
internal states
chilled state 42
effects on business performance 35–37
four important states 34–35
interoceptive awareness resilience
skill 54, 55–56
natural patterns of life and work 37–38
resilience as the ability to shift
between 43–45
shifting between 34–37
window of tolerance 39–40, 44–45
workers stuck in the stressed zone 38–40
interoceptive awareness resilience skill 54,
55–56
interpersonal relationships
compassion and care resilience skill 54,
57

social connection resilience skill 54, 57

Japan, hikikomori phenomenon 43
jogging, skill development example 111–14

leaders and managers
    anchoring business-wide habits 190
    cultivating resilience intelligence 185–86
    failure to put resilience into
        practice 180–85
    gaining their commitment to
        resilience 202–03
    having a positive impact on employee
        resilience 188–89
    'hero leader' concept 20
    impact of leadership style 181–82
    impact of the leader's stress
        mindset 185–86
    impact on employee job
        satisfaction 181–82
    impact on stress and burnout in their
        teams 180–82
    lack of awareness of resilience
        skills 183–84
    leading for resilience 187–90
    leading well 189
    less experience of stress than their
        staff 182–83
    letter to a business leader 215–16
    living resilience 187–88
    making the time for
        management 188–89
    misplaced focus on competition 6–8
    misunderstandings about resilience in the
        workplace 18–26
    performance at the expense of
        wellbeing 179–80
    prioritising performance in busy
        times 184–85
    prioritizing particular resilience
        skills 207–08
    role in creating the business
        culture 130–34
    role in staff resilience 23–24
    supporting employees 189–90
    understanding social connections at
        work 135
    use of resilience behaviours 21
leadership development, incorporating
    mindfulness 100–01
learning
    growing state 34, 35
    human capacity for 2–3
    mirroring 127

shifting between the four internal
    states 35–37
letting go 34, 35
    effects on business performance 37
'lie flat' movement (China) 42–43
lifestyle, influence on brain functioning 88
limbic system 52, 87
loneliness crisis 105–06, 107
low resilience category 79–81
    challenges facing those in 81–82
Lyubomirsky, Sonia 135

Maltz, Maxwell 118
managers see leaders and managers
mental health challenges, effects on brain
    functioning 88
mental health issues, consequences of Covid-
    19 105–08
mesolimbic (reward) system 28
    influences on 58
    stress and 33
    valence of emotions 32
mind–body integration
    challenges to 87–88
    lack of 97–99
Mindful Self-regulation competency 72–74,
    77–79, 222
mindfulness 37, 83, 84, 86–103
    as a sensor in our system 98–99
    as a skill 48–49
    behavioural effects 91
    company training programme 102
    development of physiological
        intelligence 92, 97
    difficulties experienced by beginners 89,
        98–99
    disconnect between thinking and
        feeling 87–88
    evidence for effectiveness in the
        workplace 89–91
    feeling brain (emotional processes) 87
    foundational capacity for
        organizations 100–02
    importance for leaders 100–01
    importance of breathing 95
    loss of mind–body integration
        skills 87–88
    maintaining focus 96–97
    mechanisms 91–92
    mind–body integration 97–99
    more than just relaxation 94–97
    noticing and regulating inner
        states 94–97
    organizations' need for 100–02

physiological effects 91–92
psychological effects (mindset) 91
regulating our emotional state 95–96
regulating our nervous system 95
struggling to focus (example) 92–94
thinking brain (cognitive processes) 87
time required to experience benefits 118
use of heart rate variability (HRV)
    devices 97
mirror neurons, role in empathy and
    altruism 124
mirroring
    emotional convergence 130
    learning by 127
    spreading negativity 129–30
mobile phones, addiction to
    stimulation 41–42
models for resilience 24–26
mood, emotional regulation resilience
    skill 54, 56
movement and exercise resilience skill 54
myths about resilience 18–26
    contribution to workplace stress 18–19
    endurance 19, 20
    fixed by our upbringing 20, 22–23
    immutable trait 19, 21
    someone else's responsibility 20, 23–24
    too complex to be completely
        understood 20, 24–25

nature and nurture, influence on
    resilience 22–23
negative affect 4, 5
nervous system
    arousal and 28–29
    regulation through mindfulness
        practices 95
    social bias 125–28
neuroception 126–27
    in the workplace 127–28
neurochemical level resilience skills 50–53
neuroplasticity 2–3
    shifting between the four internal
        states 35–37
    skill development 116–19
Novartis 102
nutrition, healthy nutrition resilience
    skill 54, 55

obesity 88
objective stress load 61–63
organizational culture see business culture
organizational goals, alignment of resilience
    skills 110
organizational resilience 2

awareness of employees with low
    resilience 79–82
implementing We-silience
    interventions 224–26
mindfulness as a foundational
    capacity 100–02
need for mindfulness 100–02
relevance of resilience competencies 84
shifting from 'I' to 'we' 13
steps to anchoring resilience 201–13
We-silience 60
organizational resilience skills 146–51
    attentional regulation 148–49
    clarity of goals and purpose 149
    compassion and care 150
    emotional load regulation 149
    human-centric resilience skills 147
    integration of diversity 151
    organization-wide practices 151
    physical health of employees 147
    positive work environment 149
    relaxation 148
    resilience awareness 148
    sense of energy and connection 150
    sense of meaning 149
    social connection 150
    support for healthy nutrition 147
    support for rest and recovery 147–48
    synchronization of dispersed
        employees 150
overstimulation and exhaustion 40–42
overthinking 94
oxytocin 58

parasympathetic nervous system 28
    dorsal and ventral vagal systems 126–27
    measurement of activation 97
    rest and digest response 29
perceived stress 61–63
    impact on employee mental
        health 194–95
    impact on performance 194–98
performance focus and stress 16–17
perseveration, response to chronic stress 200
personal stressors, resilience
    competencies 76–78
physical skills development, time
    required 118
physical wellbeing 107
physiological effects of resilience skills 58
physiological intelligence 92, 97
physiological level resilience skills 50–53
polyvagal theory 126–27
Porges, Stephen 126–27
positive affect 4

positive outlook, core organizational
    practices 153–54
positive outlook resilience skill 54, 56
practice frequency, impact on results 119–20
problem solving, cooperation and 124
psychological level resilience skills 50–53
psychological safety
    at work 127–30
    in teams 137, 170–71
psychology, study of resilience 18
purpose in life, connection to purpose
    resilience skill 54, 57

quiet quitting 106, 107, 108

recovery, sleep and recovery resilience
    skill 54
recovery state 33–34
regenerating state 34, 35
    effects on business performance 36–37
relaxation
    as a skill 17
    resilience skill 54, 55
    skill development example 114–15
remote working, wellbeing issues 105–08
resilience
    ability to shift between internal
        states 43–45
    as a set of skills 5
    as a trait 19, 21
    definition of 5, 43–45
    meaning in different fields 17–18
    myths about 18–26
    origin of usage in the workplace 17–18
    shifting from 'I' to 'we' 13
    shifting states 5
resilience balance score 61
resilience battery profiles
    applying to individuals 65–66
    draining and recharging 61–65
resilience behaviours 21
resilience competencies 71–85, 222–23
    authors' competencies 82–83
    combining to make resilience
        profiles 79–81
    dealing with challenging situations at
        work 71–72
    definition of 72
    distribution of types 78–79
    Healthy Habits (energy management)
        competency 72–73, 74–75, 77–79,
        222–23
    help with work and personal
        stressors 76–78

journey towards resilience 82–83
Mindful Self-regulation
    competency 72–74, 77–79, 222
Social Integration competency 72–73,
    75–76, 77–79, 223
takeaways for organizations 84
three competency types 72–79, 222–23
resilience profiles 22–23, 72
    assessment tool 60–61
    combining resilience competencies 79–81
    low resilience category 79–82
resilience screening
    individual employees 203–05
    staff-wide data gathering and
        analysis 205–07
resilience skills
    12 key skills 48–69
    assessment tool 60–61
    attention regulation 54, 56
    authors' strengths and weaknesses 58–60
    behavioural level 50–53
    compassion and care 54, 57
    connection to purpose 54, 57
    conscious breathing 54, 55
    definition of 48
    domains 53–54
    emotional regulation 54, 56
    emotional regulation example
        (Mark) 51–53
    healthy nutrition 54, 55
    identifying the most effective
        skills 53–54
    interoceptive awareness 54, 55–56
    limits in high-stress situations 142–44
    movement and exercise 54
    neurochemical level 50–53
    physiological correlates 58
    physiological impact 50
    physiological level 50–53
    positive outlook 54, 56
    psychological level 50–53
    relaxation 54, 55
    relevance in stress management 66–67
    relevance to working life 58
    skills-based approach to resilience 48–49
    skills with the highest impact 67–69
    sleep and recovery 54
    social connection 54, 57
    training at different levels 50–53
    understanding from research 49–53
resilience skills approach, comparison with
    wellbeing approaches 217–21
resilience skills balance, battery
    analogy 61–65

resilience skills building
  10-day sprint 209
  Awaris app 209
  business wide 209–10
  consistent individual skill
      building 208–09
  deepening workshops 209
  measuring outcomes 211
resilience skills development
  benefits of focusing on 108–10
  cost-effectiveness 110
  examples of learning a skill 111–15
  five-phase process 110–12
  frequency of practice 119–20
  habits 111, 112
  importance of practice 111, 112
  insights from business
      interventions 119–21
  no secret hacks or shortcuts 120–21
  preventative approach 109
  time required for benefits to
      emerge 116–19
  workplace wellbeing crises 105–08
ResilientTeam Labs approach 174–76
responsibility for workplace
          resilience 23–24 *see also* business
          responsibility for resilience
rest and digest response 29
reward (mesolimbic) system 28
  influences on 58
  stress and 33
  valence of emotions 32
reward expectation, growing state 34, 35,
      36
Rohn, Jim 105

safety cues in the workplace 127
SAP (company) 102
Sapolsky, Robert 20
sedentary lifestyle 88
self-awareness, loss of 87–88
self-reliance, benefit of resilience skills 109
shared resilience 2
sleep and recovery resilience skill 54
social bias of the nervous system 125–28
social brain, role in working life (case
      study) 125
social connection resilience skill 54, 57
social connections, importance for
      wellbeing 135
social environment, navigating 126–28
social fabric of work, component of
      resilience 128–30

Social Integration competency 72–73,
      75–76, 77–79, 223
social learning 124
social nature of humans 123–25
social signals in the workplace 127–28
societal change, influence on brain
      functioning 88
societal pressures, disengagement
      from 42–43
South Korea, Hell Joseon concept 43
stimulation, addiction to 40–42
stress
  balance between too much and too
      little 30
  benefits of employee resilience
      screening 203–05
  changes over the lifetime 206–07
  chronic 3–4, 20
  circumplex model 33
  distress 30, 33
  eustress 30, 33
  global workforce levels 3–5
  Goldilocks zone 143–45
  healthy response to 3
  help from resilience competencies 76–78
  identifying groups that face higher stress
      loads 206–07
  impact of too much (team exercise) 9–11
  impact on learning and adaptation 3
  loss of self-awareness 88
  low stress states 33–34
  misplaced focus on competition 6–8
  myths about worker resilience 18–19
  need for mindfulness 100–02
  performance focus and 16–17
  perseverative response to 20
  positive and negative stress states 33
  resilience competencies 76–78
  role of the autonomic nervous system
      (ANS) 28–29
stress load 61–63
stress management, relevance of resilience
      skills 66–67
stress response
  components of 29
  disengagement from societal
      pressures 42–43
  resilience battery profiles 61–66
stress temperature 62–63
stressed state 34, 35
  addiction to stimulation 40–42
  consequences of being stuck in 38–40
  effects on business performance 36

unhealthy coping behaviours 40–42, 52, 53
subjective stress load 61–63
sustainable performance, impact of too much stress 9–11
sympathetic nervous system 28, 126–27
    fight or flight response 29
    measurement of activation 97

team resilience 13, 160–77
    Agile teams 176
    attention regulation habit 167
    burnout in teams 169, 170, 172
    collective intelligence of teams 163–64
    connection habit 166–67
    effectiveness habit 165–66
    emotional intelligence 162–64
    emotional regulation habit 168
    five-step process towards 173–76, 177
    hybrid working challenges 135
    impact of too much stress (exercise) 9–11
    importance of teamwork 7
    influence of team habits 162–69
    influence on team performance 169–71
    innovation and 170
    integration habit 168
    interaction habit 165–66
    key skills and practices 171–73
    mastered skills and habits make a difference 169–71
    positive outlook habit 168
    predictors of team performance 162–64
    psychological safety and 137, 162–64, 170–71
    reflection habit 168
    remote working challenges 135
    ResilientTeam Labs approach 174–76
    rest and recovery habit 167
    skills and habits of successful teams 161–62
    synchronization habit 167
    synchronization of dispersed teams 150
    understanding team dynamics 160–61
TeamMind programme (Awaris) 177
technology, loss of self-awareness 87–88
theory of mind 124

threat signs in the workplace 127–28
thriving 34
trauma
    impact on learning and adaptation 3
    therapy for 18

U process 45
Unilever 102
upbringing, influence on resilience 22–23

valence of emotions 30–35
ventral vagal system 126–27
video games 40–41

wellbeing
    challenges to 88
    increased focus on 11
    regenerating state 35
wellbeing approaches
    alternative approach 13
    comparison with resilience skills approach 217–21
    limitations of 11–13, 217–21
wellbeing officers, lack of support and resources 193–98
We-silience
    approach to anchoring in organizations 224–26
    employees with low resilience 79–82
    resilience at the level of the entire organization 2, 13, 60, 84
window of tolerance 39–40, 44–45, 126, 128
work–life balance 42
workers see employees
working at home, wellbeing issues 105–08
working life
    cycling through the four states 37–38
    most relevant resilience skills 67–69
    relevance of resilience skills 58
workplace culture see business culture
workplace stress see stress
workplace wellbeing crises
    consequences of Covid-19 105–08
    tackling 107–08
World Economic Forum (WEF) 1

Looking for another book?

Explore our award-winning
books from global business
experts in Business Strategy

Scan the code to browse

www.koganpage.com/business-
strategy

Also from Kogan Page

ISBN: 9781398664706

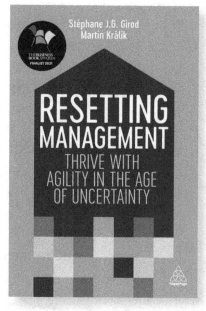

ISBN: 9781398667172

ISBN: 9781398612594

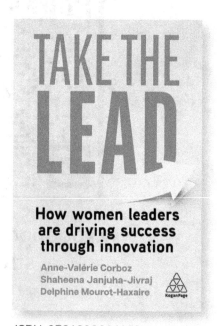

ISBN: 9781398614123

www.koganpage.com